AFTER THE ARAB REVOLUTIONS

For Jamal, a friend of freedom

AFTER THE ARAB REVOLUTIONS

Decentring Democratic Transition Theory

Edited by Abdelwahab El-Affendi and Khalil Al-Anani

EDINBURGH
University Press

Edinburgh University Press is one of the leading university presses in the UK. We publish academic books and journals in our selected subject areas across the humanities and social sciences, combining cutting-edge scholarship with high editorial and production values to produce academic works of lasting importance. For more information visit our website: edinburghuniversitypress.com

© editorial matter and organisation Abdelwahab El-Affendi and Khalil Al-Anani, 2021, 2023
© the chapters their several authors, 2021, 2023

Edinburgh University Press Ltd
The Tun – Holyrood Road
12 (2f) Jackson's Entry
Edinburgh EH8 8PJ

First published in hardback by Edinburgh University Press 2021

Typeset in 11/15 Adobe Garamond by
Servis Filmsetting Ltd, Stockport, Cheshire

A CIP record for this book is available from the British Library

ISBN 978 1 4744 8321 6 (hardback)
ISBN 978 1 4744 8322 3 (paperback)
ISBN 978 1 4744 8323 0 (webready PDF)
ISBN 978 1 4744 8324 7 (epub)

The right of the contributors to be identified as authors of this work has been asserted in accordance with the Copyright, Designs and Patents Act 1988 and the Copyright and Related Rights Regulations 2003 (SI No. 2498).

CONTENTS

FIGURES AND TABLES

Figures

Tables

PREFACE

Preparations for this volume began in the shadows of the violent counter-revolutionary assault on the burgeoning Arab democracies as they were emerging from the astonishing exuberance of the Arab Spring uprisings. The book now sees the light in skies darkened by a pandemic the likes of which humanity has never seen. This accentuated the challenges facing a project aiming to probe deeply into transition theory, a scientific enterprise defined by the paradox of having to turn inherent uncertainty into guiding rules and regularities for aspiring or struggling democrats. Adding a border-defying pandemic to the uncertainties and insecurities of high-risk competitive politics leaves little room for the reassurances of science. Related, and no less important, is the question: 'to what extent does the bio-political "state of exception" created by the Covid-19 pandemic present a threat to democracy, already threatened by other fears (of immigration, violence, pending economic ruin, climate change, etc.) that have been stoking populist fervour?'

Whether it is by coincidence/serendipity or, as we, of course, prefer, foresight, this book places these questions at the very heart of its treatment of the challenges confronting democratic transitions and transition theory. The contributions in this volume pinpoint insecurities (domestic and global) as the key variable underlying both the obstruction of transition, and the durability/revival of authoritarianism in the Arab region. As the authors strive to explain the genesis, causes, dynamics and ramifications of this improbable revival, it becomes clearer and clearer how it is driven by fear. The despots spread terror precisely because they dread the exuberance of democratic fervour observed in the Arab streets.

If the reader develops the impression, as we refer to the pandemic in the conclusion, that we have been talking about this subject all along, there is a reason for this: it is because our region has already endured a pandemic of brutal authoritarian rapacity that left vast expanses of territory strewn with its victims. But the indifference of the wider world to the millions of victims has been a vital contributor to the level of suffering. Even more harmful has been the presumptuous analyses that have tended to blame the victims, chiming with the despots' narrative that it was the people's fault for daring to revolt against their oppressors. The misunderstanding contributes to the indifference, and vice versa. We hope this work will contribute towards improving our understanding of the dynamics of socio-political change and its human context, and consequently enhance human solidarity and restore our humanity.

Like all similar endeavours in search of enlightenment, this work has benefited from the input of many. It is almost impossible to thank all those who have contributed to this project, which emerged from deliberations within the 'Project on Democratic Transformation and Transition Phases in Arab Countries'. The project was set up by the Arab Centre for Research and Policy Studies (ACRPS) in 2016 to focus on the study of Arab transitions. It has since held four conferences and continues to publish a series of volumes. ACRPS was itself founded in 2010, just in time to scrutinise the Arab uprisings. It continues to organise pan-Arab and international conferences on all aspects of the social sciences and humanities. A large number of the conferences and publications focus on democracy and democratisation, including some of the pioneering and most insightful studies of the Arab revolutions.

We are indebted to the contributions and help of the many participants in those projects, who include staff from the Centre and Doha Institute for Graduate Studies, in addition to many guest participants in the conferences and projects. We would like to offer special thanks to Mohammad Almasri, Jamal Barut, Haidar Said, Saif Abdelfattah, Morad Diani and Abdou Mousa from ACRPS for their advice and support. Gratitude is also due to Israa Batayneh and Sofia Hanazleh for their assistance with various stages of the manuscript. Thanks also to my office manager, Takwa Zweiri, and to other staff at the Dean's Office, including Engy Farid and Randa Saadi, who have been very helpful during various stages of this work. We have also benefited from the help of many research assistants, including Metodi Pachev, Abdullatif Haider, Belkacem Elguetta, Saba Khan and Somaiya Madebo. Special thanks for Dr Samah Gamar, who kindly had a sweeping last edit of the whole manuscript, to ensure it conformed to EUP's format and guidelines, and achieved this in record time.

We are indebted to the editors and EUP, Emma Rees and Nicola Ramsey for their meticulous work in seeing this volume through, and also to the diligent and helpful anonymous reviewers.

In addition to continuous support from ACRPS, the editors would also like to acknowledge the support of the Major Research Fund at the Doha Institute for Graduate Studies for supporting this research.

NOTES ON CONTRIBUTORS

Abdelwahab El-Affendi is Provost and Acting President of the Doha Institute for Graduate Studies, Doha, Qatar. He has served as Dean of the School of Social Sciences and Humanities at the Institute (2017–20), and was founder and coordinator of the Democracy and Islam Programme at the University of Westminster (1998–2015). He has been a visiting fellow at St Antony's College, Oxford (1991), the Christian Michelsen Institute, Bergen (1995, 2003) and Northwestern University, Chicago (2002), University of Cambridge (2010–12) and the International Institute of Islamic Thought and Civilization, Malaysia (2008). He is author of numerous books, including *Genocidal Nightmares: Narratives of Insecurity and the Logic of Mass Atrocities* (2014).

Luai Ali is Assistant Professor at the Doha Institute for Graduate Studies, Department of Political Science, and researcher at the Arab Center for Research and Policy Studies. He is the editor-in-chief of *Al-Muntaqa*, the first social sciences and humanities English-language journal to be released by the Arab Center, and he is also the coordinator of the academic publications in English at the Arab Center. He is currently writing a book titled *The Social Roots of Voting in the Kuwaiti National Assembly 1963–2016.*

Khalil Al-Anani is Associate Professor of Politics and International Relations at the Doha Institute for Graduate Studies. He holds a PhD in

Political Science and International Relations from Durham University, and an MA and Bachelor degree in Political Science from Cairo University. He has previously taught at Johns Hopkins, Georgetown, George Washington and George Mason universities, as well as being a Senior Scholar at the Middle East Institute and a Visiting Fellow at the Brookings Institution, Washington, DC. He has published several books (in English and Arabic), including *Inside the Muslim Brotherhood: Religion, Identity, and Politics* (2016), *Elections and Democratization in the Middle East* (co-editor, 2014) and *The Muslim Brotherhood in Egypt: Gerontocracy Fighting against Time?* (2007). He has also published articles in journals such as *Politics and Religion, Democratization, The Middle East Journal, Sociology of Islam* and *Digest of Middle East Studies*, as well as policy papers and op-ed pieces in *The Washington Post, Foreign Affairs, Foreign Policy*, CNN, Al-Jazeera, *Al-Monitor* and *Al-Araby Al-Jadeed*.

Omar Ashour is Associate Professor and the Founding Head of the Critical Security Studies Programme at the Doha Institute for Graduate Studies. He is the author of *The De-Radicalization of Jihadists: Transforming Armed Islamist Movements* and *How ISIS Fights: Military Tactics in Iraq, Syria, Libya and Egypt*, among other publications. Ashour previously researched and taught at the University of Exeter (2008–18) and at McGill University (2006–8). He served as a senior consultant for the United Nations on security sector reform, counter-terrorism and de-radicalisation issues (2009–13, 2015) and co-authored the United Nations' Economic and Social Commission for West Asia's (UN-ESCWA) document on security sector reform. He is a regular contributor to Arabic and Western media outlets.

Asef Bayat is Professor of Sociology, and the Catherine and Bruce Bastian Professor of Global and Transnational Studies at the Department of Sociology, University of Illinois, Urbana-Champaign. Before joining Illinois, Bayat taught at the American University in Cairo for many years, and served as the director of the International Institute for the Study of Islam in the Modern World (ISIM), holding the Chair of Society and Culture of the Modern Middle East at Leiden University. He also had visiting positions at the University of California, Berkeley, Colombia University, Oxford and Brown.

Azmi Bishara is the General Director of the Arab Center for Research and Policy Studies. He is also Chair of the Board of Trustees of the Doha Institute for Graduate Studies. A prominent researcher and writer, Bishara has published numerous books and academic papers on political thought, social theory and philosophy, including *Civil Society: A Critical Study* (1996); *On the Arab Question* (2007); *Religion and Secularism in Historical Context* (3 vols, 2011–13); *Sect, Sectarianism, and Imagined Sects* (Arabic 2017, English 2020); and most recently, *Democratic Transition and its Problems: Theoretical Lessons from Arab Experiences* (Arabic 2020). Some of these volumes have become key reference works within their respective field, and several are being translated for publication in English.

Hamid Dabashi has a dual PhD in Sociology of Culture and Islamic Studies from the University of Pennsylvania. He wrote his dissertation on Max Weber's theory of charismatic authority with Philip Rieff. Dabashi is the Hagop Kevorkian Professor of Iranian Studies and Comparative Literature at Columbia University, New York. He is the founding member of the Institute for Comparative Literature and Society, as well as the Center for Palestine Studies at Columbia University.

Tourya Essaoudi has a PhD in history from King Mohammed V University, Rabat, and has written extensively on issues of current history of the present, and on women's history in particular. She is a recipient of the Aladin prize for youth for co-authoring the report 'Europe Today', analysing the xenophobic and racist discourse of extreme right-wing groups in France. The prize was presented in Paris in June 2014 by Christiane Taubira, the then French Minister of Justice. Essaoudi is a secondary school vocational education instructor and a leading activist in women's and labour issues.

Marwan Kabalan is the director of political studies at the Arab Center for Research and Policy Studies (ACRPS) in Doha, Qatar. He is also chair of the Gulf Studies Forum (GSF) and adjunct professor in Diplomacy at the Doha Institute for Graduate Studies. Kabalan served as dean of the Faculty of International Relations and Diplomacy at Kalamoon University, Damascus. He taught international political theory at the University of Manchester and at the Faculty of Political Sciences, Damascus University. He was a member of the board of directors at the Damascus University Center for Strategic Studies and Research. Marwan's most recent research publications are *Qatar Foreign Policy: Elite v. Geography* (2019) and *US–GCC Relations: Politics, Economics and Security Concerns* (2020, Arabic).

Dana El Kurd is a researcher at the Arab Center for Research and Policy Studies and an Assistant Professor at the Doha Institute for Graduate Studies. She holds a PhD in Government with concentrations in Comparative Politics and International Relations, and has focused her work on authoritarian regimes in the Arab World, state–society relations in these countries, and the impact of repression on contentious politics. She has published in peer-reviewed journals such as the *PS Political Science & Politics*, *Journal of Global Security Studies*, *Middle East Law and Governance*, *Siyasat Arabiya* (an Arabic peer-reviewed journal), *Contemporary Arab Affairs* and *Parameters*. Her most recent book, *Polarized and Demobilized: Legacies of Authoritarianism in Palestine* was published in 2019.

Abdel-Fattah Mady is Professor of Political Science at Alexandria University. He studied politics at Alexandria University, Egypt and Claremont Graduate University, California, where he gained his PhD (2005). He served as a visiting scholar/ researcher at the Woodrow Wilson International Center for Scholars, University of Denver, and the UN Development Programme. He is the author of several books, including *The 2011 Revolution and the Question of Democracy in Egypt* (2019, Arabic), *Dialogues Processes after the 2011 Arab Uprisings* (2016, Arabic and English), *Violence and Democratic Transition in Egypt* (2015, Arabic) and *Religion and Politics in Israel* (1999). He is the editor of many books, including *Youth and Democratization* (2019), *Muslim Scholars and Promoting Nonviolence in the MENA and Sahel Regions* (2018, Arabic and English), *Troubled Democracy in the Arab Countries* (2014), *Towards a Historical Democratic Front in the Arab Countries* (2010), and *Arab Regime Transitions* (2009).

1

INTRODUCTION: RETHINKING TRANSITION THEORY AFTER THE 'ARAB MOMENT'

Abdelwahab El-Affendi and Khalil Al-Anani

When this book was first envisaged, the protesters that began flooding the streets of Khartoum (December 2018), Algiers (February 2019), Beirut (October 2019) and Baghdad (also October 2019) were not an inkling in the mind of even the most die-hard revolutionary optimist. After the obituary of Arab democracy was written (again) in large letters, and the funeral was over, the usual suspects were gleefully reiterating their 'I-told-you so': Arab democracy is a chimera. At that time, Sudan's military rulers appeared reasonably secure in power, having effectively and brutally quashed a popular uprising in September 2013. Egypt, Sudan's northern neighbour and ally, had set the tone a month earlier, in August 2013, when General Abdelfattah El-Sisi massacred protesters against his July military coup. The amazing and heartening horizon of hope and civility born as the 2010 winter turned into spring, was being systematically shrouded in man-made darkness. From the Gulf to the Atlantic Ocean, draconian measures were being taken to silence opposition for good, with the rest of the world watching in complicit silence. The mood turned sombre everywhere. As Syria drowned in blood, Libya disintegrated, and Yemen teetered on the verge of collapse, those who could have made a difference played dead. It was as if the 'Arab Moment', a rare occasion in recent times when the rest of the world had found political and moral inspiration from this region, was a figment of someone's imagination. Voices affirming 'Arab exceptionalism' were regaining confidence.

However, the team that gathered to discuss the idea for this book in 2016 did not share this dark mood of helpless resignation. It was impossible, it was felt, for things to go back to where the region had been before that inimitable 'Tahrir Moment'. The world-changing impact of this Arab 'miracle' went well beyond the 'Occupy Wall Street' *intifada*, transforming the intellectual, artistic, economic and, of course, the political scene in a myriad ways.

Political analysis has yet to catch up with this sea of change. The rather dramatic reversals clouding that bright sky blinded the bulk of the thinking world to the fundamental shifts already taking place. In fact, the reversals themselves were evidence that things could never be the same again. The extraordinary levels of violence and brutality unleashed on civilians highlight the unprecedented levels of resistance to the attempted return to the *status quo ante*. When Nasser affected his brutal crackdown on political opponents in 1954, Egypt was cowed into a silent submission that lasted over two decades. No dissenting voices appeared in the media, nor were street demonstrations held for years after that. Similarly, when Hafez Assad bulldozed the Syrian city of Hama into submission in 1982, the whole of Syria fell to its knees. Not a sound of protest was heard inside Syria, nor, for that matter, was much heard outside of it either. Contrast that to what is happening now. Long after the majority of Syrian cities have been demolished, defiance persists. A sign that we live in a totally different world is the proliferation of satirical Arab television shows that hinge their success almost exclusively on reproducing clips from the official media and hilarious comments by despots and their aides. This underlines the transparent implausibility of the narratives sustaining the resurgent despotisms. The draconian curb on free speech, another emergent phenomenon, is also a sign of the awareness of the new tyrants of their precarious situation.

It is interesting that, this time, it was not the people of the Middle East, but the scholarly and international policy circles that lapsed into credulity, fatalism and perplexed apathy. Initially, the multiple *intifadas* of 2011 shone a harsh light on the inadequacy of Middle East scholarship , leaving it 'as exposed and embarrassed as the Arab regimes it sought to analyse and decipher'.[1] In particular, democratic transition theorists rushed to revisit their

[1] Abdelwahab El-Affendi, 'Constituting Liberty, Healing the Nation: Revolutionary Identity

assumptions and re-examine their findings.[2] Additionally, as Hinnebusch[3] pointed out, the divergent outcomes and trajectories of the revolutions revealed the need for a radical questioning of several concepts and theories that had dominated tansitology over the past few decades. Concepts such as revolution, political pacts, democratic waves, democratic consolidation, etc. needed to be reconsidered in the light of the post-Arab Spring developments. This radical challenge to theory also offered opportunities to navigate new ways of thinking and theorising about democratisation and democratic transition.

Still, some myths of scholarship remain resistant to this sobering effect, including the alleged polarisation of scholarship on the region between two competing 'paradigms' (the 'demo-crazy' versus the fervent sceptic), both misinformed to some degree, both claiming vindication in the Arab Spring and its aftermath. This is astonishing, since pessimism versus optimism regarding the region's democratisation prospects cannot be deemed divergent methodological approaches, let alone 'paradigms'. The main distinction is the prevalence of idiosyncratic input, and the many unspoken and unexamined assumptions and biases. It is this aspect of methodology, or lack thereof, that needs to be a focus of investigation. It was no surprise that plenty of *mea culpas* and frank admissions of anti-democratic bias characterised some instances of post-uprising self-criticism.[4] This is a reminder, if one were needed, that hostility to Arab democracy remains more prevalent among Western policymakers and scholars than among the allegedly docile Arab masses.

This feverish soul-searching was also a reminder that transition

Creation in the Arab World's Delayed 1989', *Third World Quarterly* 32(7) (2011): 1255–71; Valbjørn Morten and Frédéric Volpi. 'Revisiting Theories of Arab Politics in the Aftermath of the Arab Uprisings', *Mediterranean Politics* 19(1) (2014): 134–6.

2 Alfred Stepan and Juan J. Linz, 'Democratization Theory and the "Arab Spring"', *Journal of Democracy* 24(2) (2013): 15–30.

3 Raymond Hinnebusch, 'Globalization, Democratization, and the Arab Uprising: the International Factor in MENA's Failed Democratization', *Democratization* 22(2) (2015): 335–57; Eva Bellin, 'Reconsidering the Robustness of Authoritarianism in the Middle East: Lessons from the Arab Spring', *Comparative Politics* 44(2) (2012): 127–49.

4 F. Gregory Gause III, 'Why Middle East Studies Missed the Arab Spring', *Foreign Affairs* 90(4) (2011): 81–90.

scholarship had largely ignored the Arab region, both in its input and output. As one famous 'transitologist' put it, the challenge in the region 'lies not in discerning whether a transition from autocracy will eventually result in the consolidation of some type or another of democracy, but whether such a transition has begun or will occur at all'.[5] Other reasons had been cited for advising against democratisation, predicting that the results would be a raft of 'illiberal democracies'.[6] Surprisingly, this did not prevent many from attacking a presumed 'excessive' focus on democracy and democratisation, dismissed as a Eurocentric illusion, and a conscious subservience to Western foreign policy imperatives![7]

Our team was not ready to acquiesce into the acknowledged and occasionally deplored marginalisation, even 'ghettoisation', of Middle East scholarship, nor in the despair of its democratisation prospects.[8] It was not a matter of moral indignation – despite the fact that there was a lot to be indignant about – but the simple realisation of the unsustainability of such morally bankrupt orders. We rejected the implicit assumption that the region and its people are devoid of agency, mere recipients of external blessings (in the form of knowledge, enlightenment, industrial goods, culture, petrodollars, etc.), and evils (colonialism, exploitation, colonial settlers, weapons, violence, etc.)

This narrative neglects the world-changing impact of many events and episodes in this region, starting with the Algerian revolution of 1955, which transformed the world in multiple fashions. So did the closely related 1956 Suez Crisis. Equally parochially dismissed, the Iranian Revolution continues to create waves beyond the region. The same scholarly community appeared

[5] Philippe C. Schmitter, 'Is it Safe for Transitologists and Consolidologists to Travel to the Middle East and North Africa?' Stanford University, 1995, available at: https://go.aws/2Yj4dVm, last accessed 30 April 2020.

[6] Judith Miller, 'The Challenge of Radical Islam', *Foreign Affairs* (1993): 43–56; Zakaria Fareed, 'The Rise of Illiberal Democracy', *Foreign Affairs* 76(6) (1997): 22–43.

[7] Lisa Anderson, 'Searching where the Light Shines: Studying Democratization in the Middle East', *Annual Review of Political Science* 9(1) (2006): 205–7; Morten Valbjørn, 'Reflections on Self-reflections: On Framing the Analytical Implications of the Arab Uprisings for the Study of Arab Politics', *Democratization* 22(2) (2015): 218–38.

[8] Michael C. Hudson, 'The Middle East', *Political Science and Politics* 34(4) (2001): 801–4; Lisa Anderson, 'Democracy, Authoritarianism and Regime Change in the Arab World', public lecture, London School of Economics and Political Science, 13 July 2011, available at: https://bit.ly/2Vq6lIV, last accessed 24 January 2020.

to collectively discount the international impact of numerous *intifadas* that shook the region in the following decades (Sudan 1985; Egypt 1986; Palestine 1987; Algeria 1988; Jordan 1989; etc.). The long crisis that started with Iraq's invasion of Kuwait in summer 1990, and did not exactly end with the invasion of Iraq in spring 2003, should have had a sobering impact on scholarship, even before the shocking 9/11 atrocity and the invasion of Afghanistan that followed it. Unfortunately, that has not been the case, even after ISIS and the many more bitter side-effects that followed. All these regional earthquakes remained marginal to the analyses of world events, in spite of their world-changing character. In all these cases, the scholarly approach mirrored that of policymakers: it starts with blindness/denial, turns into surprise and shock, morphs into wishful thinking, followed by over-reaction, before denial reasserts itself, this time portraying the earlier blindness as foresight, while rejecting any link between former misguided policies and current crises.

More to the point from the perspective of our current investigation, there is evidence that the trigger of at least two of the three cases that launched what Samuel Huntington called the third wave of democratisation,[9] had come from the Middle East. In Spain, the mismanagement of the consequences of the 1973 oil shock was the key trigger to the crisis that brought the Franco's dictatorship down.[10] In Greece it was Turkey's decisive reaction to the Greek junta's attempted annexation of Cyprus that was the key to its downfall.[11] What would have been a triumphant unification of Greece and Cyprus turned into a military and political fiasco, thus completely delegitimising the military regime.

After the Spring: Taking up the 'Binder Challenge'

As mentioned above, Middle East scholarship has yet to catch up with the momentous impact of developments in the region. As far back as 1988, Leonard Binder compared Middle East scholarship unfavourably with Latin

[9] Samuel P. Huntington, 'Democracy's Third Wave', *Journal of Democracy* 2(2) (1991): 12–34.

[10] Senén Florensa (ed.), *The Arab Transitions in a Changing World: Building Democracies in Light of International Experiences* (Barcelona: IEMed, 2016), p. 18

[11] Geoffrey Pridham, *The New Mediterranean Democracies: Regime Transition in Spain, Greece and Portugal* (London: Routledge, 2016), p. 21.

American scholarship, which remained unique in the Third World in its significant contribution to 'the reassertion of liberal development theory'. Neither the scholars from, nor the scholarship on, any other Third World region had a comparable impact on mainstream political and social theory. Middle Eastern scholarship, in contrast, did not even interact well with Latin American theoretical constructs, such as dependency theory or 'bureaucratic authoritarianism', nor did it produce analytical tools of its own.[12] Binder ascribes this discrepancy to Latin America's cultural proximity to the West, and the strong influences of Marxism on that region. He adds that identity defensiveness in the Middle East has militated against the integration of its indigenous scholarship into the wider pool of international research. Timothy Mitchell, however, offers a diametrically opposed explanation: it was the relative success of Middle Eastern Studies in the mid-century US academy that had 'inhibited the development of rival paradigms' from within it. In contrast, 'the lower stature of Latin American scholarship gave more room for alternative views'.[13]

Binder's claim may have been an exaggeration, since Arab contributions to mainstream social and political thought had not been that negligible. Binder has a whole chapter in his book on Edward Said's critique of Orientalism, but he failed to see its epoch-making significance.[14] Said's critique was in turn the culmination of a long line of Arab critiques of Orientalism, starting with Anwar Abdel-Malek's early critique, through Samir Amin's indictment of Eurocentrism, etc.[15] Binder's work came too early to take into account other important Arab contributions to the study of democratisation, such as those of Ghassan Salame and Bahgat Korany,[16] or to the theory of the state,

[12] Leonard Binder, *Islamic Liberalism: A Critique of Development Ideologies* (Chicago, IL: University of Chicago Press, 1988), pp. 76–8.

[13] Timothy Mitchell, 'The Middle East in the Past and Future of Social Science', in David Szanton (ed.), *The Politics of Knowledge: Area Studies and the Disciplines* (Berkeley: University of California Press, 2003), p. 94.

[14] Shehla Burney, 'Chapter Two: Edward Said and Postcolonial Theory: Disjunctured Identities and the Subaltern Voice', *Counterpoints* 417 (2012): 41–60, available at: https://bit.ly/2yTK2CT, last accessed 21 January 2020.

[15] Anwar Abdel-Malek, 'Orientalism in Crisis', *Diogenes* 44(107) (1963): 8; Samir Amin, *Eurocentrism* (New York: NYU Press, 1989).

[16] Ghassan Salame, *Democracy without Democrats: The Renewal of Politics in the Muslim World* (London: Bloomsbury, 1994); R. Brynen, B. Korany and P. Noble (eds), *Political Liberalization and Democratization in the Arab World*, vol. 1 (London: Lynne Rienner, 1995).

etc.[17] Most definitely it did not take account of later work, such as Azmi Bishara's seminal three-volume work on religion and secularism, or his more recent work on sectarianism.[18]

Thus, claims about the meagre Middle Eastern theoretical contributions may themselves be a sign of selective blindness, given the remarkable discrepancy between this marginality and the above-noted centrality of Middle East politics in many major ongoing policy and scholarship debates. In the 1990s, the 'Islamism Debate' was identified as 'one of the few remaining intellectual debates in US foreign policy'. In addition to its inherent intellectual fascination, the issue also posed significant career risks for politicians or senior diplomats who 'get it wrong'.[19] The 2003 US-led invasion of Iraq, closely linked to that earlier episode, and to 'democracy promotion', is another illustration of high impact, warped logic and horrendous consequences that were easily predictable, but were not predicted. This was partly due to the way the discipline has sought (as did policy debates) to compartmentalise these discussions, and sometimes deliberately so, to serve political ends, or because they were too embarrassing.[20]

The current volume seeks to emerge from this bind by building on earlier pioneering work, and on the opportunity offered by the still ongoing, and evolving, Arab uprisings. This is especially so since the most recent phase of the uprisings from late 2018 (in Sudan, Algeria, Iraq and Lebanon) offered another practical refutation of culturalist claims regarding lack of Arab commitment to freedom and democracy. In fact, the Arab masses took this commitment to democracy and civility to new levels, being intensely anti-sectarian and free from bigotry. In all appearances, the resistance to democratisation did not reside in the proverbial Arab street or Arab culture, but elsewhere: in the bunkers of entrenched regimes and those capitals where Arab democracy

[17] Timur Kuran, 'The Vulnerability of the Arab State: Reflections on the Ayubi Thesis', *The Independent Review* 3(1) (1998): 111–23.

[18] Azmi Bishara, *al-Dīn wal 'Almāniyya fi Siyāq Tārīkhī* (*Religion and Secularism in Historical Context*) (Beirut: Arab Centre for Research for Policy Studies, [2012] 2014); Azmi Bishara, *al-Tā'ifa, al-Tā'ifiyya wa al-Tawā'if al-Mutakhayyala* (*Sect, Sectarianism and Imagined Sects*) (Beirut: Arab Centre for Research for Policy Studies, 2018).

[19] Satloff Robert, 'Islamism Seen from Washington', in Martin Kramer (ed.), *The Islamism Debate* (Tel Aviv: Moshe Dayan Center, 1999), pp. 101–2.

[20] Mitchell, 'The Middle East in the Past and Future of Social Science', pp. 91–2.

looms as a threat: Washington, Paris, Tel Aviv, Moscow, Tehran, etc. Here, the role of theorisation becomes central. When confronted with such formidable obstacles to democracy, is it theory's role to record, describe and explain (justify?) what has become a reality? Or is it to do more: dissect, anticipate, deplore, look for alternatives?

As Guillermo O'Donnell and his colleagues embarked in the 1970s on the research that produced the seminal series of volumes, *Transitions from Authoritarian Rule* (1986), they rejected criticism that theirs was 'wishful thinking'. Rather, as one of them put it, the exercise was one of 'thoughtful wishing', leading to 'a normatively generated inquiry that was scholarly, empirically based, deliberate, and rigorous in its methods'.[21] It was also cautious, speaking about 'transition from authoritarian rule', rather than transition to democracy. This was O'Donnell's angle in an earlier work, in which he noted the fragility of Latin America's authoritarian regimes at a time when they appeared to be ascendant.[22] As he put it, the work was thus a political act in its own right: 'We were writing politics, not just an academic treatise.'[23] No less important, in the words of one of O'Donnell's co-authors, Philippe Schmitter, the work also rejected the notion that democratisation needed a 'fixed set of economic or cultural prerequisites'.

In addressing the comparable challenge to enhance understanding of democratisation, this volume seeks to confront the Weberian question regarding the truth-value distinction and the 'objectivity' of knowledge compared with the value of a presumed vantage point of an Arab-centred approach. This is in contrast to the counter-claim that a 'scientist' in the modern sense (especially a Western 'scientist') can know and understand subjects better

[21] Cynthia J. Arnson and Abraham F. Lowenthal, 'Foreword', in Guillermo O'Donnell and Philippe C. Schmitter (eds), *Transitions from Authoritarian Rule: Tentative Conclusions about Uncertain Democracies* (Washington, DC: Woodrow Wilson International Center for Scholars, 1986), p. viii.

[22] Guillermo O'Donnell, 'Tensions in the Bureaucratic–Authoritarian State and the Question of Democracy', in D. Collier (ed.), *The New Authoritarianism* (Princeton, NJ: Princeton University Press, 1979), pp. 285–318.

[23] Kees Biekart, 'Guillermo O'Donnell's "Thoughtful Wishing" about Democracy and Regime Change', *Development and Change* 46(4) (2015): 923.

than the subjects themselves![24] Another related question is whether the production of such knowledge is subject to human will, or is it the by-product of the transformation itself?

These questions merge when debating the priorities and prerequisites for democratisation. If a democratic political culture is a condition for democracy, then why is it in fact the 'uneducated' Arab masses who keep resisting oppression and revolting against it without the benefit of a 'democratic education'? In contrast, why did the 'enlightened' literati keep churning out volumes about the impossibility of defying or changing the existing regimes, precisely because the masses were not yet 'ready'? More important, why is it that the 'enlightened' and 'democratic' outsiders seem to act as brutally and oppressively as their local friends when in the region (Iraq, Palestine, etc.)? Is the impact of 'Arab culture' so powerful and instantaneous?[25]

External dynamics (regional, international) also figure incessantly in the debate, and go beyond mere 'influence', socio-economic impact or even 'neighbourhood effect'. Here, the end of the Cold War was marked not by withdrawal of the superpowers, but by their forceful reinsertion. American troops were pouring into the region to prop up autocratic regimes just as Soviet troops were leaving Eastern Europe to open the way for democratisation. Iraq was invaded, Israel kept flexing its muscles and Syria is today the locus of its own Great Game. The uprisings in Bahrain and Syria were quelled with the help of foreign troops, militias and air power.

Outline of the Book

In his critical overview of the transition debate, Azmi Bishara (Chapter 2) begins by dismissing the criticism of democratic transition research as teleological, pointing out that the very idea of 'transition' is by definition teleological, anticipating democracy as the (desirable) outcome of change. The quest to comprehend and account for transitions and transformations (towards modernity, capitalism, secularism, democracy, etc.) remains the *raison d'être*

24 Peter Winch, *The Idea of a Social Science and its Relation to Philosophy* (London: Routledge, 1990).

25 Abdelwahab El-Affendi, 'Political Culture and the Crisis of Democracy in the Arab World', in Ibrahim Elbadawi and Samir Makdisi (eds), *Democracy in the Arab World: Explaining the Deficit* (London: Routledge, 2010), pp. 12–40.

of the social sciences, making the concept of transition central to investigations in the field. Neutrality in social investigations is neither possible nor is it an essential requirement of scientific objectivity. The problem with transition theory is not its bias towards democracy, but its tendency to over-generalise from the Western experience. Generalisation is additionally problematic because it whittles down theory to trivialities. As more cases are introduced, little common features are left to generalise, except for the readiness of elites from different groups to come to an agreement. To a lesser extent, Rustow's national unity requisite, and the related commitment to the integrity of the state, also survives. In fact, a coherent state is central for the very definition of democracy and not just transition.

The challenge is thus to transcend this 'European area studies' posing as a universal theory for transition by introducing new findings and insights from outside the Western experience. The chapter seeks to do this by examining the trajectories of democratisation in Egypt and Tunisia, where the former quickly lapsed in spite of initial promise into an even more repressive dictatorship. Tunisia, in contrast, ended up as a shaky democracy that is still holding.

Significantly, Chapter 2 refutes the common perception that democracy succeeded in Tunisia but failed in Egypt because Tunisia ranked higher in modernisation indices. A closer look at statistics reveals no significant difference in per capita income, spread of education or size of the middle class between them. Rather, decisive factors related the role of the military, levels of external interventions and elite commitment to democracy and readiness to accept compromises. In Egypt the military was more politically ambitious and had more interests to defend, while the Tunisian military stayed out of politics and supported democratisation. The elite in Tunisia, including Islamists, were more flexible than in Egypt. Tunisia's relatively marginal geostrategic position, compared with Egypt, also reduced external interference and thus helped to stabilise democracy.

In addition, further generalisations can be gathered from these two cases, and the Arab scene generally. First, a party with a narrow majority cannot rule alone in a newly democratising country with a hostile state apparatus. Coalition-building becomes the only democratic option available. Second, Rustow's point regarding commitment to the polity must be heeded. Third, elections need to be approached with care, for they could trigger conflict in fragile and divided states. Finally, the Arab experience proves the impossibility of toppling a regime with a coherent military and security apparatus except with foreign support.

In Chapter 3, Abdelwahab El-Affendi proposes to stand the transition 'paradigm' on its head by taking the Arab experience as a starting point to build a robust theoretical framework. While critical of the limitations of the transition approach, the chapter defends the relevance and validity of the 'paradigm'. It proceeds to build on the theory's combative nature as a deliberately interactive approach to knowledge, exerting significant influence on both scholarship and political practice. Highlighting the interconnection between two core concepts of the theory – uncertainty and moderation – it links them to a third – insecurity. On this basis, levels of insecurity are identified as a key explanatory variable, resolving riddles both in the Arab experience and the broader international story of democracy.

Uncertainty is the paradox at the heart of the transition discourse. Its inherent fluidity, amid shifting perceptions and expectations, is what makes transitions possible. However, this same fluidity makes the derivation of generalisable rules (a 'theory' or 'rules') problematic. Democratisation, in turn, requires the reduction of uncertainty through mutual reassurances between rival actors, produced only the bounded uncertainty characteristic of democratic competition. Such processes presuppose a degree of rationality within autocratic regimes that prefer compromise and power-sharing to ruin, and an opposition sufficiently moderate as to accept the offer. But what happens if regimes are so insecure and irrational as to prefer ruin to compromise? In such cases, the concept of moderation loses its sense and utility, as the bad coin of extremism drives out the good one of moderation.

In the Middle East (and this includes Iran and Israel, and to a lesser degree, Turkey) fanatical narratives of insecurity leave little room for compromise and moderation to the extent that democracy itself is securitised, with both internal and international actors now seeing democracy as a threat. Brutal regimes thus receive ample foreign support, which enhances insecurity and generates new threats from aggrieved victims in an endless 'spiral of insecurity'. A Hobbesian universe dominated by the 'black-hole state' model dominates, with insecurity spilling over into other regions, bringing further interventions to prop up dysfunctional regimes that enhance instability. The Middle East's surplus of insecurity can thus be revealed as far from exceptional, and is in fact sustained only by substantial external input.

As an explanatory variable, the level of insecurity has universal relevance. Not only does it explain why democracy failed in Egypt and Libya, but also why right-wing populism is threatening democracies from Brazil to the United States, and from Britain to Poland. Building on this critical deconstruction, the tentative theoretical solution proposed in this chapter can help to solve some of the key the dilemmas posed by the transition paradigm, with the aim of enhancing its applicability beyond specific contexts.

In Chapter 4, Asef Bayat engages in deep intellectual and personal reflections on the nature and fate of political revolutions. Having lived through the tumult of the Iranian revolution of 1979 before witnessing the Arab uprisings of 2011 (having reflected in between on the absence of revolutionary action in Egypt), he poses and tentatively answers profound questions on the disparity between the two episodes. Why did the Arab revolutions lack charismatic leaders, unified organisations or a dominant ideology, appearing to be the acts of 'ordinary people'?

Bayat builds on his seminal work on social movements and street politics to provide a novel and compelling analysis to these upheavals and their troubled trajectories. He borrows Timothy Garton Ash's term, 'refo-lutions' (a hybrid between reform and revolution), to describe these episodes. But they were different from their East European counterparts in that no negotiations preceded the ouster of the dictators here. They were mainly 'forced out by revolutionary coercion'. The Arab variety, Bayat adds, advocated moderate change and achieved even less. Despite the meteoric speed with which dictators were toppled, mostly peacefully, old regime structures remained largely intact, making it easy for the counter-revolution to gather momentum.

The era was one where the idea of revolution became delegitimised, even in Islamist and post-colonial discourse. This influenced the preference of reform and reluctance to take over sate power, and provided an opportunity for well-organised 'free-riders' to occupy centre stage. It is thus not possible to apply the radical revolutions analytical framework in this context, where the focus would be on the struggles within the new revolutionary regimes. The transition framework may not be suitable either, since its focus is on predominantly non-revolutionary shifts from authoritarian rule. However, the paradoxical nature of the Arab 'refo-lutions', as both revolutionary and pluralist, requires special treatment. With the revolutionaries being a peaceful (if influential) minority, unable to win elections or forcefully take power, the 'free-riders' came to dominate the scene. This could – and did – open the road to slide-back and counter-revolutionary regression. In the end, Bayat concludes, the revolutions that had astonished the world 'found their deepest legacies at the grassroots, where the new awareness and imagination among the subaltern marked the post-revolutionary trajectories with unknown possibilities'.

In Chapter 5, Hamid Dabashi finds the transition debate problematic on several levels. Its Eurocentric concepts and assumptions make the theories inadequate when accounting for developments elsewhere, a fact confirmed by the shock the Arab revolutions evoked and the challenge they posed to the very foundations of the dominant regime of knowledge production. Second, questions being asked (about whether Islam/Arab culture are compatible with democracy, etc.) are irrelevant and even offensive. Third, the models against which the absences and shortcomings of Arab democracy are measured are themselves in deep crisis today (from the oldest –the United States – to the largest – India), not forgetting Europe in between. It is enough to cite as an indictment of this discourse the designation of Israel, a settler colony as being 'the only democracy in the Middle East'.

For Dabashi, such claims are instances of Ernst Cassirer's point regarding the prevalence of 'mythical thinking' within modern Western political thought, especially on the state. To pursue superficial questions about democracy, transition, etc., is a pointless distraction amid this mystification. Rather, one should go straight to the point: the violent origins and function of the modern state, and the export of this model through the colonial and post-colonial diffusion of this model.

Building on Weber, Cassirer, Walter Benjamin and Agamben, Dabashi focuses on the state, its post-colonial version, as a point of concentrated violence that is doubly bereft of legitimacy. The myth of politics as a violence-free zone, inherited from the Greeks, is contradicted by the modern realities of the ubiquity of violence. This was even more so on the colonial periphery, where the violence tended to be naked, pure, undiluted and uncamouflaged by philosophical speculation. Remarkably, Western thought is oblivious to this shocking fact, which many – including critical thinkers like Agamben – do not even seem to notice, unless the victims happen to be white Europeans! This apparent mode of collective Freudian repression prompted African authors like Aimé Césaire to argue that a Hitler unconsciously inhabits every twentieth-century humanistic, Christian bourgeois. Dabashi adds that emergence of the terrorist organisation the Islamic State in Iraq and Syria (ISIS) as the mirror image of the dysfunctional, globalised, neo-liberal state, has equally exposed the presence of an 'ISIS' inside each and every modern state. In contrast, uprisings like the Arab Spring, Occupy Wall Street, etc., are signs of a corrective global reaction to the crisis of neo-liberalism and its deficiencies and contradictions. Shifting the focus in this direction is key to disentangling political science from its imperialist genealogy and Eurocentric straitjacket.

As discussed in many of the above chapters, the 'transition paradigm' has been challenged by theorists who are pessimistic about democratic outcomes. This and other factors shifted focus towards questions relating to the durability of authoritarian regimes and 'hybrid regimes' that appear to be on a transition to nowhere. In Chapter 6, Luai Ali explores a section of the literature on typologies of authoritarian regimes, and the claim that it provides a viable alternative to the transition paradigm in terms of explaining the outcomes of the Arab Spring.

A selected number of key typological theories are assessed in term of their application to abortive Arab transitions following the recent uprisings. Regimes are classified in these theories' terms of controlling elite (military, single party or personalist) modes of maintaining political power (hereditary or lineage-based succession, actual or potential use of military force and popular election) or mode of elite selection (military involvement, restrictions on political parties, legislative selections and executive selection). In each case, hypotheses are presented on the longevity of the regime type, likely mode of demise and projections about post-regime developments.

On testing the selected theories against their regime classifications and their predictions with relation to the Arab Spring, their explanatory power appeared limited on the internal dynamics of authoritarian regimes, the mode and causes of their collapse, and the outcomes of this collapse. This was due to rigidity in classifications and errors in coding. Some theories failed to include categories such as hybrid regimes.

In addition, these theories tended to ignore the interactive relationship of authoritarian regimes with society, in particular with regard to the challenge of stateness (the coherence of the state and commitment to the political community). Thus, the extent to which each regime type had affected the state-ness issue, whether inadvertently or through purposive social engineering, was overlooked. We see, for example, the clear effects of a lack of state coherence on the transition process in Yemen and Libya.

This does mean that the theories should be abandoned; but they need to be refined and strengthened. Closer attention needs to be paid to coding and accurate classification, something that cannot be done without a careful and judicious reading of the vast literature now being produced in Arabic about these states.

In Chapter 7, Abdel-Fattah Mady focuses on the input of various key political actors in various processes leading to the collapse of authoritarian Arab regimes, and subsequently on the post-2011 transitions, using Egypt and Tunisia as case studies. He identifies and analyses the core interests and strategies of key actors, first, during the revolutionary phase and, later, during the transition phase. The actors include regime components (leader(s), ruling party, military and security apparatus, the judiciary and other bureaucracies, and popular constituencies, etc.) and the opposition (made up mainly of youth movements, civil society activists, political parties and professional organisations, etc.). More interestingly and uniquely, Mady looks at the role of what he describes as 'concealed' or 'invisible' actors, who exerted inordinate influence on the process without explicitly assuming any responsibility. These were mainly state and old regime actors, but some opposition groups also figured. External actors have similarly exerted decisive influence on the transition, often secretively and via proxies.

Regimes and the mainly civil revolutionary actors dominated the revolutionary phase, while political parties and other traditional political actors dominated the transition phase. Mady follows Bayat in lumping old regime actors and the political parties dominating the transition together as 'bad guys': the former for obstructing the transition; the latter for 'stealing' and mismanaging it and failing to reach consensus or respond to the aspirations of the protesting masses. Thus, the reluctance or inability of revolutionary actors to take power is seen as a failure, as is the success of political parties to take centre stage in running the state, which is also seen as a treachery from 'free-riders'. We will come back to this point in the Conclusion.

In both Tunisia and Egypt the fragmentation engendered by the weakness of the parties and mutual mistrust often brought democracy perilously close to the brink. The polarisation was exacerbated, and exploited, by secretive actors, including so-called 'deep state' operatives (mainly security agencies and old regime partisans), often in collusion with foreign actors. Anti-democracy 'protests', organised by security agents and paid for by foreign powers, were instrumental in triggering and legitimising the June 2013 coup in Egypt, while assassinations of prominent politicians by unknown groups almost derailed Tunisian democracy. Within the opposition, the leadership of the Muslim Brotherhood was perceived to control the leading Islamist party, the Freedom and Justice Party, as a 'puppet'. This phenomenon, Mady argues, is another Arab specificity, together with high foreign influence at a time when democracy was facing a global crisis, exacerbated by the ascendancy of anti-democratic powers. One result was to breed cynicism and widen the gap between the political elite and the masses.

The mention of 'revolutionary actors' in the context of Arab revolutions refers mainly to the youth, seen as instrumental in the uprisings. However, a large section, if not the majority, of the youth activists consisted of women. The role of women activists has been even more visible in the second wave of Arab revolutions, in particular in Sudan, Lebanon, Algeria and Iraq. Nowhere has the influence of women been more pronounced and sustained than in Morocco. In Chapter 8, Tourya Essaoudi highlights this role in relation to democratisation and transition, focusing on what she calls 'elite' women activists in Morocco during the Arab Spring and the various phases of democratisation. The term 'elite' is used in more than one sense: referring to privileged upper-class women, with connections or access to the royal court; but mostly in the sense of intellectuals and leading civil and political activists.

Essaoudi's study stands out in not only registering the key role played by women in the democratisation process, but in emphasising the intellectual and political leadership dimensions of this role and its sustained character (having started over two decades before the revolutions). The vanguard of the female component of the Moroccan political elite had even significantly contributed to the formulation of the concept of democracy within their parties. This was achieved through the struggle to penetrate male-dominated centres of decision-making during the 1980s and 1990s, and putting feminist demands at the centre of the debate. Their argument was that democracy cannot exist in the absence of the basic principle of equality.

The Moroccan female vanguard deployed many strategies and tactics to penetrate the political system and present their demands, using the media, as well as international channels, to exert pressure at the national level. While only a small portion of emerging female elite engaged in political activism, the overall impact of this activism was significant. Women's groups intensified their coordinated campaigns, undeterred by the rise of (an admittedly moderate) the Islamist-led government. In fact, they succeeded in enlisting the support of an important section of female Islamist constituency to realise many of their key demands for women-friendly legislation. While there is still a long way go to achieve full equality, the feminist elite have contributed significantly to the practice and language of democratisation. They also pose some paradoxical challenges to existing theories of democratisation and elite roles.

Together with old regime stalwarts and their foreign backers, Islamists remained key, if not *the* key, actors during the transition. They were also the target of action by all other players. They were the dominant bloc where elections were held and key actors where it was not. In Chapter 9, Khalil Al-Anani examines the role of Islamists in the Arab transitions, and the role of religion in transitions generally. He starts by outlining key empirical facts: that Islamist demands and slogans did not figure during the uprisings, in spite of the visible presence of Islamists and observant religious individuals in the protests. Second, the strategies of Islamist actors were not dictated by religious considerations, but by contingent pragmatic motives. For example, the decision by the Muslim Brotherhood to field a presidential candidate remained contentious within the group, and the decision was made on the basis of political calculus. Similarly, the decisions of Salafi hard-liners to ally with the Muslim Brotherhood in the early phase of the transition, and later to support the military coup against it, were also based on crude political calculations.

Nevertheless, contentious religious issues did impact the way the transition progressed, in particular during the constitution-making process, when the role of religion in public life became a polarising issue. This was especially the case in Egypt, where hard-line Salafis kept outbidding the Brotherhood on Islamic issues. Secular rivals were also concerned about the threat that the dominance of Islamists posed to individual liberties. Sectarian and cross-religious rivalries and insecurities also played a role, as did the rise of violent extremist groups that used religious rhetoric.

Al-Anani follows Bishara and Mady in favourably comparing the Tunisian Islamists with their Egyptian counterparts, seeing their flexibility and restraint as key to the success of the transition in Tunisia, in contrast to the rigidity and intransigence of Egypt's Islamists. Conversely, the mode the transitions took had impacted the ideologies and strategies of Islamists. Where Islamists were peacefully integrated into the political process, as in Morocco and Tunisia, this contributed to their moderation and their positive role in the transition. Where they were repressed, as happened in Egypt, they fell back on hard-line positions. While most did not engage in violence, the overall atmosphere favoured rival extremist groups. Where the demise or threatened demise of regimes led to civil wars, even moderate Islamists joined the fight. But so did 'liberals' and various secular groups.

The role of Islamists in the transition must be viewed in the broader context relating to political polarisation and mutual mistrust between key actors. The resulting fragmentation was exploited by anti-democratic forces, supported in turn by external actors concerned about the 'Islamist threat'. The incompetence and short-sightedness of most political actors, Islamist and secular, was also a major factor.

The lessons drawn from the presumed impact of religion in post-Arab Spring politics takes us back to where we started: it is a metaphor for other fears and insecurities. Trumpeting imagined or exaggerated fears about 'Islamist hegemony' by counter-revolutionary actors is often an expression of fear of democracy and change. Anti-democratic regimes and forces also often ally themselves with the ultra-conservative Salafi Islamists, and use and abuse religious rhetoric too often. This confirms what many chapters in this book have demonstrated: the way to a successful transition is mutual reassurance between key actors.

Most previous chapters have emphasised the inordinate – and not always positive – role played by external actors on Arab politics. In Chapter 10, Marwan Kabalan brings this role into focus, arguing that the likelihood of a successful democratic transition diminishes in regional and international rivalry contexts. Here, revolutions and domestic instability invite external interventions, transforming domestically originating protest movements into instruments of geo-political conflict. Examining five case studies, Kabalan concludes that 'external factors acted as the independent variable par-excellence in rendering the transition from autocratic rule to democracy a failure'. Regional and international polarisation, and major power interests in the region, meant that few could be neutral towards political change in most countries of the region. In Syria, Libya and Yemen, foreign interventions transformed peaceful protests into protracted civil wars, thus extinguishing democratic hopes. In Bahrain, the popular protests were directly suppressed by a Saudi-led military intervention. In contrast, integration contexts provide incentives and channels of support for democratic transition. Transitions in southern and Eastern Europe demonstrated how important regional integration contexts are for facilitating and consolidating transitions. Even in Turkey, the desire to qualify for membership of the European Union (EU) has contributed significantly to political reform and democratisation. The absence (or mitigation) of regional rivalry contexts in these cases has made the transition process smooth and successful. In the Arab region, the reverse effect was the more prevalent tendency.

In Chapter 11, Omar Ashour and Dana El-Kurd build on previous findings in democratic transition literature to highlight the link between democratic consolidation and security sector reform (SSR). Such reform requires the ending of impunity for crimes perpetrated by security agents, and ensuring effective and meaningful democratic control of the military, police and intelligence establishments. The focus is on the (still largely unsuccessful) quest by Arab pro-change forces (both reformists and revolutionaries) to democratically control the security sector in the aftermath of the Arab Spring. Even the relative success story of Tunisia is still lagging when compared with the achievements of other SSR transitional processes outside the region. The chapter assesses several Arab SSR reform initiatives between 2011 and 2013 in comparison with other SSR processes elsewhere. Five variables that determine the trajectory of SSR processes are analysed: levels of political polarisation; levels of internal resistance within the security sector; levels of knowledge and capacities of reformists; levels of regional/international support; and the status of demobilisation, disarmament, de-radicalisation and reintegration (DDDR). The centrality of police and intelligence organs in Arab politics was evident during the revolutions and the subsequent period, given that it was in fact police brutality that spurred the revolutions in the first place. This role became even more prominent afterwards, raising important questions about underlying causes. The failure to democratise the security sector, and the way the military and intelligence organs gained even more power, requires a very close examination that goes beyond established wisdom in this regard. This chapter thus explores the security challenges that faced nascent democracies and how old regimes used their security network and power structures to influence, and in most cases, abort, the transition.

The chapter authors outline a number of challenges that confronted SSR in the Arab Spring countries, but conclude that the whole issue became redundant as the security sector and militarised actors moved in to take over the state, thus obviating the very objective of reform, which is to safeguard democracy. In all Arab Spring states, these three related factors led to continued and intensifying political polarisation; intensive international and regional intervention; and the failure to bring the security apparatus and other militarised actors (e.g., militias) under civilian control. Matters were made worse by the politicisation of the military in countries like Egypt, and the militarisation of politics in countries where protests turned into civil war, producing militias that turned into armed political parties.

The chapters in this volume have interrogated transition studies from several theoretical and empirical angles, using the recent Arab revolutionary experience as a starting point. Rather than treating the Arab case as an 'exception' to a predetermined norm, lessons from it are shown as being key to solving many riddles of democratic transitions. The arguments converge around the point that deeper reflections on theory from another perspective could reveal more relevant and universally applicable insights into the dynamics of political change. In this process, the Eurocentric transition 'paradigm' is stood on its head, with the 'exception' explaining the 'norm'.

To achieve this, authors engaged in a dual exercise: critically re-assessing theory, and thoughtfully re-examining empirical data, accepting nothing at face value. This process revealed that repeated testing of theory by bringing in more and more new cases could end up diluting theoretical claims to near trivialities. However, this does not devalue the contribution of transition studies, which made Comparative Politics what it is today. Colleagues also reflected on the penetrating light that the Arab surprise cast on the mysteries, genesis and trajectories of revolutionary action, and explored the how events here revealed and highlighted the complex dimensions of human solidarity as well as insecurity and fragility (as well as robustness) of conflicting and narratively constructed identities. The stories being circulated and promoted, whether real or invented, play a key role in these processes. Political actors, foreign and domestic, are revealed to be motivated by a search for security, without which coexistence and solidarity (essential for any democratic order) would prove elusive. Instances of political polarisation (sectarian, ethnic or religious/secular) that appear to be region- and culture-specific, and mysteriously unique to our world, are easily deciphered as products of deep insecurities that are often induced by the insecurities of external actors.

Here, the transition discourse is again stood on its head, as a main source of the democracy phobias haunting the region is revealed to originate mainly from outside it. The object here is not to shift blame or indulge in conspiracy theory fantasies. Rather, it is an invitation to sober reflections on the enduring and still living colonial legacy in this deeply penetrated region. Major convulsions rocking this region, as we indicated earlier (revolutions, wars, oil shocks, etc.) neither start nor end exclusively here. So studying them cannot be compartmentalised geographically or disciplinarily. One can see here that the Arab region appears unique and exceptional only if some important facts about political dynamics are neglected or distorted. Otherwise, it can be seen that the United States and Europe are as susceptible to authoritarianism as the Middle East if insecurity is heightened by circulating invented horror stories about foreign-originating threats.

2

DEMOCRATIC TRANSITION STUDIES: LESSONS FROM ANOTHER REGION

Azmi Bishara

What if 'Transitology' is Teleological?

Transitional phases of history are defined as such from the perspective of a periodisation schema which ascribes to them a transitional character. This necessitates a research approach that defines eras not by their content, but rather by what precedes and follows them. Nor is research on transition to democracy born from such a periodisation, but from a purpose, a telos: that is, to bring about democracy. Accordingly, the only people who define temporal periods as periods of democratic transition are researchers with a favourable view of democracy. Such an approach is thus criticised for being teleological. Its proponents concede this point and do not consider it a shortcoming.

Although they do not constitute a theory, democratic transition studies are serious enquiries into the experience of countries in Southern Europe, then of Latin America from the mid-1970s to the mid-1980s, and, finally, the experience of Eastern Europe up to the early 1990s.

Every new experience has reduced the number of general necessary conditions for democratic transition originally extracted from the earlier experiences. The importance of supporting factors inherent in particular sets of circumstances has consequently increased. These are numerous, unpredictable or contingent, and difficult to delimit. At best, it is possible to model them through induction into patterns, which may be the aim of studies in democratic transition. Something similar has happened to so-called 'consociational democracy theory', which also drew on the institutional experiences of specific countries seeking to avoid civil war between groups making up a political entity. However, rather than accounting for new cases, it was itself continuously modified by those new cases, which added new conditions and eliminated older ones. The weight of particular conditions also increased until practically no general conditions remained, except for the readiness of elites from different major ethnicities or cultural entities (or even political ideological segments turned into identities that split a nation vertically) to sharing power.

The expression 'transition to democracy' has no meaning in a context prior to transition from an authoritarian system (regardless of the type of authoritarianism) to a democratic system, except for those who see democracy as a desirable outcome. In this sense, studies of democratic transition are not simply works of comparative politics, but are formulated within a liberal democratic discourse. Researchers of relative prominence have stated this explicitly, including authors of studies that have since come to be considered classics in modernisation theory. This applies to authors from Joseph Schumpeter to Seymour Martin Lipset, and to later critics of modernisation theory and from later waves of theory – such as transitology – which have branched off from comparative politics.

Lipset, for example, in the conclusion of an article that he hoped would help modernisation theory to reinforce democracy,[1] writes: 'To aid men's actions in furthering democracy was in some measure Tocqueville's purpose in studying the operation of American democracy, and it remains perhaps the most important substantive intellectual task which students of politics can still set before themselves.'[2] Samuel Huntington, in his study 'How Countries Democratize', adds at the end of each section, dedicated to a specific kind of

[1] But his analysis of the conditions for the consolidation of democracy misled him into considering them to be the conditions of its emergence as well. Most criticism of his article by transitology theorists focused on this point.

[2] Seymour Martin Lipset, 'Some Social Requisites of Democracy: Economic Development and Political Legitimacy', *American Political Science Review* 53(1) (1959): 103.

transition from an authoritarian regime, a series of recommendations for what democrats should do in such cases.[3]

Guillermo O'Donnell writes about the democratic transition project that he oversaw with two colleagues in the 1980s: 'I am reminded . . . of our sense of moral and political engagement as we sought ways to help rid the world of authoritarian regimes that we had very good reasons to hate.'[4] In another article in defence of the project, he responds to criticisms of the 'transition paradigm' he produced,[5] and clarifies that the project produced no such paradigm. He states that he began researching with his colleagues at the end of the 1970s and the 1980s; that their work was not a response to the democratisation process in Latin America, but an aspiration for democratic transition; and that what distinguishes the authors in their four volumes is their commitment to an anti-authoritarian position; that emphasis on the political aspect of transition at the expense of socio-economic factors will contribute to the will to topple it. They find that the majority of the studies prominent during that period disincentivise democratisation. These studies state that it is necessary to wait a long time before considering democracy, since it requires structural (yes even cultural) preconditions: economic development, high income per capita, strong middle-class spread of education, no deep social cleavages and the emergence of a proper political culture. The writers, however, assume that political work directed towards a goal may be effective, and

[3] Samuel P. Huntington, 'How Countries Democratize', *Political Science Quarterly* 106(4) (1991/2): 579–616.

[4] Guillermo O'Donnell, 'Schmitter's Retrospective: A Few Dissenting Notes', *Journal of Democracy* 21(1) (2010): 29.

[5] I will not go into Carothers' article here, whose contention that the transition paradigm is now obsolete has recently been supported by a number of specialists in the Middle East, but suffice myself with saying that in fact it does not discuss transition studies themselves, but arbitrarily equated them with theoretical analyses by government and stage agencies and NGOs which have transformed them into a paradigm, while the studies themselves do not contain what he criticises. Thomas Carothers, 'The End of the Transition Paradigm', *Journal of Democracy* 13(1) (2002): 5–21. Cf. also O'Donnell's response in Guillermo O'Donnell, 'In Partial Defense of an Evanescent "Paradigm"', in Larry Diamond, Marc F. Plattner and Philip J. Costopoulos (eds), *Debates on Democratization* (Baltimore, MD: Johns Hopkins University Press, 2010), pp. 94–100. Originally published in 2002 as Guillermo O'Donnell, 'In Partial Defense of an Evanescent "Paradigm"', *Journal of Democracy* 13(3) (2002): 6–12.

that good analysis assists this work.[6] O'Donnell recognises that their work was politicised, but does not consider it to be a shortcoming.

According to Gerardo Munck, the difference between democratic transition studies and older approaches linked to modernisation is that they were less neutral, and intended to give direction to political action. In reality, modernisation theorists were not more neutral than their critics, who openly acknowledged their pro-democracy bias. As one prominent collaborator (Abraham Lowenthal) admitted, the research on transitions led by O'Donnell and Schmitter incorporated a component of 'thoughtful wishing'. Their project rejected structural determinism (which not only was not neutral, but in some cases justified the support of dictatorships during the Cold War), adopted democracy as a value and searched for realistic possibilities for its realisation.[7]

Lack of neutrality is not a problem if the researcher acknowledges it, and adopts an objective approach in his or her research. Neutrality is not a synonym of objectivity and it is to my mind a not a condition of scientific objectivity, because the latter pertains to the scientific method and not to the intentions of the researcher or the aims that the research serves. Bias is the general condition of the social sciences, and claiming neutrality does not equate to being scientific, while taking a position does not necessarily compromise scientific objectivity.

Lisa Anderson has argued against the excessive interest in the subject of transition in Arab states, given the absence of actual democratic transitions and the existence of more pressing issues. One of the most important reasons for this, in her view, is the commitment of many Western researchers to liberal democracy, as well as their links to US foreign policy agendas. Political science in the United States has, since its birth, been keen on studying democracy and its emergence. Traces of this have formed a hereditary part of its personality.[8] Well, Huntington (like many others) certainly did not put democracy in the developing world on his research agenda. He focused on

6 O'Donnell, 'In Partial Defense of an Evanescent "Paradigm"', p. 98.

7 Gerardo Munck, 'Democratic Theory after Transitions from Authoritarian Rule', *Perspectives on Politics* 9(2) (2011): 335.

8 Lisa Anderson, 'Searching where the Light Shines: Studying Democratization in the Middle East', *Annual Review of Political Science* 9(1) (2006): 205–7.

consolidating political regimes, even despotic ones, to tame modernisation's destructive effects including political mobilisation. In the spirit of the Cold War, alliances with despotic regimes were justified.

According to Anderson, the Middle East at the beginning of the twenty-first century was not interested in discussing the presidential or parliamentary system,[9] or even transition from authoritarianism to a democracy. Rather, concern was with issues relating to nation-building, identity formation, tribal and ethnic relations, the staying power of monarchies, the dynamism of the rentier economy, the emergence of unofficial grey economies, the role of the army in politics, and environments conducive to terrorism and rebellion.[10] After the events of 2011, however – and despite the failure of democratic transitions to take off (or even to start) in most Arab countries – today the matter is a pressing item on the agenda of social scientists specialising in Arab countries.

Anderson's criticism of artificial and selective research of phenomena that transition researchers see as confirming the reality of democratic transformation is a valid one. From another perspective, however, working towards realising democracy is not an obstacle to working on other issues. No researcher working on transition to democracy in Arab countries can bypass issues like tribes, sects, the army, simply on the grounds of a shift from modernisation theory and its structural conditions, in favour of the less stringent conditions of transition studies.[11] These *necessary* conditions are not *sufficient*, and the discussion of transition in the Arab World sets out from a concrete social reality, and must lead us to discussion of the issues above.

[9] The question is, of course, what does Anderson mean by the 'Middle East'? The oppositions in Tunis, Sudan, Algeria and even in Saudi Arabia have discussed these issues since the 1980s.

[10] Anderson, 'Searching where the Light Shines', p. 209.

[11] At the end of his article, Lipset casts the prerequisites he enumerated for a stable democracy as conditions for the foundation of democracy (Eurocentrism). These were: economic development and the legitimacy of the ruling system. Economic development encompasses industrialisation, urbanisation, high average education and continuous development of the wealth of society. These are also factors in the efficiency of the system as a whole. The degree of legitimacy, meanwhile, pertains to the political system's ability to generate and preserve the belief that existing institutions are the most appropriate for the society. The degree of legitimacy of contemporary democratic systems depends to a great extent on how they deal with and solve major issues that have historically divided society: Lipset, 'Some Social Requisites of Democracy', p. 86.

Most of the social sciences, if not all of them, emerged in the West as an answer to the need to understand transitions and transformations that stimulate thinking about what distinguishes the new realities from the old (from feudalism to capitalism, and from traditional society to modern society). Investigations focus on the specificity of socio-economic systems and their structure, and the relationship of structure to process, change and development. The problem in transferring the social sciences, which had emerged mostly in the West, to other regions in different historical phases lies in their ready-made terminology and concepts such as feudalism and capitalism, traditional society and modernity, class, community and society. We use the same hegemonic Western social-scientific terms and concepts to describe and analyse different phenomena. This usage reveals the limits of such concepts as analytical and explanatory tools. None of this negates the desire to make broader use of social-scientific methodologies and their experiences in the West. The challenge is not simply to critique these sciences, but to modify them or produce different concepts by theoretical contributions derived from studying the reality in other regions.

In any case, it is possible to benefit from these experiences, as long as we do not apply 'laws' of transition derived from claims these studies did not make in the first place. The generalisations these studies do make are in fact a group of acceptable theses that border on the intuitive. Likewise, their approach refutes the position that considers scientific objectivity and political and moral neutrality to be equivalent. This is especially useful in countries where, under conditions of despotism, such an equivalence usually transforms into taking the side of the status quo.

Research on transition to democracy in Arab countries requires studying the specific circumstances in a given country. Making use of research conducted in other countries does not mean turning their conclusions into laws to be applied in one's own country.

Schmitter's contention that this sub-discipline of comparative politics arrives at a group of universal assumptions and terms that can explain transformation from autocracy to democracy[12] will be challenged later in this

[12] Philippe C. Schmitter, 'Is it Safe for Transitologists and Consolidologists to Travel to the Middle East and North Africa?' Stanford University, 1995, available at: https://go.aws/2Yj4dVm, pp. 1–2, last accessed 30 April 2020.

chapter. The universalist claim put forward by 'transitology' (which makes very few generalisations anyway) is a source of tension with area studies. It is these claims of transitology, and not its teleology, that is its problem. Transitology, like other social sciences that emerged in Europe and the United States with universalist claims, consists of regional studies that have been used to produce generalisations within a framework of comparative politics. Western social sciences in general are regional studies with universalist conclusions, and must be subject to constant testing and critique. This does not underestimate their scientific rigour, because the test of a science is its methodology, as previously stated.

Transitions in Transitology

Different categorisations of transition studies are possible. Teorel and Goa named the modernist approach (functional or socio-structural, etc.) the institutionalist (including historical institutionalism and new institutionalism), the political economy and the strategic choice approach (transitology).[13] Transitology actually deals with critical junctures defined by historical institutionalism as phases in history, where structural factors are neutralised and human agency (political actors) determines the course of events. According to Bermeo, transition studies passed through three phases.[14] The first began with Dankwart A. Rustow's article on a dynamic model of democratic transition based on the Swedish experience.[15] The distinction this chapter makes between

[13] Sujian Guo, 'Democratic Transition: A Critical Overview', *Issues & Studies* 35(4) (1999): 134–5; Jan Teorell, *Determinants of Democratization: Explaining Regime Change in the World, 1972–2006* (Cambridge: Cambridge University Press, 2010), pp. 2–3.

[14] Nancy Bermeo, 'Rethinking Regime Change', *Comparative Politics* 22(3) (1990): 363.

[15] A modernist himself, as is clear from other pessimist writings concerning democracy in newly independent states. Dankwart A. Rustow, *A World of Nations: Problems of Political Modernization* (Washington, DC: Brookings Institution, 1973), p. 227. Remember that the case he chose for building his 'dynamic model' was Sweden: Dankwart A. Rustow, 'Transitions to Democracy: Toward a Dynamic Model', *Comparative Politics* 2(3) (1970): 337–63. Dankwart Rustow begins by defining what he calls the 'background condition', a single condition that can be summarised as consensus of main social and political forces on the unity and integrity of the state. This is not a matter of romantic tales, nor is the intention 'national identity' in the psychological sense of the word. Nor is it a unifying message for the nation. He means, simply, a situation where the majority of citizens in the state do not doubt their commitment to the political community to which they belong. The translation

a functional account of democracy and its self-reproduction as a stable system, on the one hand, and the historical conditions of its emergence, on the other, is, I believe, still important today. The second stage was inaugurated in the context of the so-called third wave of democratisation by the 1986 four-volume *Transitions from Authoritarian Rule*, edited by O'Donnell, Schmitter and Whitehead, with notable contributions from Adam Przeworski on the contingent emergence of democracy.[16] The third stage began with Alfred Stepan and Juan Linz's *Problems of Democratic Transition and Consolidation: Southern Europe, South America, and Post-Communist Europe*.[17] The two also contributed to the research in the second phase, adding to the Southern European and Latin American the experience of Eastern Europe.[18] In this last phase other approaches to transitions emerged that did not make use of the conclusions of the second.

During this same period, various studies were also produced on the crisis of authoritarianism in the socialist camp and the beginning of *perestroika* liberalisation at the end of the 1980s. This again brought modernisation theory and its structural approaches back into consideration, as the key to understanding the crisis of the socialist system was in terms of failed development and an inability to compete with Western economies.[19] That is to say, the authoritarian socialist bloc regimes had become a barrier to the aspirations of the middle class produced by the relative modernisation and higher average per capita income and education levels.

The majority of the transition studies on Eastern Europe affirmed that the collapse of Soviet hegemony played a central role in the change. This

'political community' is misguided, because the intention is the political entity, i.e., the state.

[16] Guillermo O'Donnell, Philippe C. Schmitter and Laurence Whitehead (eds), *Transitions from Authoritarian Rule*, 4 vols (Baltimore, MD: Johns Hopkins University Press, 1986).

[17] Juan J. Linz and Alfred Stepan, *Problems of Democratic Transition and Consolidation: Southern Europe, South America, and Post-Communist Europe* (Baltimore, MD: Johns Hopkins University Press, 1996).

[18] Alfred Stepan and Juan J. Linz, 'Democratization Theory and the "Arab Spring"', *Journal of Democracy* 24(2) (2013): 15–30.

[19] Jordan Gans-Morse, 'Searching for Transitologists: Contemporary Theories of Post-Communist Transitions and the Myth of a Dominant Paradigm', *Post-Soviet Affairs* 20(4) (2004): 326. See Lucian W. Pye, 'Political Science and the Crisis of Authoritarianism', *American Political Science Review* 84(1) (1990): 7.

highlighted the importance of external factors in comparison with transitions in Southern Europe and Latin America. Likewise, the first studies of democratic transition did not consider complex historical ethnic cleavages like those that existed in the Balkans and Eastern European countries, which stymie the development or consolidation of democracy. These enduring issues require solutions before or after the emergence of democracy, and sometimes as a condition thereof.

The reconsideration of structural factors does not elide the importance of political will. I do not agree with Jordan Gans-Morse that emphasis of the role of political elites is inappropriate for Eastern European cases, where popular movements, unions and subnational policies played a major role in the fall of the socialist states.[20] In my view, bargaining and settlements between the opposition and the old regime elites played an important role in bringing about peaceful change in both Hungary and Poland. This occurred against the background of reform from above in the Soviet Union due to internal economic and political structural problems and internationally aggravated by the arms race with the United States and the war in Afghanistan. No country in Eastern Europe failed to experience negotiations like these in some stage of transition. Even where there was no such discussion (e.g., Romania) the elites of the old regime played a fundamental role in impeding as well as encouraging the transition process after the fall of the president.

In their introduction to the book *The Breakdown of Democratic Regimes*, Linz and Stepan write that the fall of democracy cannot be explained only by beginning from structural tensions and pressures, because this means that its collapse was inevitable. Rather, it is the practices of individuals, particularly leaders, that should be looked at, and the behaviour of political elites, particularly the failure of democratic leadership, that should be emphasised.[21] This was also Valenzuela's approach in explaining the collapse of democracy in Chile in the early 1970s,[22] through analysis of the failure of Chilean left and

[20] Gans-Morse, 'Searching for Transitologists', p. 328.

[21] Juan J. Linz, 'The Breakdown of Democratic Regimes: Crisis, Breakdown, and Re-equilibration', in Juan Linz and Alfred Stepan (eds), *The Breakdown of Democratic Regimes* (Baltimore, MD: Johns Hopkins University Press, 1978), pp. 4–5, 10–11.

[22] Arturo Valenzuela, *The Breakdown of Democratic Regimes: Chile* (Baltimore, MD: Johns Hopkins University Press, 1978), p. xiii.

centre-right political forces in coping with the consequences of polarisation of radical forces from both extremes.

The contributors to the *Transitions from Authoritarian Rule* project began to focus on the behaviour of political elites in transitioning to democracy. In the fourth volume, *Tentative Conclusions about Uncertain Democracies*, the authors argue that the positions, leanings, calculations and agreements of elites determine the fate of democratic transitions. The main engine thereof is not necessarily economic, because the driving motivation of the leadership cannot be predicted by a structuralist approach; there are circumstances, for example, where preserving one's reputation becomes as important as fulfilling material desires.[23]

O'Donnell and Schmitter's emphasis on the role of political leadership and elite decision-making processes meant de-emphasising structural factors and, likewise, external international factors. All transitions they deal with begin with splits in the ruling elite for one reason or another, most importantly, reforms initiated from above. They emphasise readiness of the opposition to bargain and moderate its demands, accepting gradual change and deals with soft-liners in the regime.[24] This conclusion or advice appears in Linz's work, as well as those of modernisation theorists like Huntington and, before him, Lipset and Robert Dahl. All emphasise gradual change and middle-ground solutions as the key to understanding the emergence of democracy.[25]

Ten years after the publication of the results of the most famous democratic transition studies project, Schmitter summarised the fundamental conclusions of this branch of comparative politics into twelve 'generic reflections', most of them negative and open to other possibilities,[26] such

[23] Guillermo O'Donnell and Philippe Schmitter, 'Tentative Conclusions about Uncertain Democracies', in Guillermo O'Donnell, Philippe C. Schmitter and Laurence Whitehead (eds), *Transitions from Authoritarian Rule: Prospects for Democracy* (Baltimore, MD: Johns Hopkins University Press, 1986), 4:19, 25, 48; Albert Hirschman, *The Passions and the Interests: Political Arguments for Capitalism before Its Triumph* (Princeton, NJ: Princeton University Press, 1977). See also Giuseppe Di Palma, *To Craft Democracies: An Essay on Democratic Transitions* (Berkeley: University of California Press, 1990), ch. 4.

[24] Bermeo, 'Rethinking Regime Change', p. 362.

[25] See Robert Dahl, *Polyarchy: Participation and Opposition* (New Haven, CT: Yale University Press, 1971), pp. 15, 33–4, 216.

[26] Schmitter, 'Is it Safe for Transitologists and Consolidologists', pp. 7–14.

as, 'transitions from autocratic or authoritarian regimes can lead to diverse outcomes', including a return to autocracy, the creation of a mixed system, the survival of a non-consolidated democracy or the anchoring of democracy – that is, transition from an autocratic system may lead to anything. This is not, in fact, a useful generalisation.

If we omit these kinds of research outcomes that are easily accepted but are not very useful, such as 'it is possible (but not necessarily easy) to move from various types of autocracy to various types of democracy', we remain with the following general conclusions/reflections after a decade of research:

1. The point that 'the eventual outcome of democratisation depends in large measure on the sequence with which actors tackle the inevitable multiple transformations that are necessary'. This means that the factor of decision-making, the ordering of priorities in considering problems, choices of political elites or influential political actors acquire added significance.
2. Another point where Schmitter offers a specific, clear conclusion on a 'prerequisite' of democratic transition: 'it is certainly preferable, if not indispensable, that national identity and territorial boundaries be established before introducing reforms in political (or economic) institutions' or democratic transition. This is, in fact, Rustow's famous precondition concerning the state, which we have already shown to be the only one that has remained solid, in addition to the capacity of political elites to make accommodations, as a prerequisite of transition itself.

Schmitter adds some general reflections about regimes acquiring experience after every transition, and the emergence of an international civil society of NGOs etc., a terminology which I do not share.

There are few theoretical outcomes that could feature as useful generalisable statements.

Schmitter believes that the problems that confront democratic transition in the Arab World are the same as in other places, with less possibility of consolidating democracy, if it emerges, by comparison with the countries of Southern Europe.[27] The first part of this last idea pertains to demo-

[27] Ibid., p. 41.

cratic transition studies, while the second part is based on modernisation approach.

The component proven to be a necessary condition of democratic transformation is almost intuitive: that the identity of the political entity should be considered a settled question.[28] As the framework for political pluralism, peaceful transfer of power and the practice of civil freedoms, the state as a given is a *sine qua non* for any definition of democracy, not one of the conclusions of democratic transition theory. This question becomes specifically pressing for the Third World, where some states have yet to acquire sufficient legitimacy: their unity is questioned as a result of arbitrary colonial borders and/or due to regime failure in integrating social and political communities in the framework of citizenship.

Experience shows that if the unity of the state is imposed only from above by force or ideological mobilisation without a corresponding economic and social integration from below, then the destabilisation of the state itself becomes likely once the despot is overthrown, with the possible establishment of a new despotism in pursuit of stability. The outcome in multi-ethnic states could also be secession and creation of new states after ethnic cleansing, or the achievement of fragile 'consociationalist' solutions that could prevent civil war, but could also obstruct the emergence of a liberal democracy.

There are cases in Eastern Europe where the collapse of authoritarianism has led to the break-up of existing states. The fact that divisions in these cases preceded democracy in every state that experienced it, as in Yugoslavia or some former Soviet Union republics,[29] does not mean that democracy is impossible in multi-ethnic states.

[28] As the source of this idea, Rustow did not claim to be establishing a theory of democratic transition, but called his a 'dynamic model'.

[29] This does not mean that democracy was the goal of those calling for separation, nor that it was a driving motivation behind it or a reason thereof, contrary to what one could conclude from Michael Mann's work. See Michael Mann, *The Dark Side of Democracy: Explaining Ethnic Cleansing* (New York: Cambridge University Press, 2005). Dissolution of states is the result of the failure of authoritarian regimes in nation-building on citizenship and of rising ethnic nationalism. Indeed, the division and ethnic cleansing that accompanied the separation process in some cases created a nation-state with a legitimacy derived from the congruence between ethnic nationalism and the state, which makes it easier to form consensus on pluralism within this new state.

Arab Lessons

It is not a hasty generalisation to state that all Arab revolutions since 2011 began as wide popular uprisings (generally resulting from spontaneous anger), which moved on to demand the ouster of the regime. Undoubtedly, there was mutual influence within the shared linguistic and national (pan-Arab) framework and regional proximity. This might reinforce my scepticism concerning so-called 'international' waves of democratisation that were actually *regional* in nature.

These popular uprisings were referred to as revolutions, because they were broad-based, persistent popular movements that demanded regime change. The truth is that revolutions oust regimes and do not *demand* that they be ousted. The Arab revolutions, however, demanded that regimes be changed, actually by reforming themselves. They did not present ready alternatives, nor did they bring to the fore a leadership that intended to seize power. The Libyan case (where the regime fell after foreign intervention) notwithstanding, in the states where the revolution succeeded in overthrowing the head of the regime, the reins of government were taken over by personalities or institutions from inside the regime itself immediately after the dictator was toppled.

Among the states of the Arab revolutions, only Tunisia and Egypt went through a process of democratic transition (with a short, fragile experience in Libya). The transition in Egypt failed before the consolidation process could even begin, while Tunisia enjoyed relative success, but with no consolidation yet. Transition studies could benefit theoretically from these two experiences. The findings of transition studies do not, meanwhile, apply to Yemen, Libya or Syria (and likewise Bahrain if we consider what happened there to be a revolution, rather than simply a broad-based protest against sectarian discrimination).[30]

[30] What use is it to Arab researchers with democratic inclinations to understand, with assistance from previous studies on democratic transition in other countries, that revolution in their own country will not lead to democracy because of the nature of society, the existing system and the political culture of the elites? Does that exempt them from taking a position with the revolution against despotism? Will they stop and analyse that this revolution will not lead to democracy and, as such, there is no use in taking part in it? Or will they support

In Syria, a civilian revolution demanding reform and then the ouster of the regime transformed into a civil war for various reasons: (1) the closed authoritarian regime's fear of any reform and its determination to violently suppress its peaceful beginnings,[31] and its use of even more excessive, and continuously escalating, violence that was deployed when earlier attempts failed to deter demonstrators; (2) the sectarian affiliation of the security apparatus' leadership, and its linking of its fate to that of the head of the regime; (3) the regime's exploitation of religious minorities' fear of Islamist control; (4) the impact of the increasingly sectarian discourse of the armed opposition, and the ascendancy of extremist Islamist militias; and (5) the impact of regional power struggles and Iranian and Russian direct intervention.

The regime 'won'[32] this war after direct Iranian–Russian military intervention, using superior air power. The states referred to as the 'friends of the Syrian people' – particularly the United States – meanwhile, lost the will to support and arm the opposition for various reasons. The most important of these was the lack of will to get involved militarily after the Iraq experience of 2003, the uncertainty regarding alternatives to the regime, and the negative example of Libya after the revolution.

In Yemen, the revolution failed to oust the regime, settling instead for a power-sharing agreement sponsored by Gulf countries. The agreement culminated, after a UN-sponsored national dialogue, in a consensus over a federal democratic system, but was soon overtaken by a coup carried out by a political–sectarian movement (Houthis). Yemen was then transformed into a theatre of civil war, with the intervention of regional forces, first indirectly

it and spread the seeds of democratic discourse in its ranks through their pro-revolutionary stance? Social theory has no answers to this sort of question (nor, in my view, does philosophy). They are moral questions, but they are the important and definitive ones at specific historical crossroads.

31 Authoritarian despotic regimes like Syria or Libya suffer from the 'Gorbachev Syndrome', evinced in their conviction that any reform in a regime that rests on total control will lead to its collapse. Likewise, the Syrian regime learned from the Algerian experience that: (1) the regime tends to lose control of reform and is unable to control its dynamism; and (2) that despotic regimes must do anything necessary to present the conflict in terms of a stark choice between the regime and its Islamist adversary, thus forcing Western powers to choose the former.

32 There are no winners in the Syrian civil war, and the 'victorious' regime is not able to rule the broken, shattered country.

via support to the Houthis (Iran) and then directly (the military intervention by the Saudi–Emirati coalition).

For the last half century, oppressive Arab regimes have depended for survival to a great extent on the excessive harshness of their security apparatus, and on the closure of the public sphere. The Arab experience proves that it is impossible to topple a regime whose loyal army and security apparatus work together in crushing popular movements. Unless the army refuses to carry out orders, defects, or sides with the revolutionaries, it is not possible for any revolution to survive except by turning to arms or benefiting from external intervention. The people who take up arms are not the same people who demonstrate peacefully. Militarisation changes the character of the revolution and does not guarantee its success, as in any civil war.

After success in ousting the regime with the help of an external armed intervention, Libyans attempted to cross the threshold of democratic transition by holding parliamentary elections (on 7 July 2012). However, the process quickly stumbled on the difficulty of building state institutions, the hold of armed militias (with no democratic agenda) over political life and the obstruction of parliamentary life. The political polarisation took a regional form between eastern and western Libya after the legislative elections that followed (on 26 June 2014). Inasmuch as there is something of theoretical relevance here, it pertains to two points: (1) to national unity prerequisite, the Libyan experience adds that the issue is not simply one of loyalty and commitment to the polity. It is also about the viability of major state institutions, such as the army, the judiciary, etc., and the capacity for building them should they be absent. In the case of Libya, the dictator left behind a state that was lacking in institutions. The new elite struggled to build new ones – particularly a security apparatus and an army – in the presence of armed militias resistant to institutionalisation. Libyan patriotism has not (yet) managed to overcome the divisions of the armed formations, and (2) elections are not always a priority after overthrowing an authoritarian regime. When institutions are fragile and the elites divided, reaching consensus on building new institutions should be the priority. Elections in these cases are the fastest way to activate social and political divisions, and ultimately civil conflict. Nonetheless, elections are usually the first thing to occur to political actors, NGOs and international agencies after the ouster of an authoritarian regime.

We now turn to the two Arab experiences of democratic transition: Egypt and Tunisia. Although the Egyptian experience advanced quite far in the transition process (election of a parliament, the writing of a democratic constitution, election of a president, registration of parties, establishment of civil and political freedoms), it ended with a military coup against the elected president. This initiated a retreat from the democratic process to an authoritarian security regime more oppressive than the old one, albeit under an electoral cover. Organised opposition was either prosecuted or was effectively banned from taking part in the elections, freedoms were trampled upon and the media put under draconian control. In short, the ruling regime closed the public sphere. The Tunisian experience, in contrast, led to a – still fragile – liberal-democratic regime. The variation between these two similar cases that led to different outcomes makes them so useful in understanding the transition process, and testing and contributing to theory.

Going back to Rustow's model, we find an additional prerequisite of 'a conscious adoption of democratic rules' and habituation to them by both politicians and the electorate. The model also suggests 'a sequence from national unity as background, through struggle, compromise, and habituation, to democracy'.[33] Rustow reiterates that agreement on the procedures and rules of managing pluralism, competition and conflict takes place before agreement on political principles.[34] Przeworski continues Rustow's effort in this regard by considering agreement between elites on the rules of democracy to be a contingent result of conflict.[35]

The national unity precondition was met in both Egypt and Tunisia,

[33] Rustow, 'Transitions to Democracy', pp. 361–2.

[34] Ibid., p. 362.

[35] Przeworski's idea regarding transition can be summarised as follows: it begins with conflict and balance within the ruling elite, and between it and the opposition. A section of the ruling elite may arrive at the conviction that it is in their interest to initiate reform and seek a peaceful compromise. This may also take place, however, against the will of ruling forces after a defeat in war, as a result of an economic crisis or a victory of pro-democratic forces in elections the regime held as part of reforms. In such cases, the democratic transition process depends on the existence of elites in the opposition and the regime that are able to bargain, find compromise solutions, etc. Adam Przeworski, 'Democracy as a Contingent Outcome of Conflicts', in Jon Elster and Rune Slagstad (eds), *Constitutionalism and Democracy* (Cambridge: Cambridge University Press, 1988), pp. 59–80.

because in both cases the state is deeply rooted and has strong institutions. The historical roots of the modern polity go back to the end of the Ottoman era, with the construction of modern state institutions predating colonialism. Likewise, within the ideology of post-colonial regimes and their emphasis on state nationhood (*wataniyya*). This is well known in the case of Bourguiba, but it also applies in my view even to (Egyptian-led) Nasserite pan-Arabism, which did not contradict Egyptian nationalism, but in fact enhanced Egypt's standing in the Arab World.

It is also the case in both countries that change did not take place by reform from above. The reforms that were put in place three decades ago were ultimately understood as the regime's attempt to improve its image and enhance its survival, using economic liberalisation to form clientalist networks and benefit its social base.[36] Its political reforms did not lead to splits within the elite that follow a popular movement to deepen reforms according to transition studies. The capitalist class that emerged from top-down liberalisation in Egypt and Tunisia did not yearn for democracy; rather, it preferred a combination of political authoritarianism and economic liberalisation.

Furthermore, the revolutions of 2011 were not related to these reforms, but were triggered by oppressive and humiliating practices and deteriorating living conditions after a phase of rapid growth that raised expectations but widened the gap between rich and poor, and did not create enough job opportunities to rising numbers of young people, especially university graduates. I say this because researchers mechanically applying transitology – mistakenly – consider the 2011 revolutions in terms of a sequence of reform (beginning with Sadat's reforms, and creating divisions within the regime).[37] The 25 January 2011 revolution was not a popular revolution seeking to deepen a reform process that began in 1974–9 with Sadat's liberalisation policies (*infitah*) that were continued under Mubarak. Rather, it was the revolution that split the regime and not the reforms from above. The revolution ultimately launched a totally different track of reforms that could have led to democracy.

[36] Much has been written about this phenomenon. See, e.g., Steven Heydemann, 'Upgrading Authoritarianism in the Arab World', Saban Center for Middle East Policy at the Brookings Institution, Analysis Paper, No. 13, October 2007.

[37] Amel Ahmed and Giovanni Capoccia, 'The Study of Democratization and the Arab Spring', *Middle East Law and Governance* 6(1) (2014): 20.

Mubarak's regime was leaning, on the eve of the revolution, towards intensification of its repressive policies against the opposition. Corruption was widespread, and preparations were under way for the president's son to inherit his father's position. The rigging of the 2010 parliamentary elections was equally provocative, as was the widespread practice of torture in prisons. Popular mobilisation was encouraged by the revolutionary tremor from Tunisia's uprising, and National Police Day was chosen to protest police brutality. The Tunisian revolution made the possibility of ousting the head of the regime realistic. But the revolutionary youth gathered in 'Tahrir Square' did not seek to take control of government, calling instead for the president's resignation and making a series of demands that meant nothing less than the realisation of democracy. It beat on the walls of the regime from outside so that it would dispose of Mubarak and reform itself.

In both cases, the revolution succeeded in ousting the president within a relatively short period. Although both regimes used lethal force, with a comparatively high number of victims within a short duration,[38] they were less violent than the Syrian and Libyan cases. In Yemen, sections of the army defected, whereas in Tunisia and Egypt the commanders of both armies refused to carry out regime orders.

In both Egypt and Tunisia, the authoritarian regime had permitted a narrow margin of political action for 'safe' parties, while banning parties deemed threatening. There was a greater margin of freedom for the press, unions and societies in Egypt than in Tunisia. But in both cases – contrary to Syria and Libya – political parties and unions had a deep history. Similarly,

[38] In Egypt the official death toll reached 846 people and a further 6,467 were injured according to reports by both Human Rights Watch and Amnesty International: 'Egypt Rises: Killings, Detentions and Torture in the "25 January Revolution"', Amnesty International, 19 May 2011, p. 28; 'World Report 2012: Egypt – Events of 2011', Human Rights Watch, available at: http://bit.ly/2CyCR4r. In Tunisia, the UN put the number of those killed as high as 300 citizens, with 700 others injured. See Adéle Aranki Nassar, 'Events of the Tunisian Revolution: The Three First Years', Department of Peace and Conflict Research, Uppsala University, Report No. 108, p. 9, available at: https://bit.ly/2MeC9sm; Amna Guellali, 'Flawed Accountability: Shortcomings of Tunisia's Trials for Killings during the Uprising', Human Rights Watch Report, 12 January 2015, available at: https://bit.ly/2MaSWfX; 'Tunisia: Country Reports on Human Rights Practices for 2011 United States Department of State', Bureau of Democracy, Human Rights and Labor, available at: https://bit.ly/2N2cRD4, all last accessed 30 April 2020.

the margin of freedom for the activism was wider in Mubarak's Egypt than in Ben Ali's Tunisia.

What, then, was the difference? Why did we arrive at a democracy in Tunisia, while the process of democratic transition in Egypt was sharply cut off by a military coup on 3 July 2013?

Contrary to a widely held conviction, the difference cannot be accounted for by modernisation theory's propositions about indicators like wealth, size of middle class and level of education. Although, at first glance, the conditions for strengthening democracy in modernisation theory serve to account for the variation in the results of the transition in the two countries. Eva Bellin believes that the conditions that facilitate transition from an authoritarian regime to a democratic regime (she is careful not to say *necessary* conditions) are as follows: 'a certain level of economic development, higher levels of literacy, the existence of a sizeable middle class, and the absence of deep sectarian and/or ethnic cleavage . . . [and m]ost important of all is the existence of a credible elite that is committed to adopting the defining institutions of democracy: free and fair elections, universal suffrage, and guaranteed civil liberties'.[39] Many have the impression that these requisites of the modernisation theory were met in Tunisia to a greater extent than in Egypt. Our investigation reached a different conclusion: there is no significant difference between both countries in per capita income, spread of education and size of the middle class (see Tables 2.1–2.3 and Figures 2.1–2.5). So, the variation between both countries that may explain the different results of the transition process should be looked for elsewhere.

Anyway, structural factors have long-term effects that will influence the process of consolidation and sustainability, and not at critical junctures like revolutions and democratic transitions that neutralise their role. It would have been possible to utilise these factors had the *transition* succeeded in both countries, while the consolidation failed in Egypt. But it was not the consolidation but the second phase of transition that failed in Egypt and continues to advance in Tunisia.[40] I lean towards considering the transition

[39] Eva Bellin, 'Lessons from Jasmine and Nile Revolutions: Possibilities of Political Transformation in the Middle East?' *Middle East Brief – Brandeis University's Crown Center for Middle East Studies*, No. 50 (May 2011), p. 6.

[40] Transition to democracy according to this thesis passes through two major phases: (1) the

Table 2.1 Poverty headcount ratio at national poverty lines in Tunisia and Egypt, 1999–2015

	Tunisia (%)	Egypt (%)
1999	–	16.7
2000	25.4	–
2004	–	19.6
2005	23.1	–
2008	–	21.6
2010	20.5	25.2
2012	–	26.3
2015	15.2	27.8

Source: National poverty headcount ratio is the percentage of the population living below the national poverty line. National estimates are based on population-weighted subgroup estimates from household surveys. 'Poverty Headcount Ratio at National Poverty Lines (% of population) – Egypt, Arab Rep., Tunisia', World Bank Data, available at: http://bit.ly/2B6eozL, last accessed 30 April 2020.

Table 2.2 Income share held by lowest to highest subgroups in Tunisia and Egypt, 1985–2015

	Income share held by lowest 20%		Income share held by second 20%		Income share held by third 20%		Income share held by fourth 20%		Income share held by highest 20%	
	Tunisia	Egypt	Tunisia	Egypt	Tunisia	Egypt	Tunisia	Egypt	Tunisia	Egypt
1985	5.5	–	9.6	–	14.2	–	21.0	–	49.6	–
1990	5.9	8.7	10.4	12.5	15.3	16.3	22.1	21.4	46.3	41.1
1995	5.7	9.5	9.9	13.0	14.7	16.4	21.8	21.2	47.9	39.9
1999	–	8.9	–	12.5	–	15.8	–	20.7	–	42.1
2000	6.0	–	10.2	–	14.9	–	21.6	–	47.3	–
2004	–	9.0	–	12.7	–	16.1	–	20.8	–	41.4
2005	6.4	–	11.2	–	15.6	–	22.1	–	44.7	–
2008	–	9.2	–	13.0	–	16.2	–	20.8	–	40.8
2010	6.7	9.1	11.6	12.9	16.1	16.1	22.6	20.8	42.9	41.2
2012	–	9.5	–	13.3	–	16.4	–	21.0	–	39.8
2015	7.8	9.1	12.3	12.8	16.5	16.0	22.5	20.6	40.9	41.5

Sources: 'Tunisia: Income Share Held by Lowest 20%', World Bank Data, available at: https://bit.ly/2K8YngG; 'Tunisia: Income Share Held by Second 20%', World Bank Data, available at: https://bit.ly/2JYWDrd; 'Tunisia: Income Share Held by Third 20%', World Bank Data, available at: https://bit.ly/32TJY0i; 'Tunisia: Income Share Held by Fourth 20%', World Bank Data, available at: https://bit.ly/330wqjR; 'Tunisia: Income Share Held by Highest 20%', World Bank Data, available at: https://bit.ly/2Oq6ElL; 'Egypt, Arab Rep.: Income Share Held by Lowest 20%', World Bank Data, available at: https://bit.ly/3170BUF; 'Egypt, Arab Rep.: Income Share Held by Second 20%', World Bank Data, available at: https://bit.ly/2K9Yrwv; 'Egypt, Arab Rep.: Income Share Held by Third 20%', World Bank Data, available at: https://bit.ly/2Gxboj6; 'Egypt, Arab Rep.: Income Share Held by Fourth 20%', World Bank Data, available at: https://bit.ly/2YbcjAk; 'Egypt, Arab Rep.: Income Share Held by Highest 20%', World Bank Data, available at: https://bit.ly/2JXFTRe, all above last accessed 30 April 2020.

Table 2.3 The size of the middle class in Tunisia and Egypt, 1985–2015

	Tunisia	Egypt
1985	44.8	–
1990	47.8	50.2
1995	46.4	50.6
1999	–	49.0
2000	46.7	–
2004	–	49.6
2005	48.9	–
2008	–	50.0
2010	50.3	49.8
2012	–	50.7
2015	51.3	49.4

Sources: The middle class is measured as those whose income lies between the second, third and fourth quintiles (20%) of income distribution according to William Easterly's definition. The ratio of the middle class does not differ between Tunisia and Egypt even if we only include the third and fourth quintiles. See William Easterly, 'The Middle Class Consensus and Economic Development', *Journal of Economic Growth* 6(4) (2001): 317–35. See: United Nations Economic and Social Commission for Western Asia (ESCWA), *Arab Middle Class: Measurement and Role in Driving Change* (Beirut: United Nations, 2014), p. 29.

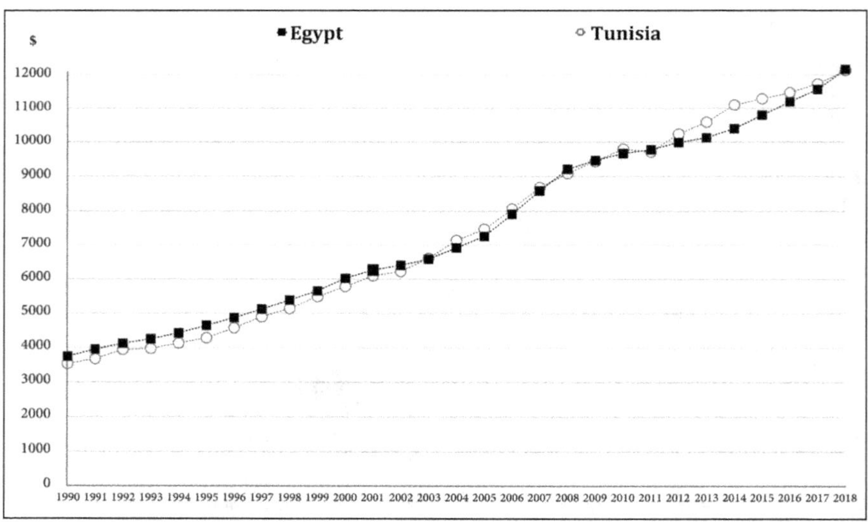

Figure 2.1 GNI per capita, PPP in Tunisia and Egypt, 1990–2018 (current international $)

Source: 'GNI per capita, PPP (current international $) – Tunisia and Egypt', World Bank Data, available at: http://bit.ly/2nlgrNd, last accessed 30 April 2020.

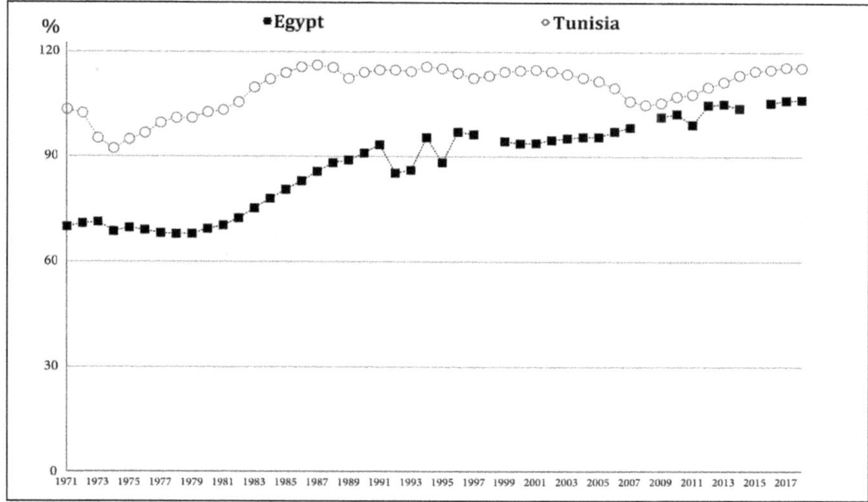

Figure 2.2 School enrolment: primary in Tunisia and Egypt, 1971–2018 (% gross)

Source: 'School Enrollment, Primary (% gross) – Tunisia and Egypt', World Bank Data, available at: http://bit.ly/336MOhW, last accessed 30 April 2020

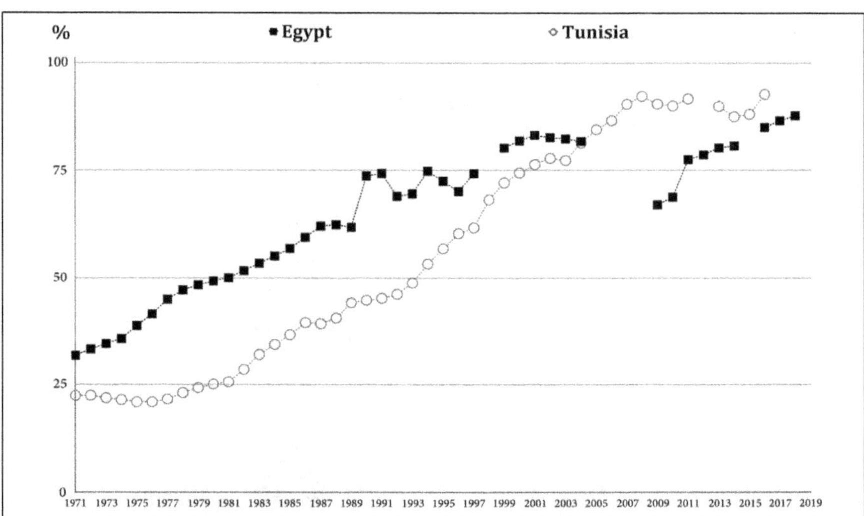

Figure 2.3 School enrolment: secondary in Tunisia and Egypt, 1971–2018 (% gross)

Source: 'School Enrollment, Secondary (% gross) – Tunisia and Egypt', World Bank Data, available at: http://bit.ly/332vPNB, last accessed 30 April 2020.

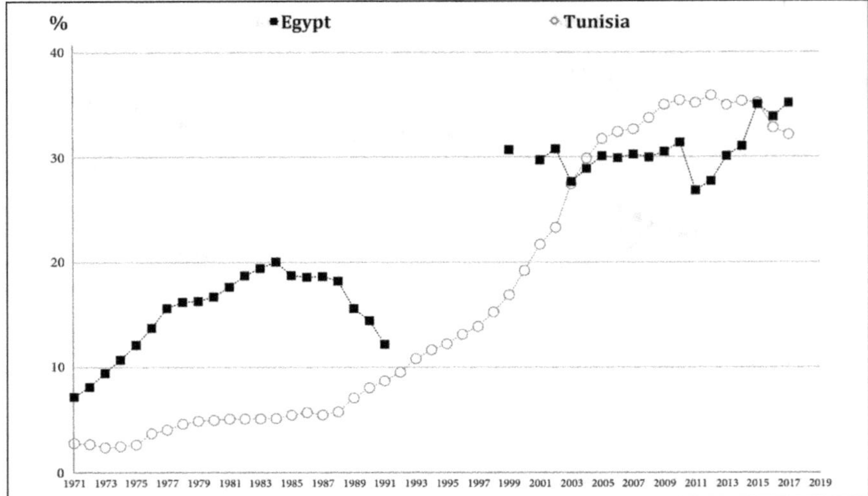

Figure 2.4 School enrolment: tertiary in Tunisia and Egypt, 1971–2017 (% gross)
Source: 'School Enrollment, Tertiary (% gross) – Tunisia and Egypt', World Bank Data, available at: http://bit.ly/30LbJ8T, last accessed 30 April 2020.

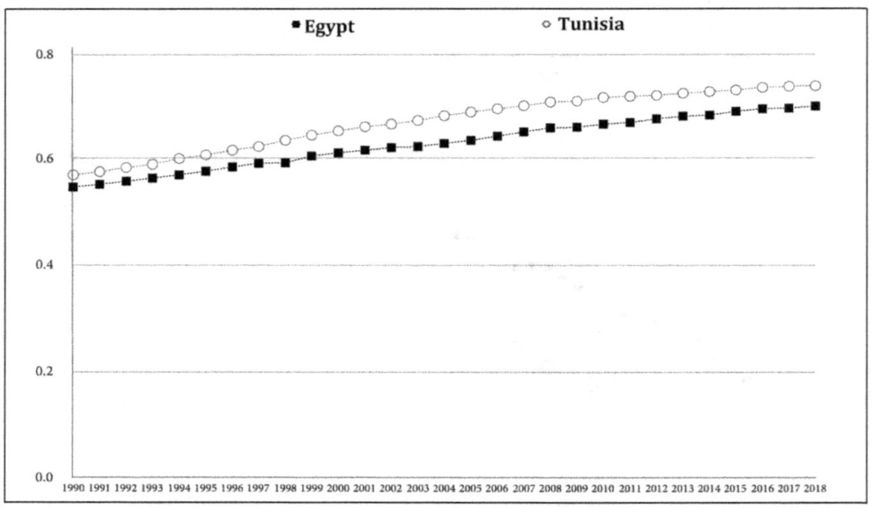

Figure 2.5 Human development indicators in Tunisia and Egypt, 1990–2018
Sources: 'Tunisia: Human Development Indicators', *Human Development Reports – United Nations Development Programme (UNDP)*, available at: http://bit.ly/2VBd3uj; 'Egypt: Human Development Indicators', *Human Development Reports – United Nations Development Programme (UNDP)*, available at: http://bit.ly/31c7nYA, all last accessed 30 April 2020.

process itself to have failed in Egypt, despite the holding of fair and free elections and the drafting of a democratic constitution. Elected institutions were constructed only for a very brief period in which they were not, practically, able to govern.

In this chapter, I argue that the difference between the Egyptian and Tunisian experiences in the transition period relates to other factors: (1) the role of the military, the extent of its politicisation and its ambitions; (2) the political elites' readiness to bargain and arrive at compromise solutions and joint commitment to the transition process; and (3) the varying roles and effect of external factors due to the difference in the geo-strategic importance of the two countries.

In democratic consolidation, on the other hand, economic factors such as growth and per capita income,[41] policies regarding distribution, and the government's capacity to deal with people's socio-economic problems and their rising expectations, are still decisive – perhaps *the* decisive factor – for the future of Tunisian democracy. Regional and international economic support for the new democracy may become crucial in this phase.

Learning from Difference: Egypt and Tunisia

In Tunisia the military declined to participate in the violent suppression of the revolutionary movement and, in practical terms, sided with the people. This forced the president to depend solely on the security forces, and in the end to leave the country on the advice, it seems, of his Republican Guard. In Egypt, too, the military refrained from violent suppression of the

ousting of the rulers of the old regime and agreement on the procedures for choosing new rulers; and (2) building the institutions of democracy. The attitudes of the new elites and the degree of their commitment to democracy become clear in the second phase.

41 Przeworski notes that Lipset's observation in 1960 that most developed countries are democracies and the majority of poor countries are dictatorships is true with regard to the sustainability of a democratic regime. But there is no greater possibility of the emergence of a democracy in a more developed country, but if democracy does emerge, regardless of the reasons for its emergence, it will be more capable of surviving in developing countries. Adam Przeworski, 'Capitalism, Development, and Democracy', *Brazilian Journal of Political Economy* 24(4) (2004): 488; Seymour M. Lipset, *Political Man* (Garden City, NY: Doubleday, 1960). For statistical details, see Adam Przeworski and Fernando Limongi, 'Modernization: Theories and Facts', *World Politics* 49(2) (1997): 155–83.

revolutionary movement, but did not side with the people. Rather, it sided with itself. The difference between the Egyptian and Tunisian military is that the former had a major political and internal security role. This was reduced by Sadat and Mubarak in favour of the presidency, which relied on the Ministry of the Interior and the security forces on issues of internal security, in a deal that granted the army autonomy in running its affairs. The Egyptian military seems to have maintained political ambitions, if not to rule directly, then to prevent the hereditary transfer of the presidential office planned by Mubarak, and thus to preserve its economic privileges threatened by economic neo-liberal policies associated with his son and probable heir. For these considerations, and for the preservation of the stability of the country, the military went beyond non-compliance with Mubarak's orders, issuing a series of public statements. These acts of rebellion against the regime paved the way to launch a coup against it,[42] placing the initiative in the hands of the military at the expense of both the regime and opposition. The military was thus able to manage at least the first part of this transition stage.

The small and non-politicised Tunisian military, in contrast, did not attempt to manage the transition. Rather, it returned to barracks, throwing the ball into the court of ruling and opposition civilian political elites. Under popular pressure, the ruling elite was forced to vacate power, and elections were held and won by the opposition after the dissolution of the ruling Democratic Constitutional Rally (RCD). The majority then formed a coalition that agreed on establishing a democratic system in the country.

In Egypt, the military was forced to hand power to civilians and set dates for parliamentary and presidential elections, but only after a failed attempt to enshrine its privileges as part of a package put to a referendum.[43] It became

[42] For details, see Azmi Bishara, *Thawrat Masr 2: Min al Thawra Ilā al- inqilāb* (*The Egyptian Revolution, Vol. II: From Revolution to Coup d'Etat*) (Beirut and Doha: Arab Centre for Research and Policy Studies, 2016), pp. 51–7. This two-volume work is also the source of my narrative in this chapter of the events of the Egyptian Revolution.

[43] On 30 October 2011, the Deputy Prime Minister for Political Development and Democratic Transition, Ali El Salmi, invited political parties and actors to discuss a document announcing the fundamental principles of the constitution of the modern state and the selection criteria for members of the Constituent Assembly that would draft a new constitution for the country. This was later dubbed the 'El Salmi Document'. Most of the political, civil and human rights movements rejected this document, mainly in protest against its provi-

clear that competition between opposition forces had driven them to reject even a temporary compromise with the military that would have allowed it to keep its privileges (even though every opposition force individually would have accepted such a compromise had the military supported them in rule).[44]

In the period that followed Mubarak's resignation, revolutionary legitimacy was stronger than the legitimacy of the military, and a real movement emerged against military rule.[45] When the parliamentary elections were held, the Islamist movements taken together (the Muslim Brotherhood's Freedom and Justice Party and the Nour Party) won a majority.[46] The Brotherhood alone could not win a majority in any country where elections were held, despite being at the height of its popularity, and in a period when other opposition parties were at their weakest. Unlike in Tunisia, no broad parliamentary coalitions were formed in Egypt due to its presidential system, and because the Islamists had a majority.

In Tunisia the Islamist party, Ennahda, did not win a majority of seats. It was thus forced into a coalition with two other (democratic secular) parties

sion for broad powers for the armed forces in internal affairs, while the Islamist forces, who were only interested in holding the elections as soon as possible, rejected any notion of 'supra-constitutional principles'. The forces opposed to the document claimed that accepting it would place the armed forces in a position to dictate to the Egyptian state. On 18 November 2011, a protest of millions of people was called to demand that the Military Council hand over power to civilians, abolish the document and dismiss El Salmi. The next day saw bloody confrontations between security forces and demonstrators in Muhammad Mahmoud Street, which resulted in many deaths and injuries. Confrontations continued until 25 November 2011. As a result of the protests, dates were set for the transfer of power to civilians. See Bishara, *Thawrat Masr 2*, pp. 192–202.

44 The Egyptian military has historically considered itself the 'Father of the Republic', setting itself apart from other elements of the political regime. The prevailing culture among the military elite is contemptuous of political parties, has a low opinion of the civilian administration, and believes that the military is more capable of discerning both the security needs and the interests of the country. See Bishara, *Thawrat Masr 2*, pp. 55, 79, 82.

45 See Bishara, *Thawrat Masr 2*, pp. 84–5, 173, 192–202, 211–13.

46 The Freedom and Justice Party won 44 per cent of the vote, but had no majority of seats in parliament. Al-Nour Party came second, with half this percentage. The two parties jointly held two-thirds of the seats in parliament. Liberal and leftist parties did not exceed 25 per cent of the seats. The Wafd Party alone won one-third of this figure, i.e., 8 per cent of the seats, while the parties whose base was the non-Islamist revolutionary youth sustained a marked defeat, having failed to organise and create a real popular base outside Tahrir Square.

from among many that emerged in the revolutionary atmosphere, but did not have strong popular bases. Nevertheless, this was an alliance between religious and secular forces that were in agreement on the establishment of a democratic system. In Egypt, meanwhile, no such alliance was formed, even though the electoral list supported by the Brotherhood included secular forces and independents. Surprised at the strength of the Salafist-Islamist representation in parliament, the Brotherhood chose to outbid them in deploying Islamist discourse, rather than forming an alliance with secular parties that were fellow revolutionaries. Likewise, the tendency favouring the exploitation of this opportunity to rule the country gradually came to prevail within the Brotherhood's own ranks. Political and electoral action was accompanied by an Islamist mobilisation behind Islamic slogans, which alarmed broad social demographics.

The Brotherhood's political thought has seen a development towards the adoption of some of the principles of democracy into its conceptual terminology, without abandoning its ideology and goals. Its language has changed and its vocabulary has been acclimatised to become closer to the terminology of democracy. This appears clearly in the reform documents and political and electoral programmes that it produced, particularly in 1994 through to the Freedom and Justice Party's (FJP) 2011 manifesto.

The FJP participated in the first parliamentary elections in Egypt after the January 2011 Revolution. It announced that it had no ambition to win a majority in parliament and establish control over it, recalling its slogan, 'participation not domination' (*musharaka la mughalaba*). It justified this by saying that the coming period would require the cooperation of parties and movements to build the new Egypt, and it thus sought to form a political and electoral 'democratic alliance' in which it included various secular political forces. The Brotherhood also affirmed that it would not seek to implement Sharia law, or limit individual rights and freedoms, as already stated in its 1994 declaration. The movement decided to contest half of the seats in parliament.[47] But mobilisation in the struggle for rule after the Revolution was accompanied by the marginalisation of the Islamists' democratic discourse in

[47] Khalil Al-Anani, *Inside the Muslim Brotherhood: Religion, Identity, and Politics* (Oxford: Oxford University Press, 2017), p. 156.

favour of their old slogans. After the parliamentary elections the Brotherhood competed with the Salafists, who explicitly rejected the principles of democracy. The FJP also changed its position on its earlier commitment not to contest the presidency in the first presidential elections, announcing a nominee on 7 April 2012. The candidate won the second round with a narrow majority (51.8 per cent) after receiving 24.7 per cent of the vote in the first. They decided to rule with this narrow majority in a transitional period where it was necessary to establish the widest possible national unity to protect the transition, given that the state bureaucracy was still loyal to the old regime and the army held its political ambitions.

This is one of the important lessons of the Egyptian case that can be generalised: it is not possible to rule a country where democratic traditions are not deeply rooted by a narrow majority, especially if the state apparatus is hostile to the elected government. If the state apparatus unites with a socially and economically strong opposition against it, an administration with a slim majority will not be able to rule with democratic instruments. It will either fall or must establish a broad coalition. To succeed in holding onto power without such a coalition can be achieved only by undemocratic means: liquidating enemies and/or purging the state apparatus. However, these steps do not usually lead to democracy, and, anyway, they were not possible in Egypt without confronting the army. If the aim is to consolidate democracy, there is no alternative to a broad national unity that imposes its legitimacy until the state apparatus undergoes gradual change, together with the military and the security apparatus' culture.

The elected president and the Brotherhood did not form alliances with rival secular forces. The latter were quick to establish their own alliances to oppose what they referred to as 'Brotherhood rule'. Every step taken by the president soon came to be explained as a step towards Ikhwanisation (from *Ikhwan*, Brotherhood) of the state. The opposition asked the judiciary to dissolve parliament and to impede the steps taken by the president. Only a small fraction of the judiciary supported the new regime, with the rest divided between previous regime loyalists and many fearful for the independence of the judiciary.[48]

[48] On 22 November 2012, President Morsi issued a Supplementary Constitutional Declaration

Every step taken by what might be considered the 'deep-state apparatus' to impede the rule of the elected president was welcomed by the secular opposition (including some elected to parliament on the Brotherhood list itself), even though its purpose was to obstruct democratisation. An implicit alliance between the two emerged to fight elected institutions. Moreover, a competition developed between the Brotherhood and its rivals to win the military over to their side – thus re-legitimising the military's political role at the expense of retreating revolutionary legitimacy.

Shared responsibility for the success of the transition was abandoned. The struggle produced an atmosphere of political chaos and disrupted state services during a period of high expectations, particularly as the protests against the previous regime had been driven by social demands. Fear of instability came together with disappointment that demands had not been met quickly enough. This instability was public opinion's greatest concern when a great part of the Egyptian people supported the army's coup on 3 July 2013. The security regime that emerged from the coup continuously reminded Egyptians of the chaos and lack of security, citing the examples of Libya and Syria. Chaos and insecurity may be the worst types of despotism as far as the daily life of citizens is concerned.

We must not ignore the effect of the instability of 'public morale' resulting from people's unfamiliarity with open, sometimes ruthless, political competition that can easily deteriorate into populism. This influenced Egypt and is still threatening the Tunisian experience. Parties do not bear in mind people's unfamiliarity with political pluralism when throwing around non-validated accusations of corruption, conspiracy etc., or spreading rumours. Media outlets that use their newly-granted freedoms irresponsibly to muckrake or incite also play a part. This includes media loyal to the old regime,

under which he abrogated the Constitutional Declaration published on 17 June 2012, which gave legislative powers to the Supreme Council of the Armed Forces, and protected its members from dismissal or any change in its membership. He also attempted to use this declaration to prevent the Constitutional Court from dissolving the Constituent Assembly (which was busy preparing the constitution), a plan that was already afoot in the court, and to dissolve the Shura Council after dissolving the People's Assembly in accordance with its method of besieging elected institutions. The Declaration stirred up much controversy and criticism, and a strong rejection from the secularist parties, which announced the formation of a new umbrella, the National Salvation Front.

with funding by anti-democratic regional powers. Broad demographics start to become alienated from the democratic process, and political parties in particular. A feeling that no one is better than anyone else, and that none are better than the old regime arises. In such cases, the military appears as a clean pair of hands, not part of the competition, and the media are hesitant to criticise it.

In Tunisia, a tripartite alliance (the troika) between the Ennahda Movement and two secularist parties, the Democratic Forum for Labour and Liberties (*Ettakatol*) and the Congress for the Republic (CPR), jointly ruled the country. An alliance began to form between secular opposition parties that had remained outside the coalition in order to bring it down, along with remnants of the former ruling party and elites that had rid themselves of Ben Ali, but not of the Bourguibist legacy. These parties started to warn of the risks of Ennahda taking control, Islamising the country, and changing the character of state and society and way of life (incomparably more secular than that of Egypt). Ennahda's allies did not enjoy a huge following that might have convinced secularist circles, and the Ennahda Party itself was the strongest within the coalition. The crisis worsened as news spread that Salafist youth (especially in universities) had attempted to impose religious strictures on campus life, and as extremism and terrorism developed on the edge of Tunisian society. Leaders of two secularist parties – Chokri Belaid and Mohamed Brahmi– were assassinated (in February and July 2013) under circumstances that still remain unclear. A broad movement emerged that might have led to chaos or a military coup had Ennahda held fast to majority rule, as did the Brotherhood in Egypt. This, however, is where the importance of the political choices of elites play a crucial role. Prominent here was the importance of the readiness of former opposition elites (Ennahda) and regime elites (that were organised into the Nidaa Tounes Party) to bargain and arrive at a compromise. Ennahda knew that it was not possible to rule by electoral weight alone, faced by a hostile media, uncooperative economic and political elites, and without support from the state apparatus.[49] It should also be

[49] According to Przeworski, negotiation between the old regime factions and the opposition becomes urgent for political forces after a crisis that rocks the existing system, or reform that splits it into extremists and moderates. Moderates in both the regime and opposition then realise that it is not possible for either one to defeat the other and the extremists at the

noted that the presence of broad organised social forces from the previous era came to the fore. Forces like the Tunisian General Labour Union were able to bring together political actors to protect the country's stability and prevent the return of the old regime. The Tunisian political elite in general, however, knew that there was no alternative to democracy, while Ennahda had already launched a campaign to convince the wider society that it would not use the state to dictate religion. This is what the Brotherhood in Egypt, whose discourse in the public sphere was entirely contrary to this, failed to do.[50]

After Ben Ali's fall, the old regime elite in Tunisia were prepared to arrive at compromise solutions until power was handed over after the general election. The opposition were also prepared to make compromises. In the second phase of transition, when it became clear that electoral majority was not sufficient to overcome deep discord and contentions that could split society and threaten the democratisation process, the political leaders of both camps were ready to compromise and share power. In Egypt after the Revolution, the opposition was not ready to accept any gradual reform, nor were its components prepared to suspend their disagreements to form a unified front against the old regime, which still controlled the institutions, security apparatus and bureaucracy of the state. Sensing their inability to secure a decisive victory, rival forces began to compete to win the military and old regime loyalists to their side. This re-legitimised the military's involvement in politics and offered it the opportunity to return to power.

Stepan and Linz explain the success of Islamists and secularists in reaching a compromise in Tunisia (as opposed to Egypt) with reference to a previ-

same time. Negotiations lead to agreement on settlements as a tactical choice to avoid total defeat, and they satisfy themselves with a share in power or the right to obtain power in future elections – not on the basis of democratic principles.

[50] Abdelwahab El-Affendi goes into expansive detail on the question of trust between political groups, distaste with the uncertainty surrounding the results of democracy, and the point that anxieties must be overcome by arriving at styles of mutual assurance. This process might begin with the larger Islamist movements putting together a very clear and widely accepted programme. See Abdelwahhab El-Affendi, 'The Challenges of Theorizing of the Transition towards the Unknown: Reflections on the outcomes of the Arab Revolutions and the Theories of Democratic Transition', in Idris LiKrini et al. (eds), *Phases of Historical Transition: The Outcome of the Arab Revolutions* (Beirut and Doha: Arab Centre for Research and Policy Studies, 2015), p. 163.

ous experience of a secular–Islamist alliance against Ben Ali. The reference is to the 18 October Committee of 2005. But it seems that the authors did not consider this example sufficiently, because some of the forces that formed an alliance against the Ben Ali regime on that committee were not the same forces that joined the coalition with Ennahda. Most of them, in fact, rejected any compromise with Ennahda after the Revolution. The real bargain took place after the second election and it was not between old oppositional forces who struggled against authoritarianism, but between Ennahda and secular pragmatic circles of the old ruling elites.

Throughout the period of competition and conflict between secular opposition and the ruling troika, parliamentarians from all parties continued working on the constitution together despite their differences. Thanks to this cooperation, the Tunisian parliament was able to produce a liberal democratic model constitution unlike any Arab states had ever seen – despite the opposition demonstrations against the government outside. In Egypt, by contrast, some opposition actors boycotted the drafting of the Egyptian constitution, even though it had taken place democratically and through open and lengthy discussions.

Finally, we come to the third factor: variation in geo-strategic importance between Egypt and Tunisia. Tunisia is geo-strategically less important than Egypt. But as it says in the Quran: 'And you may hate something, yet it is good for you' (Quran, 2:216). The geo-strategic marginality of Tunisia in comparison with Egypt saved it from intervention by regional powers opposed to democracy. In Egypt, on the other hand, reactionary regional forces that feared democratic transformation in the region saw a great danger in Egypt's transition to democracy. They recognised its influence and the possibility that the experience might pass to other countries by contagion or by example, or by direct influence on the stability of conservative regimes. I consider the regional effect more important than what Huntington referred to as 'global waves'.

Here I refer in particular to some Gulf states, such as Saudi Arabia and the UAE, which made use of their economic power and Arab ethnic and cultural commonality to intervene using their financial means against democratic transformations in other Arab countries. In Egypt, they played an active role in funding the counter-revolutionary media and movements calling for a military coup. There is also considerable evidence of intervention in Egypt to fund the military and the security forces directly, and of funding demonstrations and petitions to destabilise the transition process.[51] Similar attempts were made in Tunisia,[52] but not on the level seen by Egypt. Tunisia's distance from Israel has also contributed to the stability of the democratic process, reducing external support to potential coup plotters. Unlike Egypt, where Israel and its Western supporters fear any unexpected or unpredictable developments with regard to the peace agreements with Israel. There is a preference on the part of America – sometimes covert, sometimes overt – for the rule of strongmen they 'can make deals with' in Egypt and other states close to Israel, as people. Israeli officials still speak in glowing terms about the Syrian regime's respect for the separation of forces and ceasefire agreements in the Golan Heights since the 1973 war. With regular elections, however, there is no guarantee as to who may take power as a result. In addition to considering Israel's security a criterion for approaching any political development in Arab states, the West has moved from considering terrorism to be a product of despotism and seeking democracy as a solution during the neo-conservative period, to forming alliances *with* despotism on the grounds that fighting terrorism is the most important issue to the West.

[51] David Kirkpatrick has written about his experience in Egypt at the time of the coup, in particular during his time there as the *New York Times* Cairo bureau chief, about the role of Saudi Arabia and the UAE in supporting the coup by providing secret financial support for protests against the Morsi presidency, and how they managed to convince Washington that Morsi and the Brotherhood represented a threat to American interests. He notes statements made to him in an interview in early 2016 by the then the US Secretary of Defense, Chuck Hagel, to the effect that he was besieged by complaints about Morsi from the Israeli government, Saudi Arabia and the UAE. Neil Ketchley, an expert on Middle Eastern politics at King's College London, has likewise published a book on this subject – specifically, how the Egyptian military engineered the protests of 30 June 2013 in cooperation with the UAE and Saudi Arabia, detailing the financial support provided to leaders of *Tamarrod* (Rebellion) movement, based on a series of leaked voice recordings. See Neil Ketchley, *Egypt in a Time of Revolution: Contentious Politics and the Arab Spring* (Cambridge: Cambridge University Press, 2017); Neil Ketchley, 'How Egypt's Generals Used Street Protests to Stage a Coup', *Washington Post*, 3 July 2017, available at: https://wapo.st/2N57Rh9, last accessed 9 November 2018; David D. Kirkpatrick, 'The White House and the Strongman', *New York Times*, 27 July 2018, available at: https://nyti.ms/2O5KJf2, last accessed 11 September 2018.

[52] In the Tunisian case this information remains on the level of allegations as yet unsupported by definitive evidence.

Conclusions

For purposes of clarity and brevity, concluding remarks of this chapter are classified and condensed in three categories.

A: Concerning democratic transition studies:

1. It is possible to benefit from transition studies on the methodological level – which this chapter considers, like all social sciences, to be Area Studies with universal claims – to analyse democratic transition in other countries and regions, on the condition that the approach taken and their conclusions are not treated as a paradigm or laws ready to be applied to other countries.
2. Experience shows that the few 'universal' generalisations that can be derived from these studies concerning the consensus on the state and the importance of the political choices of elites and influential political actors maintain their relevance.
3. The researchers' bias towards democracy is not an obstacle. Democratic researchers in the Arab World can benefit from the analysis of democratic researchers in other areas and countries in service of transition to democracy.
4. The analysis of the cases of Tunisia and Egypt shows that requisites of modernisation theory do not explain success or failure of transition to democracy.
5. Critiquing modernisation theory in an approach to democratic transition does not mean not making use of it during the period of consolidation of democracy.

B: What follows are broad theoretical conclusions drawn from Arab case studies. These are not laws, nor do they constitute a paradigm.

1. If the military and repressive state apparatus are bound together and are ready to use ultimate force in the service of the regime, with no limits imposed on its use of force either internationally or locally, then it will be difficult to get rid of an authoritarian regime.

2. Revolution in circumstances of deep social and political divisions, such as sectarianism or tribalism, may stir deep-seated cleavages, so that group fears may become a tool in the hands of the authoritarian regime. Reform, it seems, is a more suitable way of effecting change in these circumstances.
3. Some authoritarian regimes consider any reform to threaten their existence, and will not opt for gradual reform. Nor would they provide any option for organised political action demanding reform. Under these regimes, spontaneous revolutions could erupt under certain political, local or regional conditions.
4. The absence or fragility of institutions frustrates the process of democratic transition after the authoritarian regime has been removed.

C:

1. The political ambition of the military threatens democratic transition. It cannot be confronted without national unity among civil forces opposed to military rule and/or ready for temporary compromise accepting some privileges for the military.
2. As stated in A2 above, choices made by political actors are of great importance during the transformation period. The democratic culture of political elites, or at the very least their willingness to bargain and come to compromise solutions, are decisive factors in transition.
3. It is impossible to rule a country during a transition period with a small majority, especially if the core state apparatus, supported by significant social sectors hostile to this ruling numerical majority, is opposed to democratic transformation. Here, building broader coalitions and national unity on the basis of consensus on democratic procedures become essential to the success of transition.
4. Polarisation between total ideological camps (such as a religious and a secular camp) could stymie democratic transition.
5. Political chaos and intensive social protests due to rising expectations after a revolution may generate a public mood of fear of uncertainty, and a desire for stability that, before the majority went through habituation to democratic pluralism, could threaten the transition process.
6. Regional factors are important in obstructing or supporting the demo-

cratic process, especially in the case of prevalent cultural commonalities. It becomes exceedingly important if the dominant regional states rely on financial power and can invest money in countries at times of transitions and uncertainties.

7. The less important a state is geo-strategically, the less the external factor will be in impeding democratic transformation.

3

THE MODERATION OF INSECURITY: STANDING THE EUROCENTRIC DEMOCRATIC TRANSITION PARADIGM ON ITS HEAD

Abdelwahab El-Affendi

The democratic transition debate embodies and evokes multiple paradoxes, starting with the challenge of deriving generalisable rules from processes characterised by inherent uncertainty and fluidity, amid shifting perceptions and expectations.[1] It is, as Sydney Tarrow put it, tantamount to 'aiming at a moving target'.[2] Paradoxical also are the persistent claims and critiques treating transition theory as the 'hegemonic paradigm', framing debates on major political transformations, even when evidence points to the contrary.[3] Nowhere is this paradox more salient than in the Middle East, a region that had remained on the margins of theoretical debates on democratisation, becoming instead a focus of 'a distinct sub-debate about the dynamics of authoritarian resilience'.[4]

1 Guillermo O'Donnell, 'Schmitter's Retrospective: A Few Dissenting Notes', *Journal of Democracy* 21(1) (2010): 29–32.

2 Sidney Tarrow, "'Aiming at a Moving Target': Social Science and the Recent Rebellions in Eastern Europe', *Political Science and Politics* 24(1) (1991): 12–20

3 Jordan Gans-Morse, 'Searching for Transitologists: Contemporary Theories of Post-Communist Transitions and the Myth of a Dominant Paradigm', *Post-Soviet Affairs* 20(4) (2004): 320–49.

4 Frédéric Volpi, 'Explaining (and Re-explaining) Political Change in the Middle East during the Arab Spring: Trajectories of Democratization and of Authoritarianism in the Maghreb', *Democratization* 20(6) (2013): 969–90 at 973; Raymond Hinnebusch, 'Authoritarian Persistence, Democratization Theory and the Middle East: An Overview and Critique', *Democratization* 13(3) (2006): 373–95 at 374

While the Arab revolutions temporarily destabilised existing frameworks and cast new light on the problematics of democratisation in the region, the problematic 'tribal' character of the debate persists, as does its apparent triviality. On the face of it, treating the democracy question in the region from the angle of how democracies emerge and falter is no different from examining it from the angle of the resilience of autocracies. Unless, of course, one is implicitly biased one way or another. The pioneers of the transition and democratisation theory usually did both, studying both the collapse of democracies and autocracies. The problem with authoritarian resilience focus is that it smacks of partiality to authoritarianism, either because they fear 'chaos' or worse, or because of belief in Middle Eastern 'exceptionalism'. The latter angle suffers (like the alternative recent appeal to 'contextualisation')[5] from a circularity regarding the causes, nature and alleged durability of the 'exception'. The same goes for the relevance of 'context'. Whether this be cultural/hereditary along Orientalist lines,[6] or structural/economic according to more sophisticated accounts,[7] the question remains: why here and nowhere else?

This refers back to Leonard Binder's point explored in the Introduction, regarding Latin American scholarship's pioneering contributions to transition theory in contrast to the meagre contributions of Middle Eastern Studies.

Binder's analysis betrays an implicit partiality to a Eurocentric vocabulary: failure to share the Western cultural and historical experience, and 'misgivings' about Western-led modernity, become self-explanatory determinants of theoretical impoverishment, as well as democratic lag. Other authors fault the transition discourse as an 'ill-fitting framework for understanding dynamics in the Middle East', blaming its adoption for the failure of Middle Eastern Studies to contribute to 'the development of general theory about democratization'.[8] Implicit (explicit?) in this argument is that there is a strong

[5] Sanford F. Schram, Bent Flyvbjerg and Todd Landman, 'Political Science: A Phronetic Approach', *New Political Science* 35(3) (2013): 359–72.

[6] Ernest Gellner, *Conditions of Liberty: Civil Society and Its Rivals* (London: Hamish Hamilton, 1994), p. 8.

[7] Lisa Anderson, 'Arab Democracy: Dismal Prospects', *World Policy Journal* 18(3) (2001): 55.

[8] Ibid.

reason why democracy should not be expected in the region or desired for it.

A Troubled 'Paradigm'?

In this chapter, we challenge this demo-scepticism by reclaiming and 'Arabising' the 'transition paradigm', showing not only its relevance to the Arab case, but the centrality of this case for a more advanced analytical framework. We build on the broader theoretical introduction in Chapter 2 above, and its tests of applicability to Arab politics, and move critically to challenge and further develop the basic theoretical framework. We do this by re-examining five key issues in the theory: uncertainty, moderation, regime type, consolidation and cultural specificity (especially with relation to Islamism and sectarianism), and the 'securitisation' of democracy. Finally, we propose a tentative theoretical proposal to the dilemmas posed by the paradigm that enhancing its wider applicability.

Despite sustained critiques of the democratic transition 'paradigm', it is difficult to contest Gerardo Munck's assertion that contemporary political science 'would be unimaginable' without it.[9] In fact, the very vehemence of the protests against its 'hegemony'[10] highlights its importance. The designation 'transition theory' (or 'transitology') refers to a loosely interconnected discourse within comparative politics, consisting mainly of deriving lessons and generalisations from the empirical examination of democratisation experiments. The label 'paradigm', however, comes mainly from critics, and is rarely espoused by practitioners. Donald L. Horowitz pointedly interjects that the discourse 'is not really a concept, and it certainly wasn't a paradigm'.[11]

The focal reference of this debate is Dankwart A. Rustow's seminal article, which dropped socio-economic prerequisites for democracy. For Rustow, the only indispensable 'background condition' for successful transitions is national unity (that the bulk of citizens should have 'no doubt or mental

[9] Gerardo Munck, 'Democratic Theory after Transitions from Authoritarian Rule', *Perspectives on Politics* 9(2) (2011): 355–75 at 333.

[10] Gans-Morse, 'Searching for Transitologists', pp. 320–49.

[11] Larry Diamond et al., 'Reconsidering the Transition Paradigm', *Journal of Democracy* 25(1) (2014): 89.

reservations as to which political community they belong to').[12] He cites Ivor Jennings' remark that 'the people cannot decide until somebody decides who the people are'.[13] The transition discourse henceforth focused mainly on 'elite dispositions, calculations and pacts'.[14] However, Rustow added another 'requisite': that the protagonists in a democratic game 'must represent well-entrenched forces (typically social classes), and the issues must have profound meaning to them'. This is necessary to weather the 'prolonged and inconclusive political struggle' accompanying democratisation.[15] This idea was further developed by Adam Przeworski in terms of democratisation being the 'contingent outcome of conflict', where much depended on actors' calculations about realistically achievable outcomes.[16] The moderation of opposition demands, together with mutual assurances, is also crucial for this process.[17] Successful transitions thus typically require a strong commitment to a given political community, dominated by cohesive blocs with authoritative representation and identifiable (moderate and flexible) demands. Intransigence or excessive fragmentation (or both) could be a significant hindrance to democratisation.

The acknowledged pioneers in this discourse were very modest about their 'tentative conclusions',[18] and wary of ambitious generalisations. Schmitter even called the exercise a 'pseudo-science'.[19] Critics, however, continue to

[12] Dankwart A. Rustow, 'Transitions to Democracy: Toward a Dynamic Model', *Comparative Politics* 2(3) (1970): 351; cf. Seymour Martin Lipset, 'Some Social Requisites of Democracy: Economic Development and Political Legitimacy', *American Political Science Review* 53(1) (1959): 69–105.

[13] Rustow, 'Transitions to Democracy', p. 351.

[14] Nancy Bermeo, 'Rethinking Regime Change', *Comparative Politics* 22(3) (1990): 361; cf. Lisa Anderson (ed.), *Transitions to Democracy* (New York: Columbia University Press, 1999), pp. 7–15.

[15] Rustow, 'Transitions to Democracy', p. 352.

[16] Adam Przeworski, 'Democracy as a Contingent Outcome of Conflicts', in Jon Elster and Rune Slagstad (eds), *Constitutionalism and Democracy* (Cambridge: Cambridge University Press, 1988), pp. 59–80; John Waterbury, 'Fortuitous By-Product', in Lisa Anderson (ed.), *Transitions to Democracy* (New York: Columbia University Press, 1999), pp. 200–17.

[17] Bermeo, 'Rethinking Regime Change', p. 363.

[18] Guillermo O'Donnell and Philippe Schmitter, *Tentative Conclusions about Uncertain Democracies* (Baltimore, MD: Johns Hopkins University Press, 1986).

[19] Philippe C. Schmitter, 'Reflections on "Transitology" – Before and After', in Daniel Brinks, Marcelo Leiras and Scott Mainwaring, *Reflections on Uneven Democracies: The Legacy of*

ascribe to it greater ambitions (and faults), deploring the model's 'teleological' assumptions regarding an automatic linear democratic progression from collapsed autocracies, and its apparent belief in the transformative power of elections.[20] Critics also questioned the dismissal of structural prerequisites, arguing that they remain highly relevant, despite the transitologists' 'wishful thinking'.[21] The latter disavowed any belief in the magical powers of elections, or in a universal linear course for transitions. However, they remained defiant in their dismissal of structural prerequisites. Otherwise, one would have had to accept that Latin America needed decades to become democratic.[22] As Bishara points out in Chapter 2, there is nothing wrong with the teleology embedded in the transition discourse, since preferences are inherent in all research, and do not necessarily entail lack of objectivity. One should add that an important factor in the collapse of autocracies is awareness of the democratic alternative.

The case of transition theory is complicated by the way the constitutive uncertainty of the process equally shapes social scientific knowledge, revealing the limitations of normal science (in the Kuhnian sense). While consciousness of this contingency entails limitations on scientific enquiry, it also enables a re-conceptualisation of theory construction as 'a form of political intervention'.[23] The paradox is that, while this 'activism' owes its existence to 'the irregular and unpredictable moment' of the transition, it simultaneously depends for its scientific credentials on 'the normal and regular processes whose existence it needed to assume'. Thus, it is forced to perpetually straddle the gap between the two: assuming uncertainty while claiming to predict definitive outcomes.[24]

Guillermo O'Donnell (Baltimore, MD: Johns Hopkins University Press, 2014), pp. 71–86.

20 Thomas Carothers, 'The End of the Transition Paradigm', *Journal of Democracy* 13(1) (2002): 5–21.

21 Ibid., pp. 15–17.

22 Guillermo A. O'Donnell, 'In Partial Defense of an Evanescent "Paradigm"', *Journal of Democracy* 13(3) (2002):6–12; Schmitter, 'Reflections on "Transitology"'.

23 Rafael Khachaturian, 'Uncertain Knowledge and Democratic Transitions: Revisiting O'Donnell and Schmitter's "Tentative Conclusions about Uncertain Democracies"', *Polity* 47(1) (2015): 114–39.

24 Khachaturian, 'Uncertain Knowledge and Democratic Transitions', p. 130; see also pp. 125–7 on Machiavelli as inspiration.

We can conclude from the above that the transition discourse is a deliberately interactive approach to knowledge, proactively questioning and reshaping existing theory, while exerting significant influence on both scholarship and political practice.

Beyond Eurocentrism

Critiques of the transition 'paradigm' often dwell on its Eurocentric genealogy and limitations,[25] a problem that leading transitologists readily acknowledge.[26] The theory's decidedly Eurocentric focus (and the related implicit 'end of history' rationale) had deep roots reflected in both the historiography and pantheon of modern democratic theory. Valiant attempts to set the historiographical record straight, such as John Keane's recent history,[27] remain preliminary exercises in exploratory 'archaeology', with limited impact. However, many critiques seeking to unmask this 'provincialism' tend to reproduce it under new guises.[28] The narratives of modernity are intimately interwoven into the hegemonic vocabulary and its 'universalisation' through colonial expansion and integrative globalisation. That is why modern knowledge, as exemplified in the social sciences, is 'not just a way of grasping modernity in thought, or recognising and registering the changes it brought about, but has been a force in bringing about the changes that it catalogues and characterises'.[29]

[25] Laurence Whitehead, 'Maghreb, European Neighbour, or, Barbary Coast, "Constructivism in North Africa"', *Journal of North African Studies* 20(5) (2015): 691–701.

[26] Alfred Stepan and Juan J. Linz, 'Democratization Theory and the "Arab Spring"', *Journal of Democracy* 24(2) (2013): 15–30. The pioneering work of O'Donnell and his colleagues focused on transitions in southern Europe and Latin America, while Stepan and Linz's work added transitions in post-Communist Eastern Europe. See Guillermo O'Donnell, Philippe C. Schmitter and Laurence Whitehead (eds), *Transitions from Authoritarian Rule: Comparative Perspectives*, 4 vols (Baltimore, MD: Johns Hopkins University Press, 1986); Juan J. Linz and Alfred Stepan, *Problems of Democratic Transition and Consolidation: Southern Europe, South America, and Post-Communist Europe* (Baltimore, MD: John Hopkins University Press, 1996).

[27] John Keane, *The Life and Death of Democracy* (London: Simon & Schuster, 2009).

[28] Zeynep Gülşah Çapan, 'Enacting the International/ Reproducing Eurocentrism', *Contexto Internacional* 39(3) (2017): 655–72.

[29] Sanjay Seth, 'Is Thinking with "Modernity" Eurocentric?' *Cultural Sociology* 10(3) (2016: 385–98 at 395. See also Anne-Charlotte Martineau, 'Overcoming Eurocentrism? Global History and the Oxford Handbook of the History of International Law', *European Journal of International Law* 25(1) (2014): 329–36.

Concerns about the Eurocentric bias of the theory and its hegemonic vocabulary could be neutralised if the Western political experience is taken as just another set of case studies in a comparative perspective, and the findings consciously posited as a provisional/'provincial' starting point. One must start somewhere. Theorists like Stepan sought to address these flaws through a critique of liberalism's 'secular bias', together with a dismissal of Huntington's claim regarding democracy's exclusive origins in Western 'Christian civilisation'.[30] In his important history of democracy, John Keane has also highlighted the role of religion as a crucial component in all major steps in the 'life of democracy'.[31] However, Stepan's recipe for a 'twin toleration' between religion and democratic politics still privileges a liberal conception of democracy that trumps religion. For here it is (the liberally delineated) citizens' rights that set the limits of religious freedoms for minorities and majorities alike, ruling out by default any alternative to liberalism.[32]

Again, this liberal bias is not a problem if critically interrogated. It is certainly preferable to some condescending critiques of liberal transition theory that presume the unreadiness for (unworthiness of?) democratisation. Such perspectives denounce academic interest in democratisation in these societies as misguided 'parochialism', reflecting political science's 'disciplinary bias', and/or its subservience to American foreign policy.[33]

In this chapter, we seek to stand Eurocentrism on its head (to paraphrase Marx on Hegel) by highlighting the universal relevance of other experiences. Arab 'exceptionalism' will be shown as easily explicable in terms of universal concerns and conditions, such as insecurity and complexity: a larger number of factors, in more unique and specific combinations, including an exceptional level of external input, tends to generate high levels of uncertainty, mistrust and insecurity. The problem with transitology's provincialism is

[30] Alfred C. Stepan, 'Religion, Democracy, and the "Twin Tolerations"', *Journal of Democracy* 11(4) (2000): 37–57; Alfred Stepan, 'Tunisia's Transition and the Twin Tolerations', *Journal of Democracy* 23(2) (2012): 89–103; Stepan and Linz, 'Democratization Theory and the "Arab Spring"'.

[31] Keane, *The Life and Death of Democracy*.

[32] Stepan and Linz, 'Democratization Theory and the "Arab Spring"', p. 17.

[33] Lisa Anderson, 'Searching Where the Light Shines: Studying Democratization in the Middle East', *Annual Review of Political Science* 9(1) (2006): 205–7 at 209.

precisely to miss such key variables, resulting in the failure to evolve generalisable regularities. In thus responding to Binder's challenge, we contend that the Arab experience can provide an explanatory paradigm accounting for the erosion of democracy in other regions, including the West, where rising populism and extremism are destabilising 'established' democracies by heightening perceptions of insecurity.

We start by exploring the impact of the uncertainty inherent in the transition, a process that is by definition an interregnum between a dying old regime and the birth of a new one. In this 'transition' the rules, practices and expectations associated with the old system falter, while the emerging order has yet to take shape.[34] Taking this dimension of uncertainty seriously entails factoring in the (fast shifting) expectations of actors, and the significant impact of this fluidity on actors' responses and choices.[35] Then we tackle the serious challenges facing the demand of 'moderation' and the related convergence of positions among rivals on the Arab scene. We then look at the unique regime type that continues to thrive in this region, consolidating itself in bizarre and grotesques forms in the post-Spring era, with no little help from outside actors, who also behave along similar patterns to acquire some of its repulsive characteristics. This is one more reason to study the Arab case with great care. Then follows an exploration of supposedly indigenous impediments to democratic consolidation, where the uncertainty and contingency of transition are supposed to give way to more sedate politics, permitting 'structural' factors (the economy, former regime type, ethnic/sectarian polarisation, etc.) to regain importance.[36] The recent Arab experience highlights the challenges facing consolidation in the face of scepticism (from both theoreticians and policymakers) about prospects for democratisation. Contrary to claims by critics of the 'transition paradigm', the enthusiasm among theoreticians is far

[34] O'Donnell and Schmitter, *Tentative Conclusions*, p. 6.

[35] A. Schedler, 'Taking Uncertainty Seriously: The Blurred Boundaries of Democratic Transition and Consolidation', *Democratization* 8(4) (2001): 6.

[36] David J. Galbreath, 'Securitizing Democracy and Democratic Security: A Reflection on Democratization Studies', *Democracy and Security* 8(1) (2012): 28–42; Philippe C. Schmitter, 'Some Basic Assumptions about the Consolidation of Democracy', in Takashi Inoguchi, Edward Newman and John Keane (eds), *The Changing Nature of Democracy* (Tokyo: United Nations Publications, 1998), pp. 23–36.

from general, in contrast to the diligence of anti-democracy actors, including a multiplicity of outside actors, in both undermining democracy and sustaining (costly) autocratic regimes. Too many actors and interests see democracy as a threat, and their insecurity translates into active interventionism and endemic instability. As shown in many chapters in this book, external actors, including key figures in the Obama administration, saw democracy in Egypt as a threat, and encouraged the military coup there.[37] The 'securitisation of democracy' thus becomes another key variable.

We conclude by examining the reality and consequences of the securitisation of democracy as a result of all the above factors.

Rethinking Uncertainty in Transitions

Uncertainty, deemed by Schmitter and O'Donnel as a defining feature of transitions,[38] is a paradoxical feature of the transition process, as noted earlier. Adam Przeworski sees it as inherent in democracy's subjection of all interests to uncertainty, thus depriving authoritarian regimes of intervention mechanisms against 'undesirable' political outcomes.[39] A defining feature of the democratic process is that it is neither wholly predictable, nor totally controlled by one specific actor.[40]

Scott Mainwaring counters that autocratic regimes offer even less certainty, given the absence of checks and balances.[41] One could add that democracy's desirability stems from its core claim as a system where everyone is a winner (even when one loses). The guarantees of full and equal participation for all citizens offer protection against severely adverse outcomes. The rule-

[37] See David D. Kirkpatrick, *Into the Hands of the Soldiers: Freedom and Chaos in Egypt and the Middle East* (New York: Penguin, 2019)

[38] O'Donnell and Schmitter, *Tentative Conclusions*, p. 3.

[39] Adam Przeworski, 'Some Problems in the Study of the Transition to Democracy', in Guillermo O'Donnell, Philippe C. Schmitter and Laurence Whitehead (eds), *Transitions from Authoritarian Rule: Comparative Perspectives*, 4 vols (Baltimore, MD: Johns Hopkins University Press, 1986), pp. 47–63.

[40] Gerard Alexander, 'Institutionalized Uncertainty, the Rule of Law, and the Sources of Democratic Stability', *Comparative Political Studies* 35(10) (2002): 1145–70 at 1146–50.

[41] Scott Mainwaring, 'Transitions to Democracy and Democratic Consolidation: Theoretical and Comparative Issues', University of Notre Dame, Helen Kellogg Institute for International Studies, November 1989, available at: https://bit.ly/3aMweao, last accessed 30 April 2020.

of-law dimension additionally ensures that losing elections does not mean losing basic rights or individual and group security. 'It is the very nature of democratic decision making that renders substantive outcomes relatively predictable.'[42]

Even Przeworski's formula of '*institutionalised* uncertainty', indicates 'controlled' (or 'bounded') uncertainty.[43] In this instance, the predictability of the rule of law (in contrast to the arbitrariness of non-democratic systems) is not the opposite of 'institutionalised uncertainty', but the other side of that coin. For while uncertainty is inherent in the freedom to organise, contest and change one's mind, this freedom is protected (and restricted) by law to safeguard basic rights and shared values. To achieve this, a minimal consensus is essential to mitigate the negative impact of political polarisation and mutual mistrust.

Uncertainty is confronted not just as a practical challenge facing political actors; nor merely as a theoretical challenge facing observers grappling with this unpredictability and its consequences. It also enables the interactive/interventionist dimension of the work of pro-democracy theoreticians, including their 'thoughtful wishing'.[44] This knowledge could also be used by anti-democracy actors for reverse engineering: destroying civil society, undermining national solidarity and eliminating the public sphere. At a metatheoretical level, the nature of knowledge being sought or produced, and the epistemological and conceptual challenges involved, are impacted and shaped by this interactive loop. Seminal events (such as the Arab Spring or the revolutions of 1989) force a radical rethink of theoretical assumptions and expectations, even occasioning a Kuhnian paradigm shift. Theoretical elaborations in turn impact political practice, which in turn affects future theorisation, while highlighting the paradoxicality of scientific claims.

42 Alexander, 'Institutionalized Uncertainty', p. 1149.

43 Philippe C. Schmitter and Terry Lynn Karl, 'What Democracy Is . . . and Is Not', *Journal of Democracy* 2(3) (1991): p. 82.

44 'Thoughtful wishing' (as opposed to 'wishful thinking'), was, in spite of its conscious interventionist inclinations of its proponent, described by some of them as 'a normatively generated inquiry that was scholarly, empirically based, deliberate and rigorous in its methods'. See Cynthia J. Arnson and Abraham F. Lowenthal, 'Preface', in Guillermo O'Donnell and Philippe C. Schmitter (eds), *Transitions from Authoritarian Rule: Tentative Conclusions about Uncertain Democracies* (Baltimore, MD: John Hopkins University Press, 2013), p. viii.

Uncertainty heightens insecurity, thus endangering democracy, which cannot function, *pace* Robert Dahl, where electoral outcomes pose fundamental threats to 'very highly ranked values' of key actors. This is especially the case in societies divided into large groups that fear the victory of rivals,[45] thus confirming Rustow's above point on the indispensability of national unity. To address this challenge, additional institutional safeguards are needed to mitigate polarisation. These include devolution and/or complex, multi-layered electoral processes, multiculturalist concessions, robust courts and multiple levels of decision making, etc.[46] Democracies are usually more suited to addressing deep divisions than any alternative, but they need more elaborate devices to help stabilise them.[47]

Intense conflicts accompanying democratisation (as in Yugoslavia) may not thus be a mere coincidence, but inherent in the insecurities generated by the democratisation process itself.[48] Michael Mann links democratisation, and the distinctly modern phenomenon of politicised nationalism, to genocide and ethnic cleansing. If democracy means rule of the 'people', narrowly defined in ethno-nationalist terms, then for the people to rule its own state, 'outsiders' must be removed (by obtaining independence, autonomy, mass expulsions, etc.). The resulting 'perversion of modern aspirations to democracy and the nation-state' would entail sacrificing 'the kind of citizen diversity that is central to democracy'.[49] Critics contend that the problem is with 'majoritarianism', or failed democracy, rather than democracy as such. Mann himself refined his thesis by blaming democratisation (i.e., transitions), rather than democracy, for the mass violence.[50]

In a related early warning about possible conflictual outcomes of the

[45] Robert Dahl, *A Preface to Democratic Theory* (Chicago, IL: University of Chicago Press, 2006), pp. 97–8.

[46] Donald L. Horowitz, 'Democracy in Divided Societies', *Journal of Democracy* 4(4) (1993): 18–38.

[47] Nathan Glazer, 'Democracy and Deep Divides', *Journal of Democracy* 21(2) (2010): 19.

[48] Jeffrey C. Isaac, *Democracy in Dark Times* (Ithaca, NY: Cornell University Press, 1998), pp. 187–96.

[49] Michael Mann, *The Dark Side of Democracy: Explaining Ethnic Cleansing* (Cambridge: Cambridge University Press, 2005), p. 3.

[50] Daniel Conversi, 'Demo-skepticism and Genocide', *Political Studies Review* 4(3) (2006): 258.

Arab revolutions of 2011, Azmi Bishara acknowledges that revolutions have a tendency to produce 'disasters and ethnic cleansing'. However, they could also be internationalist, as was the case in Europe's nineteenth-century democratic revolutions, when Giuseppe Mazini participated in several European revolutions, convinced of the compatibility of each people's specific mission with the universal human mission.[51] In the Arab case, the actual existence of a shared 'Arab identity' could temper the centrifugal tendencies generated by conflicting representation claims and rival liberation projects. Sufficient evidence of this cohesive Arab identity is evident in the galvanising impact on the Arab World of the Tunisian revolution, passing, as it did, 'like an electric current through an Arab body that was weak, but highly conductive of concerns and hopes' (unlike others, such as the Indonesian one of 1998).[52]

It is indeed the case that revolutions can forge new collective identities of 'citizens' and 'democrats', as happened in the myriad revolutionary squares of the Arab Spring. Just as the French and American revolutions forged new national identities through the revolutionary process itself, the Arab revolutions displayed and constructed new national identities. This was symbolised by displaying the national flag to downplay old and new schisms (religious, sectarian, ideological, political, class, etc.). The 'revolutionary' identity became the primary one, as actors embraced each other in the squares, repeating scenes we have seen in earlier revolutions (1919 in Egypt, the Algerian war of liberation, the Palestinian struggle, etc.).[53] In contrast, the counter-revolutions sought to deliberately divide and fragment nations, generating high levels of 'induced insecurities'.[54] The newly circulated narrative depicts the shift in solidarities from co-revolutionaries who were ready to die to defend you in Tahrir Square from the mortal enemy, the military whose snipers were targeting everyone in the square, to the split which saw

[51] Azmi Bishara, *Fi al-Thawra wa 'l-Qābliyya li 'l-Thawrah* (*On Revolution and Susceptibility to Revolution*) (Doha: Arab Centre for Research and Policy Studies, 2012), pp. 72–3.

[52] Ibid., pp. 77–9.

[53] Abdelwahab El-Affendi, 'Constituting Liberty, Healing the Nation: Revolutionary Identity Creation in the Arab World's Delayed 1989', *Third World Quarterly* 32(7) (2011): 1255–71.

[54] Abdelwahab El-Affendi, 'Overcoming Induced Insecurities: Stabilising Arab Democracies after the Spring', in Ibrahim Elbadawi and Samir Makdisi (eds), *Democratic Transitions in the Arab World* (Cambridge: Cambridge University Press, 2017), pp. 75–104.

some revolutionaries side with the military to protect themselves from their former co-revolutionaries.

To sum up, the uncertainty inherent in the transition process offers opportunities and challenges for both theorists and political actors. In the context of democratic evolutions, the challenges are already framed within narratives of democratic solidarity, mutual trust and shared democratic expectations. This should lead to the institutionalisation of this uncertainty through mutual guarantees for core values and interests, and imaginative forms of constitutional accommodation. Democracy's point of strength stems from this 'institutionalised uncertainty', where sufficient flexibility permits the accommodation of changing demands, while pacts and constitutional guarantees offer protection for the fundamental values and basic interests of key players. But both theoreticians and actors could do the opposite: contribute to narratives of mistrust that undermine democratic solidarity and spread mistrust and fear. But sometimes this could be hard work!

The Question of Moderation

This links to the issue of 'moderation', a key feature of successful transitions (and a maxim of transition theory). The transition 'paradigm' not only foregrounded 'moderation'; it embodied it in the political and intellectual biographies of its key theoretical protagonists. As Khachaturian notes, the 'conversion' experienced by O'Donnell and Schmitter from adherence to dependency theory and similar radical propositions was crucial for evolving their theories. Key here was their radical shift during the 1970s towards 'a microanalysis of political elites and an emphasis on the autonomy of political outcomes from structural determinants'. This in turn 'dovetailed with the [Western] foreign policy establishment's traditional goal of "promoting democratic elites that would be moderate, respectful of capitalistic interests, and pro-American"'. Such policies required the emergence of 'a moderate, professional, and non-threatening conception of democratization'.[55] The transitologists were happy to oblige.

[55] Khachaturian, 'Uncertain Knowledge and Democratic Transitions', pp. 114–39. See also Nicolas Guilhot, *The Democracy Makers: Human Rights and the Politics of Global Order* (New York: Columbia University Press, 2005), pp. 137–54.

Does this label the 'transition paradigm' as the theoretical framework for capitulation to the dominant international interests that tended to prefer certainty and stability to democracy? Nancy Bermeo sums up the 'moderation argument' as the claim that 'too much popular mobilization and too much pressure from below can spoil the chances for democracy', especially pressure of the 'extremist' kind.[56] She cites various versions of the argument (Terry Karl, Myron Weiner, Samuel Huntington, Robert Dahl, Daniel Levine and Juan Linz, and Larry Diamond, among others) that 'popular participation sometimes harms rather than enhances democratization'. Successful transitions are usually conservative, where the traditional ruling classes retain a significant share of power, with minimal popular mass action or pressure from the radical left, helped by a 'docile' working class.[57]

It is true that only with the weakening of radical trends, and the 'compacting of the political spectrum', have the dominant conservative establishments begun to find democracy less threatening.[58] Democracies tended, in any case, to reflect existing power imbalances, and only a marked reduction in threats to the prevalent order would induce those holding the levers of social power to tolerate pluralism and power-sharing. Here, institutional safeguards were not deemed sufficient, but extra-institutional assurances were also needed, including 'the stable compacting of political spectrums', as exhibited in the 'gradual diminishing of policy differences between left and right'.[59] As happened in Latin America with the defeat of armed insurgencies, improved economies and leftist 'moderation', the 'costs of democratisation' for the dominant elite began to decrease substantially.[60]

Both the collapse of democracies in inter-war Europe and post-war Latin America, and their subsequent restoration, could thus be explained with reference to one factor: the quest by dominant political and economic interests for certainty and security. In this regard, the consolidation of (liberal) democracy

[56] Nancy Bermeo, 'Myths of Moderation: Confrontation and Conflict during Democratic Transitions', *Comparative Politics* 29(3) (1997): 305–22.

[57] Bermeo, 'Myths of Moderation', pp. 305–6.

[58] Alexander, 'Institutionalized Uncertainty', p. 1167.

[59] Gerard Alexander, 'Institutions, Path Dependence, and Democratic Consolidation', *Journal of Theoretical Politics* 13(3) (2001): 265.

[60] Mainwaring, 'Transitions to Democracy and Democratic Consolidation', p. 28.

has gone hand in hand with the consolidation of capitalism and the weakening of anti-capitalist dissent. The process also included the incorporation of class and cultural dissidents, the weakening and 'domestication', even virtual capitulation, of major radical tendencies. Thus, in Europe the radical left was displaced by social democrats, and later by even more centrist parties, not to mention the emergence (and eventual meltdown) of Eurocommunism. Radical groups within African American communities were also marginalised in favour of 'moderates', while the retreat and 'moderation' of the radical left in Latin America, together with significant improvement in the economies, became the main impetus behind democratisation. Similar processes unfolded in Africa and Asia.

However, Bermeo also points to counter-evidence from the transitions in Portugal, Spain and several Latin American countries, where radicalism, and even violence, failed to derail the transition, contrary to predictions by O'Donnell and Schmitter's key threats to transitions by 'extremist' actions or positions (including threats to the military hierarchy, the territorial integrity of the nation-state, the country's key international alliances, or capitalist property rights). While Bermeo concludes that moderation is 'not a prerequisite for the construction of democracy', she still restates the 'moderation argument' in a new form. Starting from Dahl's point on the increased likelihood of democratisation proportionate to the rise in the cost of suppressing opposition, she argues that sections of the governing elite might choose democratisation, not only despite, but *because of*, apparent 'extremist' risks and threats. The elites in Portugal and Spain saw in democratisation the best strategy to contain 'extremism' while re-legitimising the existing order.[61] This tended to reproduce the same result of moderation as virtual capitulation by the opposition. For the contention is not about 'extremism' being a challenge to democratisation, but about how to contain it: through suppression or co-optation? 'Extremism' is, of course, in the eye of the beholder. At various stages, movements like feminism, working-class activism and civil rights agitation, were deemed threatening 'extremism'.

Moderation is thus both relative and contextual. Radical liberation organisations like South Africa's ANC and the PLO in Palestine were

[61] Bermeo, 'Myths of Moderation', p. 315

regarded as terror groups, but their leaders later became heroes who won Noble peace prizes, because contexts changed. More radical groups emerged, and the leaders were needed to avert bigger threats. However, 'moderation' could be a problem. The PLO's deal with Israel made the Palestinians worse off, as happened with earlier attempts in South Africa to segregate blacks into 'Bantustans'. In Turkey, to be considered 'moderate' Islamists had earlier to compromise with anti-democratic hegemonic secular forces, thus skewing the whole system in a non-democratic direction.[62] In this regard, moderation in Syria today would be submitting to a genocidal regime.

'Moderation', interpreted as the minimising of threats from extra-systemic challengers is crucial for inducing the ruling elite to share power with a wider section of the population. This might lead to a rapprochement in the positions, but also reflects the existing power balance, at least temporarily, in the favour of powers that be.

On the face of it, this might sound disturbing: democracy can be achieved only when those fighting for equality and inclusion virtually capitulate to the hegemonic order. However, even a nominally inclusive political process usually takes on a life of its own, moving progressively towards more genuine inclusion. Examples abound, including the inclusion of the working class, women and minorities. The acceptance of capitalism led to important social change, including the application of moderate socialist reforms and the establishment of the welfare state.

Regime Types: From 'Black Hole State' to the 'Blackwater State'

The designation 'extremist' depends on the orientation of the regime and its ruling elite. While positing regime disintegration as its starting point, most transition theories still hold that the outgoing regime type and related legacy matter for transitions.[63] Linz and Stepan distinguish four non-democratic regime types: totalitarian (eliminating pluralism and engaging in intensive mobilisation); post-totalitarian (relaxing control and mobilisation, and accepting some limits on its powers); authoritarian (with limited political

[62] Murat Somer, 'Moderation of Religious and Secular Politics: A Country's "Centre" and Democratization', *Democratization* 21(2) (2014): 244–67.

[63] Munck, 'Democratic Theory after Transitions from Authoritarian Rule', pp. 355–75.

pluralism but substantial economic pluralism); and sultanistic (with personal control of all areas of the state, and a 'high fusion of the public and the private').[64] An authoritarian regime might thus leave behind a functioning state, market, civil society and a rudimentary political society. However, where the rule of law and political pluralism had been absent or weak (as in totalitarian or sultanistic regimes) not much infrastructure exists on which to build.[65]

In the application of their theory to Arab Spring countries, Stepan and Linz make three important additional points. First, secularism is not necessary for democratisation; second, regimes in these countries are mainly sultanistic, with some (Syria and Libya) more sultanistic than others; and, third, the character of some post-Spring regimes (such as that of Egypt under Morsi), may make it necessary to specify a new regime type: authoritarian–democratic hybrid.[66] Additional regime categories posited by theorists included 'illiberal democracies' (as in Iran),[67] or 'political grey zones', where such category may jostle with other types of 'qualified democracies' that had been labelled 'semi-democracy, formal democracy, electoral democracy, façade democracy, pseudo-democracy, weak democracy, partial democracy, illiberal democracy, and virtual democracy'.[68] The term 'defective democracy' has also been used.[69]

The question of regime type will be tackled in more detail in Chapter 6 of this volume. But here we want to re-visit the 2004 *Arab Human Development Report*'s concept of the 'black hole state', which features a constantly expanding zone of state influence, linked to a fast-shrinking power centre. The regime, nominally controlled by a dynasty or a ruling party, tends to progressively concentrate power in the hands of a small clique of confidants around the individual ruler and his immediate family. The model is a hybrid between sultanism and totalitarianism (with additional features from authoritarian-

[64] Linz and Stepan, *Problems of Democratic Transition*, ch. 3.

[65] Ibid., ch. 4.

[66] Stepan and Linz, 'Democratization Theory and the "Arab Spring"', pp. 15–30.

[67] Fareed Zakaria, 'The Rise of Illiberal Democracy', *Foreign Affairs* 76(6) (1997): 22–43.

[68] Carothers, 'The End of the Transition Paradigm', pp. 9–10.

[69] Wolfgang Merkel and Aurel Croissant, 'Conclusion: Good and Defective Democracies', *Democratization* 11(5) (2004): 199–213.

ism). It is totalitarian in its ideological militancy and aggressive drive to maximise social control. Additionally, unlike 'classical' sultanism (such as Bokassa's in the Central African Republic or Haiti under the Duvaliers), its rule is neither purely whimsical nor chaotic. Coherent state institutions do exist, in the form of an extremely efficient, well-funded and relatively institutionalised repressive apparatus. Relying on corruption and brute force, it also benefits from plausible levels of ideological religious/sectarian legitimation ('resistance' to imperialism or foreign enemies, fighting religious or political extremism, protecting against 'sectarian' enemies, upholding religious orthodoxy and tradition, etc.). It is thus not entirely accurate to describe these institutions as 'patrimonial', in the sense of being predatory, self-interested and based on 'primordial' ties, while lacking rule-governing behaviour or meritocracy.[70] In fact, its security institutions are perversely 'professional' and result-oriented. When 'patrimonial' considerations get in the way of efficiency, decisive action is taken. Former Syrian president Hafez Assad forced his over-ambitious and unruly younger brother Rifat into exile in 1985 to protect regime interests. The current Saudi monarch is ruthlessly eliminating rival family, political, economic and religious power centres to consolidate his personal power and his 'modernising' project. These regimes also benefit from significant external support, often from supposed 'democracies', in a bizarre re-creation of the colonial project as a 'civilising mission' of a region deemed to be inherently anti-modern.

As economically dysfunctional, politically unstable and socially corrosive, this model is ruthlessly destructive. However, it tends to develop fiercely loyal constituencies: personnel of the security apparatus, militias, vested economic interests, political and ideological enthusiasts, co-opted 'sects', opportunistic political and civil actors, and significant foreign support. This (temporarily) reduces the exorbitant cost of sustaining regimes that operate close to Charles Tilly's 'organised crime' model in early modern West Europe.[71] Like good protection rackets, they manufacture (in both senses of fabricating and

[70] Eva Beilin, 'Robustness of Authoritarianism in the Middle East: Exceptionalism in Comparative Perspective', *Comparative Politics* 36(2) (2004): 145–8.

[71] Charles Tilly, 'War Making and State Making as Organized Crime', in Peter B. Evans, Dietrich Rueschemeyer and Theda Skocpol (eds), *Bringing the State Back In* (New York, Cambridge University Press, 1985), pp. 169–91.

producing) threats against which they then offer protection. Especially when resource-endowed such states can create a huge differential between brutal repression and generous rewards, a highly effective combination. Even 'stable democracies' can be snared by this combination, where the offer or withdrawal of lucrative weapons contracts worked magic in ensuring partiality to repulsive despots. Often these regimes play an internationally prescribed role, bringing substantial economic and political 'rents' that are crucial for keeping otherwise unsustainable political edifices afloat. However, as seen by the 'side-effects', such as the mounting threats of violence and wars, and inherent instability, the hidden costs may turn out to be phenomenal.

For all these factors, this model displays features that could not be subsumed under any of the others. As a hybrid model, it is extremely resilient and adaptive, responding to threats by quickly re-inventing the regime, often within its original legitimising narrative. As the 'totalitarian' dimension of Baathist, Nasserite or socialist ideologies lost appeal and utility, the impacted regimes quickly compensated by deploying authoritarian/sultanistic, sectarian, tribal, 'Islamist' or even 'liberal' strategies (open market, social permissiveness, etc.). Thus, sectarian Syria continues to use 'radical' rhetoric of anti-colonial pan-Arabism, while Nasserism continues to be applauded by a repressive Egyptian kleptocracy that simultaneously boasts 'liberal' credentials. The current regime also deploys anti-Israeli rhetoric and anti-Americanism, even when it is in bed with both. Saudi Arabia remains a strict 'Wahhabi' kingdom, as well as a post-modern consumerist enclave. Dissidents can be arrested, even killed, for transgressing strict Wahhabism, or for championing it independently of regime guidelines.

However, the problematic resilience of this model is as terrifying as it is indicative of fragility. In the Syrian and Egyptian cases, its attempted resurrection after virtual collapse is a reminder of the 'zombies' of horror movies. The half-dead sectarian Syrian terror-state morphed into a more heinous 'warrior-state', maliciously enlisting sectarianism, religious extremism, rogue militias, xenophobia and the international power balance on its side. In Egypt, the regime's repressive apparatus donned a messianic garb as saviour of state and nation, mobilising chauvinism (fascism?), personality cult, religion, clientelism, raw fear and gang violence in its campaign of terror. In both cases, the totalitarian dimension of the 'black hole state' assumed new bizarre and grotesque characteristics that do not promise long-term viability. The sheer level of brutality needed to sustain such models, and massive external subventions required, are not a recipe for longevity.

Regrettably, this level of brutality has become internationally acceptable, even normalised, given the narratives of insecurity in which it is wrapped. The threat of 'Islamic terrorism' and similar spectres of instability have been trumpeted with such vehemence as to make these 'zombie' regimes the proverbial 'lesser evil'. It is *this* that is the real horror; the more so given that these entities are likely to enhance the threat, rather than combat it.

It is possible that we may soon have to speak of a new clone of this model, what I would like to provisionally dub 'the Blackwater state' (after the notorious American private security company, Blackwater). Founded by Erik Prince in 1997, the company was linked to many atrocities while working for the US military in Iraq. The brand became so toxic that Prince had to change its name in 2009 and sell it in 2010. He has since relocated to the United Arab Emirates (UAE), where he has been helping set up mercenary units made up mainly of Columbians on behalf of his new hosts.[72]

In this context, offering the UAE as the epitome of the 'Blackwater state' is more than a metaphor. The *New York Times* sees the UAE 'outsourcing critical parts of [its] defence to mercenaries' as a harking back to medieval times, or at least the late colonial era, introducing 'a volatile element in an already combustible region'. However, this mutation threatens to turn a state itself a largely private outfit, virtually a family firm hollowed out politically. Still, this 'un-political' entity engages in hyperactive politicking in multiple arenas, punching well above its weight as a quasi-colonial entity. It fights ideological battles, mobilises and funds various militias around the region, plots coups and various intrigues, stokes regional rivalries, and lavishly underwrites a myriad quixotic schemes. Paradoxically, an outfit bent on banishing politics from the scene in favour of pure economics becomes one of the most politicised entities of the age. It is what the East India Company would have probably become, had the Empire stayed at home. What is more unsettling

[72] Mark Mazzetti and Emily B. Hager, 'Secret Desert Force Set Up by Blackwater's Founder', *New York Times*, 14 May 2011, available at: https://nyti.ms/3bQukqw, last accessed 30 April 2020.

is that both Prince and the UAE figure prominently in the scandals that engulfed the Trump administration, raising the spectre of the 'Blackwater state' becoming more international, rather than merely Arab, or 'coming back home', so to speak.

The Challenge of 'Sectarian' Insecurity

Based on the above, it can be argued that the Arab region's insecurities provide the missing explanatory variable needed to bridge the massive gap between the *actual exceptional status* in terms of democratic lag, and the failure of tentative explanations that posit an inherent regional *exceptionalism*. The recent resurgence of right-wing populism in the West further illustrates the point when intense polarisation around insecure and mutually threatening identities continue to hinder democratisation. In such contexts, few are prepared to play a democratic 'game' that looks more like a game of Russian roulette. For democracy to work, the major players should feel comfortable enough with the relative uncertainty of electoral processes, and not feel threatened by electoral outcomes, nor by their partners in the political game.

The new revolutionary era in the Arab World appeared at first to transcend the multiple dichotomies and lines of ideological and cultural polarisation.[73] In 'remapping the imaginative geography of liberation' the revolutions announced the transcendence of the post-colonial ideologies.[74] Moreover, as indicated above, the revolutionary tide has actually helped to forge new solidarities and shared identities, transcending the divisive labels promoted and exploited by the failed regimes.

However, as those opposed to change began to fight back, deliberate attempts were made to shatter this solidarity, first by invoking and constructing Islamist 'ghosts' amid these celebrations of a 'post-ideological' age. As an unlikely coalition of influential external and internal interests threatened by democracy began to form, the revolutions were denounced by some as 'a creeping Islamist resurgence'.[75] Israel was among the first to raise the outcry,

[73] Hamid Dabashi, *The Arab Spring: The End of Postcolonialism* (London: Zed Books, 2012).

[74] Hamid Dabashi, 'New Texts Out Now: Hamid Dabashi, The Arab Spring: The End of Postcolonialism', *Jadaliyya*, 6 June 2012, available at: https://bit.ly/3brM8Iw, last accessed 10 July 2013.

[75] Asef Bayat, *Post-Islamism: The Changing Faces of Political Islam* (Oxford: Oxford University

depicting the Arab Spring as less like Eastern Europe in 1989, and more like Iran 1979.[76] Bizarrely, two anti-democratic blocs (Western-backed Gulf states and Russian-backed Iran) vied with each other to destroy the prospects for democracy and stability in the region. It was Iran that achieved more success, helping to stall the revolutions in Syria, Lebanon, Iraq and Yemen. The circle was closed by the emergence of a third party: rogue terrorist entities such the Islamic State in Iraq and the Levant (ISIL) and rival Al Qaeda affiliates. They helped to destroy the democratic movements in Syria and Iraq, offering the two rival blocs pretexts to cooperate to extinguish the flame of democracy. The 'international community' contributed by virtually condoning genocide as a legitimate policy option in violation of *the* cardinal norms of the post-war consensus.[77]

This loss of Rustow's national unity requirement was not predetermined. True, the region is a mosaic of tribes, sects and ethnicities, but many overlapping identities have been mobilised in the past to overcome these cleavages. However, these very overlapping identities were used to destabilise, rather than enhance, existing solidarities. Arabism could have united Shia and Sunni Iraqi communities, but it was used instead to camouflage new forms of sectarianism. Pan-Islamism was also subverted by the emergence of heavily politicised sectarian identities, espousing (divergent) and conflicting pan-Islamic projects. In Lebanon and Syria, 'imagined' and constantly shifting sectarian identities trumped both the shared Arab identity and the constructed national identities. Bishara makes the perceptive point that these sectarian divisions are the outcome of sectarianism, and not its cause. Political actors construct and promote 'imagined' sectarian identities to achieve contingent political goals.[78]

To complicate matters further, emerging 'sectarian' identities (ethnic,

Press, 2013), p. 3.

76 Daniel Byman, 'Israel's Pessimistic View of the Arab Spring', *Washington Quarterly* 34(3) (2011): 123–36.

77 See Abdelwahab El-Affendi, 'When Genocide becomes the "Lesser Evil": The Bystander–Collaborator in the Era of "Savage Politics"', paper presented at the Political Studies Association's Annual Conference, 27 March 2016, available at: https://bit.ly/2SntyK9, last accessed 30 April 2020.

78 Azmi Bishara, *al-Tā'ifa, al-Tā'ifiyya wa al-Tawā'if al-Mutakhayyala* (*Sect, Sectarianism and Imagined Sects*) (Beirut: Arab Centre for Research for Policy Studies, 2018), pp. 31–59.

e.g., Kurdish), political (liberal, Islamist, etc.) evolved cross-border aspiration solidarities and outside alliances, which in turn overlapped with equally globalised conflictual identities (left and right, West and East), complicated by further fragmentation (Sunni–Shia among Muslims, Maronite versus the rest among Christians), again with cross-border ramifications. In this incendiary atmosphere, all identities (including 'secular' identities or even 'civil society' associations) were 'sectarianised' in the sense of acting paranoid and 'claustrophobic', with very little room for compromise or cross-group cooperation. This tended to undermine national coherence, and the related requirement of 'state-ness' (the existence of an authoritative, autonomous and coherent state on a given territory), deemed vital for democratic consolidation. Robust 'state-ness' is elusive where a territory is contested by more than one political community.[79] The resulting turmoil undermined other key requirements for a successful transition, such as the existence of a usable state bureaucracy, 'an institutionalised economic society', a lively civil society, a 'relatively autonomous and valued political society', and the rule of law.[80]

The Securitisation of Democracy?

Proponents of the 'culturalist' approach ascribe the region's apparent hospitality to dysfunctional regimes to peculiarities such as the rise of Islamic extremism and sectarianism, evidence that the region is struggling under the weight of its history. However, Bishara's above point about sectarianism being a constructed and imagined modern phenomenon offers a more plausible account of developments. Externally backed, shrewd political strategists deliberately promote sectarianism as a tool for political survival. However, these strategies tend to backfire. Clumsy attempts to contain Islamism or even banish politics tend to encourage more radicalism and to intensify politicisation. The promotion of sectarianism tended to create monsters that regularly went out of control. It has also motivated the recent wave of anti-sectarian Arab revolutions.

The resulting polarisation and fluidity of positions pose a unique problem, making it extremely difficult to offer (or abide by) guarantees of protec-

79 Linz and Stepan, *Problems of Democratic Transition*, ch. 2.

80 Linz and Stepan, *Problems of Democratic Transition*, Kindle edn, loc. 406.

tion for key actors' core interests and values. For instance, popular support for Islamist groups kept growing despite draconian measures to suppress them. Most of these gains were a surprise even to Islamists, a factor that makes it difficult to contract or sustain political deals and alliances. Dissent within Islamist ranks, together with the proliferation of competing and mutually hostile Islamist factions and trends, exacerbates this unpredictability.

The liberal/secular scene of Arab politics also suffers from fragmentation, shifting positions and conflicting views. The dramatic decline, fragmentation and loss of credibility by secular political movements (liberalism, radical Arab nationalism and the left) contributed to unwise political choices, such as siding with brutal regimes.[81] This saps the diminishing credibility and moral standing of these rivals to Islamism, seeming like admission of defeat.[82] Where the size of relevant blocs, as well as their positions and demands, remained uncertain, it is difficult to speak of national unity or of 'well-entrenched forces' as parties to the political contest. The fluid lines of demarcation between severely polarised identities create a deep sense of uncertainty and insecurity. Factional fragmentation and mercurial alliances tend to exacerbate the problem, even where identities may be relatively stable. Regional rivalries, international meddling and the proliferation of terror groups and sectarian militias further contribute to the deep sense of insecurity.

Concerns about such uncertainties resulted in a problematic 'securitisation of democracy', seen alternatively as a threat or a safeguard against threats. 'Securitisation' is the successful labelling of an issue or field by key political actors as a security concern. An issue like immigration can be 'securitised' through a 'speech act', which transfers it from an administrative to a national security issue, if and when the relevant audience accepts this label.[83] Trade

[81] See David Gorvin, 'Hala Mustafa and the Liberal Arab Predicament', *Middle East Quarterly* 17(2) (2010); Sohrab Ahmeri, 'The Failure of Arab Liberals', *Commentary* 133(5) (2012): 21–5; Jon Alterman, 'The False Promise of Arab Liberals', *Policy Review* 125 (2004): 77–85.

[82] Joseph Glatzer, "Three Questions for Liberals and Progressives Who Support the Egyptian Coup', *Mondoweiss*, 10 July 2013, available at: https://bit.ly/2xlO1HJ, last accessed 30 April 2020.

[83] Rita Taureck, 'Securitization Theory and Securitization Studies', *Journal of International Relations and Development* 9(1) (2006): 53–61; Barry Buzan, Ole Wæver and Jaap De Wilde, *Security: A New Framework for Analysis* (London: Lynne Rienner, 1998); Thierry Balzacq, 'The Three Faces of Securitization: Political Agency, Audience and Context',

can also be securitised, as we have observed in Trump's America. Liberal orders are usually minimal securitisation systems, favouring free trade, free speech, free elections, and minimal state intervention in the economy and social and personal life.[84] However, since 9/11 the level of securitisation in liberal polities has been rising steadily, as immigration, religious beliefs and even free speech became security concerns. Democracy could be 'securitised' via rhetoric linking democratisation to peace-building and counter-terrorism strategies, as was the case in Iraq. But democracy did often figure as a threat, as was the case when democracies were toppled by Western powers in Iran (1953) and Chile (1973). More recently, as Islamism replaced left-wing radicalism as *the* threat, Arab democracy became a threat because it could benefit Islamists.

The dual and mutually reinforcing securitisation of Islamism and democracy involved a bizarre coalition of actors, not to mention the weirdest construction of narratives. United States' and other Western (and Israeli) officials worked with Gulf despots and Egyptian and Middle Eastern generals and despots (and even intellectuals and the media) to portray democracy as a dire threat. The bumbling Muslim Brotherhood was demonised, but at the same time depicted as invincible. The dynamics and devastating outcome of these machinations were meticulously documented and analysed by a few prominent academics and journalists, providing a lesson in how story-telling, even when crooked and deceptive, could generate nightmares that justify all forms of insanities.[85]

In such a context, it becomes redundant to speak of moderation as a prerequisite for successful democratic transition, especially when the goalposts are being constantly moved. The problem may thus be one of too much Arab moderation, with the opposition bending over backwards to

European Journal of International Relations 11(2) (2005): 171–201; Jef Huysmans, 'Revisiting Copenhagen: Or, On the Creative Development of a Security Studies Agenda in Europe', *European Journal of International Relations* 4(4) (1998): 479–505.

84 Abdelwahab El-Affendi, *Genocidal Nightmares: Narratives of Insecurity and the Logic of Mass Atrocities* London: Bloomsbury, 2014), pp. 34–7.

85 See Kirkpatrick, *Into the Hands of the Soldiers*; Nicola Pratt and Dina Rezk, 'Securitizing the Muslim Brotherhood: State Violence and Authoritarianism in Egypt after the Arab Spring', *Security Dialogue* 50(3) (2019): 239–56; Rasha Abdulla, *Egypt's Media in the Midst of Revolution*, vol. 1 (Washington, DC: Carnegie Endowment for International Peace, 2014)

accommodate the most unreasonable demands of despots and their foreign allies.[86] 'Moderate' political movements and civil society organisations dutifully followed the prescriptions of security organs about how, where and when to organise, if at all. Sham elections were accepted as the norm, and the arbitrary dissolution of civil or political organisations and arrests of activists became routine. This docility may have contributed to enhancing the grip of the black hole state, encouraging its increasing rapacity and intransigence.

In a supreme irony, a recent article on the website of an international TV station withheld the identity of its reporter on the Egyptian state's intimidation of mourners on the death of Egypt's first and only freely elected president, Mohamed Morsi in June 2019, 'to avoid state reprisals'![87] The most recent annual human rights report released by the US State Department accused the Saudi regime of torturing human rights activists and religious scholars for their views, and seeking the death penalty for some, even though their 'offences' were exclusively peaceful, such as expressing support for political detainees.[88] In both countries, many key supporters of the new regimes, even those who applauded its brutal crackdown (and in Saudi Arabia, key members of the royal family), are currently in jail.

Ironically, as the black hole state politicises and securitises everything, including private thoughts and communications within families, no one can ever be *politically* 'moderate'. Thus, even complete capitulation will not suffice. For example, many intellectuals and activists in Saudi Arabia have been arrested, and some charged with capital offences, for keeping silent about the new 'reforms' or for a tweeting a prayer for peace and reconciliation! While Islamists had been the main target of initial crackdowns in Egypt and some Gulf countries since 2013, human rights advocates are now also fair game.

[86] Francesco Cavatorta and Fabio Merone, 'Moderation through Exclusion? The Journey of the Tunisian Ennahda from Fundamentalist to Conservative Party', *Democratization* 20(5) (2013): 857–75 at 862.

[87] 'Morsi's Death Triggers Passive Rage against Egypt's Surveillance State', *TRT World Magazine*, 21 June 2019, available at: https://bit.ly/34UY6rz, last accessed 1 May 2020.

[88] '2018 Report on International Religious Freedom', *US State Department*, 21 June 2019, available at: https://bit.ly/2KrcTAY, last accessed 1 May 2020.

Towards a New Theoretical Framework

In addition to destabilising the region and contributing to violence, the intensifying 'securitisation' of Arab politics is now also undermining established democracies. By reinforcing the narratives of insecurity fed by right-wing populist tendencies in the West, at a time when both the left and liberal trends are in decline, the region's multiple crises are being imported (back?) to the countries that had exported them in the first place. Pleading democracy promotion (problematically if not disingenuously) as one reason for invading Iraq in 2003, countries of the US-led alliance are currently experiencing blowback, including refugee flows. In a bitter irony, key US figures who played a pivotal role in undermining Egypt's democracy, such as generals James Mattis and Michael Flynn,[89] later played (equally problematic) roles in the Trump administration. This 'interactivity' provides the key entry point into our proposed theoretical solution: a more universalistic framework, transcending the habitual dichotomy between established and burgeoning democracies.

Democratic stability depends on certain levels of institutionally guaranteed security. When people go to vote, not everything is up for grabs. One may not know who will be elected, but there has to be reasonable assurance that whoever is will not proceed to overthrow the constitution or upset the basis of the economic system. However, when the stakes become too high, as we see now with issues like terrorism, immigration, globalised economic insecurity, etc., things begin to change. Leaders whose democratic credentials are questionable find it easier to get elected. Levels of insecurity among citizens are thus the key variable for the consolidation or stabilisation of democracy.

Many indicators and requirements cited above for a successful transition and consolidation, such as national unity, 'moderation', the compacting of the political spectrum, etc., work through mitigating insecurity. This is equally the case for 'structural' factors such as levels of education and per capita income. Generalised economic security reduces polarisation, while the spread (of usually state-sponsored) education helps to improve communication across communities and enhances national identity through a shared lan-

[89] Kirkpatrick, *Into the Hands of the Soldiers*, pp. 207–14.

guage and culture. While perceptions of insecurity are not wholly subjective, they are narratively constructed and socially mediated. It is usually easy for agitators to inflate risks and stoke fears when actual threats become the focus of attention. However, as mentioned above, narratives of insecurity could be spun out of the flimsiest of yarn.[90] When slavery was the norm, the idea of an end to slavery as a grave threat to the established order was promoted even by prominent 'liberals' like de Tocqueville.[91] In the colonial era, the very idea of 'independence' for colonies was anathema to many, with 'radical' leaders like Egypt's Nasser, Iran's Mosaddeq or Ghana's Nkrumah seen as 'rogue' actors threatening peace and stability. Even then, however, counter-narratives were emerging to neutralise such 'paranoid' narratives and the resulting excessive securitisation. The civil rights movement did precisely that in 1960s America, as did Nelson Mandela's ANC in 1990s South Africa, and moderate Islamists in post-Spring Tunisia. The process was helped by other factors, such as the materialisation of bigger threats, major structural shifts (economic, ideational, socio-political, as when slavery and colonialism became economically, politically and morally untenable).

Sobering and 'moderation' could also be the contingent outcome of conflict:[92] failing to vanquish the other may reveal the opponent as a fellow human after all. Again, African majority rule in South Africa did not signal the end of civilisation, as some had warned. Many other instances of post-conflict accommodation exemplified sobering up to realities, but often too late for many victims. The extension of the vote to women or the 'lower classes', let alone blacks or Catholics, did not produce the threatened doomsday scenarios either. Knowledge of this should contribute to reassurance.

[90] I have elaborated at length elsewhere on how narratives of insecurity are constructed, disseminated and deployed to incite and justify genocide and other forms of mass violence. That also applies to undermining democracies. See El-Affendi, *Genocidal Nightmares*, esp. chs 1, 2 and Conclusion.

[91] Curtis Stokes, 'Tocqueville and the Problem of Racial Inequality', *Journal of Negro History* 75(1/2) (1990): 1–15.

[92] Adam Przeworski, 'Democracy as a Contingent Outcome of Conflicts', in Jon Elster and Rume Slagstad (eds), *Constitutionalism and Democracy* (Cambridge: Cambridge University Press, 1988), pp. 59–80.

Conclusion

In this chapter, we sought to address the core issue of reducing uncertainty and mitigating insecurity as key to successful transitions at several levels, bringing an Arab focus to the debate without assuming Arab exceptionalism. Side-stepping the habitual wrangling over the theory's Eurocentrism, we take the Arab case as a starting point towards broader generalisations, with a focus on the interconnected variables of insecurity and uncertainty, and moderation. We have started this discussion by querying the type of knowledge the transition 'paradigm' seeks to provide, critically engaged with its many valid findings, while acknowledging its shortcomings. In exploring the challenge of uncertainty, we conclude that democratisation should in fact reduce insecurity when successful, rather than increase it as many argue. While moderation and readiness to compromise are necessary for democratisation, it cannot work with the prevalence of precarious and insecure regimes that live in panic, rule by terror and radiate fear. The 'black hole state', a hybrid and highly adaptable regime type unique to this region, played a paradoxical role in this intersection of terror and despotism. By isolating itself from society, relying largely on external support to offset tenuous legitimacy, these regimes united the elite and masses against them, a key factor in facilitating the Arab Spring.

The misguided reliance on these regimes by equally insecure outside actors (including major democracies) engendered a hyper-securitisation of democracy.[93] In the period between 9/11 and the invasion of Iraq in 2003, democracy was touted as a panacea and an antidote to terrorism, before later being treated as a threat. This explains the lack of enthusiasm for the uprisings and the acquiescence in the increasingly desperate tactics adopted by collapsing regimes (with some morphing into a new hybrid, the 'Blackwater state') to maintain or regain power from the people. The dynamics of foreign interventionism created vicious 'spirals of insecurity', where foreign insecurities exploited internal ones, exacerbating both. This interactive loop has now impacted 'established democracies', where insecurity has encouraged support for foreign despots, only to generate more insecurity at home. This confirms

[93] For more on the concept of hyper-securitisation, see El-Affendi, *Genocidal Nightmares*.

that the crucial variable of levels of insecurity can simultaneously explain the absence of democracy *and* the undermining of established democracies, an important theoretical breakthrough.

Democracies reflect a delicate and precarious balance between values and aspirations on one side, and configurations of social power, on the other. If the system loses its adaptability, those on the margins will act disruptively, creating revolutions and civil wars. In contrast, the despotic Arab regimes and their sponsors chose an odd way of adapting: opting to banish politics and resist all change in an area that cannot afford stagnation or regression. The attended intense securitisation, demanding the dedication of vast resources to sustain unsustainable regimes, can only generate more insecurity. The resulting 'international cooperative of repression', where adversaries such as Russia and the United States, Iran and Israel, Saudi Arabia and the UAE compete over which repressive regime to support, is hardly a recipe for peace and stability.

As a result, the regimes ironically feel too powerful to compromise, but too insecure to adapt. In the light of the increasing fluidity and unpredictably of political trends, the obsession with an elusive total control is creating even more instability and uncertainty. As explained above, the 'black hole state' has no room for moderation. Its paranoia about change, and its obsession with securitising everything, perpetually keep the political temperature near boiling point. Rather than facilitating the total control objective, this intense securitisation tends to ultimately unite the disparate squabbling political forces against this type of regime. However, the resulting democratic consensus was shattered due to misjudgements and faux pas on the part of the democratic forces, but also by deliberate acts of sabotage by the enemies of democracy. It is both possible and desirable to restore that consensus and build on it. The 'zombie' successors to the 'black hole state' are becoming even more paranoid and acting more irrationally, which is very promising from a democratisation perspective since collapse looks imminent. The recent wave of Arab revolutions is further proof of this.

The current sectarian antagonisms (including the Islamist–secularist polarisation), and the international paranoia feeding it and feeding upon it, are more likely to resolve themselves in the long run in a contingent fashion. Most likely, this will happen after too much suffering (where there is more than enough already), after too much good money has been thrown after bad in futile bids to sustain the unsustainable; and certainly too late for too many victims.

In the meantime, the role of theorists is to map possible roads towards that end, indicating shorter and less costly routes to stability. Given that influential actors would most likely come around to rational options after having exhausted all others, theorists will need more than deep insights – they will need patience, and plenty of it. Our contribution here is to highlight a central variable with tremendous explanatory power.

4

AFTER THE ARAB SPRING

Asef Bayat[1]

On 16 December 2010, Mohammed Bouazizi, a poor street vendor set himself on fire in the depressed Tunisian town of Sidi-Bouzid after the police abusively confiscated his scales and vegetables because he lacked a permit. The incident set the stage for the spectacular Arab uprisings that were to engulf the Arab region in a ferocity and scale unseen before. In Tunisia, the uprising involved mostly ordinary people – workers, educated unemployed youths, provincial populations, and, later, middle-class professionals as the street protests moved northward to the capital Tunis. Within a month the long-standing dictator, Zein al-Abedin Ben Ali, was toppled, opening the way for the formation of a democratic government. Egyptians were watching the events in Tunisia with great interest and enthusiasm. Within two weeks, they had begun their own uprising when on 25 January 2011 tens of thousands of ordinary people poured into Tahrir Square in Cairo from different parts of the city, including the poor informal communities. The crowd, spearheaded by young activists, occupied the Tahrir for the following days and nights, while massive street protests spread into other cities and towns. Within two weeks President Hosni Mubarak, who had ruled Egypt for some thirty years, was

[1] This chapter draws on my book, Asef Bayat, *Revolution without Revolutionaries: Making Sense of the Arab Spring* (Stanford, CA: Stanford University Press, 2017); as well as my article, Asef Bayat, 'Revolution in Bad Times', *New Left Review*, No. 80, March/April 2013.

forced to step down. Egyptians were still relishing their revolutionary honeymoon when mass revolts engulfed Libya, then Yemen, Syria and then Bahrain, in total nineteen Arab states toppling four dictators and brought one (Bashar al-Asad) to the brink. Those monarchies and sheikhdoms that deeply felt the shockwaves of the revolutions began to appease their citizens with handouts or reforms, while attempting to sabotage the revolutions elsewhere in the region.

I have lived through and witnessed two revolutionary episodes; first, the revolutions of 1979 in Iran and Nicaragua when I was a student activist; and then the Arab revolutions of 2011, in particular in Egypt where I lived and worked for many years prior to its revolution. As I eagerly observed the Arab revolutions unfolding, I became increasingly perplexed by how different they were from those I had seen and studied before. To begin with, the Arab uprisings were happening in a region which the prevailing social science and media had quite confidently deemed to be stable and ensured by the authoritarian durability. Second, these revolutions were generated mostly by ordinary people – with virtually no charismatic leaders, no unified organisations, no particular ideology and no intellectual precursor; there was no one like Lenin or Trotsky, Ayatollah Khomeini or Ali Shariati, or Vaclav Havel and Lech Walesa. Third, all were unfolded by spectacular mobilisation and mass revolts in the key urban streets and *maidans* (squares) in the mode and manner that became a standard reference for the global 'Occupy Movements' that spread through some 500 cities around the world. And yet, this is the key point, these revolutions caused only a slight break from the old orders – little changed from the structure of the old states and their power networks that nurtured them.

What type of revolutions were those in Tunisia, Egypt or Yemen? And what did their novel character mean for the idea and experience of 'transition'? Rich in terms of movement but poor in terms of change, these political happenings, I suggest, were 'reformist revolutions' with their particular paths of transition distinct from those known to us. While the transitions were less disruptive and more peaceful, little changed in the structure of the old order; while the transitional governments were far less repressive and more pluralistic, they remained more vulnerable to counter-revolutionary restoration, as we saw in Egypt which experienced the return of the counter-revolution. But a relatively democratic transition became possible, as in Tunisia, largely thanks to attempts to build a coalition between the Islamic (al-Nahda) and liberal, secular political forces, which, unlike Egypt, remained organised and influential. Yet, in general, the trajectory of transition remained open because the uprisings instigated among many citizens new ideas about power and renewed expectations about governance – a condition that could follow unforeseen outcomes.

What Kind of Revolutions?

Many observers have indeed pointed to certain novelties that characterised the Arab Spring and the global Occupy Movements alike; they were deemed to be the political happenings of peculiar nature – 'something totally new', the 'movement without a name', and the revolutions that heralded a novel path to emancipation.[2] On these they drew largely on the revolution as movement or in terms of mobilisation – focusing invariably on Cairo's Tahrir Square. What transpired in Tahrir – protesting, barricading, debating, camping, connecting, catering and caring for the wounded – constituted no less than the 'communism of movement', according to the French philosopher Alain Badiou. Tahrir exhibited a model of alternative polity to the conventional state of both liberal or authoritarian character – a universal concept that heralded a new possibility to practice democratic politics. For Badiou, the Tahrir communitas represented a true revolution,[3] while Slavoj Zizek saw the 'magic of Tahrir' in the novelty of these movements that had no hegemonic organisation, charismatic leadership or a party apparatchik. For Negri and Hardt, the 'Arab Spring', like the European Indignado and Occupy Wall Street, expressed the longing of the 'multitude' for a 'real democracy', a different kind of polity that aimed at overriding the hopeless liberal democracy entrapped by overpowering corporate capitalism.[4] In short, most observers saw them as the 'new global revolutions'.[5]

[2] Keith Kahn-Harris, 'Naming the Movement', *Open Democracy.net*, 22 June 2011.

[3] Alain Badiou, 'Tunisia, Egypt: The Universal Reach of Popular Uprisings', available at: https://bat020.com/2011/03/11/badiou-on-the-revolutions-in-egypt-and-tunisia, last accessed 10 May 2020.

[4] Antonio Negri and Michael Hardt. Mathijs Van de Sande, 'The Prefigurative Politics of Tahrir Square: An Alternative Perspective on the 2011 Revolutions', *Res Publica* 19(3) (2013): 223–39.

[5] Paul Mason, *Why It's Kicking off Everywhere? The New Global Revolutions* (London: Verso, 2012).

There is certainly much to appreciate in these observations, and even more to learn from the actual episode of the Tahrir moment; for it represents an extraordinary time in every revolutionary mobilisation when attitudes, behaviours and visions transform in a dramatic fashion; these are the moments when sectarian divides dissipate, gender equality reigns and selfishness diminishes; when grassroots exhibit unprecedented innovations in activism, self-organisation and democratic decision-making. These represent the revolution as movement. However, we cannot escape the hard question of what happens when the dictators abdicate and people go home; how to sustain the 'communism of the movement'; and how to institute such twenty-first-century modes of self-governance in society at large and beyond the confines of the squares? After all, how are we to break from the past order? What to do with the state power? And how to manage the counter-revolution? In short, a more fruitful reading of revolutions has no choice but to examine them in their spatial, temporal, strategic and ideational totality. In other words, we need to assess the revolutions in terms of change, with the revolution defined as the rapid and radical transformation of the state pushed by the popular movement from below to usher change at the broader societal level. Looking from such an outlook, the revolutions in Tunisia, Egypt or Yemen espouse a more complex, novel and a highly paradoxical reality. Indeed, their trajectories resemble none of the pathways for political change that are known to us – be they reform, insurrection or implosion. The Arab revolutions had characteristics of their own.

In the 'reformist' course, broadly speaking, social and political movements mobilise in a usually sustained campaign to exert concerted pressure on the incumbent regimes to undertake reforms through the institutions of the existing states.[6] Resting on their social power – the mobilisation of the grassroots – the opposition movements compel the political elites to reform themselves, their laws and institutions, often through some of kind of social pact. So, change happens within the framework of the *existing* political arrangements. The transition to democracy in countries like Mexico and Brazil in the 1980s was of this nature. The leadership of Iran's Green move-

[6] The following few paragraphs draw heavily on Bayat, *Revolution without Revolutionaries*, pp. 155–8.

ment pursued a similar reformist path. In this trajectory, the depth and extent of reforms vary. Change may remain superficial, but it can also be profound if it is materialised cumulatively by legal, institutional and politico-cultural reforms.

Such a reformist trajectory is very different from the 'insurrectionary' mode, where a revolutionary movement builds up in a fairly extended span of time during which a recognised leadership and organisation emerge along with some blueprint of future political structure. At the same time that the incumbent regime continues to resist through police or military apparatus, a gradual erosion and defection begin to crack the governing body. The revolutionary camp pushes forward, attracts defectors, forms a shadow government, and builds some organs of alternative power. In the meantime, the regime's governmentality becomes paralysed, leading to a state of 'dual power' between the incumbent and the opposition, which usually enjoys commanding charismatic leaders as in the figures of Lenin, Mao, Cory Aquino, Khomeini, Lech Wałęsa or Nelson Mandela. The state of 'dual power' ends in an insurrectionary battle in which the revolutionary camp takes over the state power via force or negotiation; it dislodges the old organs of authority and establishes new ones. Here we have a comprehensive overhaul of the state, with new functionaries, ideology and mode of governance. The Iranian Revolution of 1979, the Sandinista Revolution in Nicaragua or the Cuban revolution of 1952 exemplify such an insurrectionary course.[7] Qaddafi's Libya faced an insurrection by the revolutionary insurgency under the leadership of the National Transitional Council, which eventually advanced from the liberated Benghazi to capture the capital Tripoli.

There is still a third possibility: 'regime implosion'. Here a revolt may build up through general strikes and broad practices of civil disobedience, or through a revolutionary warfare progressively encircling the regime, so that in the end the regime implodes, collapsing in disruption, defection and total disorder. In its place come alternative elites and institutions, often in a state of confusion and disorder, hurriedly forming new organs of power manned

[7] Ervand Abrahamian, *Iran between Two Evolutions* (Princeton, NJ: Princeton University Press, 1982); Henry Weber, *Nicaragua: The Sandinista Revolution* (London: Verso, 1981); James Defronzo, *Revolutions and Revolutionary Movements* (Boulder, CO, Westview, 2011).

by people with little experience of running public offices. Ceausescu's regime in Romania imploded in dramatic political chaos and violence in 1989, but gave rise eventually to a very different political and economic order under the newly established political structure, the National Salvation Front led by Ion Iliescu following the dictator's escape and subsequent capture.[8] In both 'insurrection' and 'implosion', and unlike the reformist mode, attempts to reform the political structure take place not through the existing institutions of the state, but largely *outside* them.

Neither the Egyptian, Tunisian nor Yemeni revolutions resembled any of these trajectories. In Egypt and Tunisia, the rise of powerful political uprisings augmented the fastest revolutions of our time. Tunisians in the course of one month and Egyptians in just eighteen days succeeded in dislodging long-serving authoritarian rulers, dismantling a number of institutions associated with them, including the ruling parties, the legislative bodies and a number of ministries, in the meantime establishing a promise of constitutional and political reform. And all these were achieved in ways that were remarkably and relatively civil, peaceful and fast. But these astonishing rapid triumphs (unlike the fairly prolonged revolts in Yemen, Libya or Syria) did not leave much opportunity for the opposition, if they ever intended, to build parallel organs of authority capable of taking control of the new states. Instead, the revolutionaries wished the institutions of the incumbent regimes, for instance, the military in Egypt, to carry out substantial reforms on behalf of the revolution – that is, to modify the constitution, ensure free elections, guarantee free political parties and in the long run institutionalise democratic governance. Here lay a key anomaly of these revolutions – they enjoyed enormous social power, but lacked administrative authority; they garnered remarkable hegemony, but did not actually rule. Thus, the incumbent regimes continued more or less to stand; there were few fresh state institutions or governing bodies, or adequately novel means and modes of governance that could altogether embody the will of the revolution. And if there were new institutions, they were filled less by revolutionaries and more by the free-riders – those traditionally well-organised constituencies,

[8] Victor Sebestyen, *Revolution 1989: The Fall of the Soviet Empire* (New York: Vintage, 2009), pp. 380–400.

like religious groups, many of whom had remained on the margins of the revolutionary initiative and battles.

It is true that, like their Arab counterparts, the Eastern European revolutions of the late 1980s were also non-violent, civil and remarkably rapid (East Germany's revolution took only ten days, and Romania's five days)[9]; but they managed, unlike in Egypt, Yemen and even Tunisia, to completely transform the political and economic systems. This was possible because the difference between what East European people had (a one-party communist state and command economy) and what they seemed to demand (liberal democracy and a more open economy) was so distinctly radical that the trajectory of change had to be revolutionary. Half-way, superficial and reformist change would have been easily detected and resisted. This was a pattern very different from the Yemeni, Tunisian and Egyptian revolutions in which the demands of 'change, freedom, social justice' were so broad that they could be claimed even by the conservative forces. The Arab Spring revolutions also differed from the anti-Marcos revolution of 1986 in the Philippines, which enjoyed popular leaders like Corazon Aquino and General Fidel Ramos, organisation, and hard military power. Likewise, the remarkable non-violent protests in Sudan that brought down two military dictators – General Abboud in October 1964 and General Nimeiri April 1985 – had their own particular characteristics. They built on the organised opposition of political parties, trade unions, professional associations, the student movement, as well as the support of some army officers. The absence of any hostile international actor and the presence of what Abdelwahab El-Affendi called the 'legendary Sudanese civility' eased the non-violent operation of these uprisings.[10]

The Arab revolutions looked more like Georgia's Rose Revolution of 2003 and Ukraine's Orange Revolution of November 2004–January 2005 where in both cases a massive and sustained popular protest brought down incumbent fraudulent rulers.[11] In these instances, strictly speaking, the

[9] Ibid., p. 380.

[10] See an excellent analysis, Abdelwahab El-Affendi, 'Revolutionary Anatomy: The Lessons of the Sudanese Revolutions of October 1964 and April 1985', *Contemporary Arab Affairs* 5(2) (2012): 300.

[11] Defronzo, *Revolutions and Revolutionary Movements*, pp. 81–3.

trajectory of change looks more reformist than revolutionary. But in reality there was a much more promising side to the Arab political upheavals. One cannot deny the operation of a powerful revolutionary drive in these political episodes, which made them more profound than those in Georgia or Ukraine. In Tunisia and Egypt, the departure of despotic rulers and their apparatus of coercion opened up an unprecedented free space for citizens, notably the subaltern subjects, to reclaim their societies and assert themselves. As is the case in most revolutionary turning points, an enormous energy had been released and an unparalleled sense of renewal emerged in the societies' body politics. Banned political parties came to the surface and new ones were established. In Tunisia, some 100 political parties came to life, and in Egypt a dozen new ones emerged. Societal organisations became more vocal and extraordinary grassroots initiatives began to be forged. Working people, free from fear of persecution, aggressively followed their violated claims. Unofficial industrial action and protests raged. In Tunisia, the labour unions began to play a much greater role; and in Egypt labourers pushed for new independent unions, some of them forming the 'Coalition of the 25 January Revolution Workers' to assert the revolutionary principles of 'change, freedom, and social justice'. While small rural farmers called for independent syndicates, Cairo's slum dwellers poised to set up their first organisation ever. For their part, youth groups organised to upgrade slum areas, got engaged in civil works and reclaimed their civic pride. Students poured into the streets to demand that Ministry of Education revise the curricula. And the Tahrir Revolutionary Front in Egypt, and the 'Supreme Body to Realize the Objectives of the Revolution' in Tunisia were formed to exert pressure on the new rulers for meaningful political reforms. Of course, all these represented popular engagement of exceptional times. But the extraordinary sense of liberation, the urge for self-realisation, the dream of a new and just order – in short, the desire for 'all that is new' – were what defined the very spirit of these revolutions. In these turning points, these societies moved far ahead of their elites, exposing the major anomaly of these revolutions – the discrepancy between a revolutionary desire for the 'new', and a reformist trajectory that led to harbouring the 'old'.

Arab Refo-lution

How then can we make sense of the Arab revolts? I have suggested that the Arab revolutions were neither revolutions in the sense of the twentieth-century popular mobilisation that would inaugurate a radical makeover of the state to pave the way, in turn, for societal transformation; nor were they simply reformist trajectories in the mould of democratic transitions in Brazil or Chile in the late 1980s. Rather, they embodied a mix of revolutionary mobilisation and reformist trajectory. They were, in a word, 'refo-lutions' – a novel trajectory, quite distinct from the epochal events of Eastern Europe in 1989, which Timothy Garton Ash described by coining the term 'refo-lution'.[12] Originally, Garten Ash was referring to the process of political reform in Poland and Hungary in June 1989 that resulted from negotiations between the Communist authorities and the leadership of the opposition movements, but rapidly entailed a profound structural transformation, including the end of the Communist system, one-party arrangement, socialist economy and Warsaw Pact, and their replacement with new elites, ideas and institutions. In Garten Ash's 'refo-lution', there is no 'reform' of the existing arrangement. Rather, his is a description of revolutions brought about through peaceful negotiations – a model very different from the Arab 'refo-lutions' wherein no Arab dictator agreed to far-reaching reform through negotiation; they were either forced out by revolutionary coercion (Ben Ali and Mubarak) or tried to trick the revolutionaries into superficial 'change', as in the case of the military rulers in Egypt after Mubarak or Ali Saleh in Yemen. In all of these experiences, the key facets of the old orders continued to persist.

Thus, here in my formulation, refo-lution refers to those revolutionary movements (e.g., in Tunisia, Egypt, Yemen or Bahrain) that emerged to compel the incumbent regimes to reform themselves; it describes the revolutions that wished to push for reforms in and through the institutions of the existing states. In this trajectory, the revolutionaries enjoyed enormous social power, but they lacked administrative authority; they garnered remarkable hegemony, but they did not actually rule, with the consequence that the

[12] Timothy Garton Ash, 'Refolution, the Springtime of Two Nations', *New York Review of Books*, 15 June 1989.

protagonists remained on the margins, while the mostly organised free-riders ascended to the helm of power. Thus, the old elites and their networks of patronage, as well as the key institutions of governance such as the judiciary, police, intelligence apparatus and the military, remained more or less unaltered. For instance, in Yemen, the ruling families and tribal leaders mostly kept their positions, as did the political networks controlled by Ali Saleh. The Saudi-led initiative of the Gulf Cooperation Council (GCC) largely sought an exit strategy for Saleh without ensuring a democratic reform of the governance. When the Houthi rebels marched through Aden to unseat President Hadi in September 2014, Saudi Arabia deployed its own forces to protect the president, thus prompting a deadly civil war. In Egypt, President Mubarak's downfall allowed for a new parliament, president and a new constitution. But the institutions and the power base of Mubarak's regime, even though challenged, remained largely unreformed; in fact, they sheltered the forces of counter-revolution that forcefully took power from President Morsi in a military coup on 3 July 2013. Things appeared better in Tunisia, where a peaceful transition entailed a political shift from the old autocratic rule into a pluralist democracy, and ensured a democratic constitution. Yet some key operators of the Ben Ali regime returned to power in the 2014 presidential elections, presiding over an economic system that continued with its pre-revolution neo-liberal legacy. In addition, the old 'parallel state', the de facto authority before the revolution including the security sector, certain business elites and local mafia made a come-back.[13] When the 'Economic Reconciliation' law – passed and supported by both the ruling Nidaa Tounes and the Islamic al-Nahda in September 2017 – gave amnesty to some 2,000 businessmen accused of corruption under the old regime, it indicated that the old elites were back in business.[14]

Why did the revolutions in Tunisia, Egypt and Yemen broadly assume a 'refo-lutionary' character? Why did some key institutions of the old regimes remain unaltered while revolutionary protagonists became marginalised?

[13] Nicholas Noe, 'Another Middle Eastern State Could Collapse, and More Cash and Weapons Won't Save It', *tabletmag.com*, 22 September 2015, available at: https://bit.ly/3aMTPYw, last accessed 1 May 2020.

[14] 'Tunisians March against Contested Corruption Amnesty', *New York Times*, 16 September 2017.

Many observers have pointed to the domestic and regional counter-revolution intrigues – 'conservative coup', the 'deep state'[15] and foreign meddling. There is certainly a truism in these arguments. The region's geo-political exceptionalism, shaped by oil and Israel, rendered the revolutions prone to geo-political diktats. Foreign meddling, coming chiefly from Saudi Arabia and United Arab Emirates, took the form of protracted sabotage, economic blackmail and support of counter-revolution. Yet the question is not whether the counter-revolution tried hard to stall or hijack the Arab revolutions, which they did; in fact, all revolutions carry within themselves the germs of counter-revolutionary intrigues. The question, rather, is whether the revolutions were 'revolutionary' enough to offset the perils of restoration.

I have suggested that the revolutionaries in these countries remained outside power because they were not planning to take over the state; and when in the later stages the protagonists realised that they should, they lacked the means and resources – organisation, powerful leaderships and a strategic vision – to wrest power both from the old regimes and the well-organised 'free-riders', like Salafis who managed to ascend to institutions of power. Without such resources, the protagonists lacked sufficient bargaining power to negotiate powerfully (as did, for instance, Polish Solidarity) for democratic transition, and were ill-equipped to win parliamentary or presidential elections. In this sense, the Arab revolutions differed considerably from their twentieth-century counterparts primarily because they occurred in different ideological times.

Revolutionary Times

Until the mid-1990s or so, three major ideological traditions carried the idea of revolution as the strategy of fundamental change in societies: anti-colonial nationalism, Marxism-Leninism and Islamism. Anti-colonial protagonists (such as Frantz Fanon, Ho Chi Minh, Sukarno or Abdel-Nasser) imagined post-colonial states as something new – states that could eject the political and economic domination of colonial powers and comprador bourgeoisie.

[15] See, for instance, Gilbert Achcar, *The People Want* (Berkeley: University of California Press, 2013); Jean-Pierre Filiu, *From Deep State to Islamic State* (New York: Oxford University Press, 2015). These are against those such as Bernard Lewis who attribute the despairing Arab Spring to the absence of democratic culture.

But the nationalist revolutions had come to a halt in the post-colonial era, and many nationalist revolutionaries turned into administrators of the post-colonial states. Despite some achievements in state-building, distributive measures and modernisation, most of the states failed to secure the democracy, social justice and independence that they had anticipated. Some turned into autocracies, military populist and later embraced neo-liberal transformation, if they were not overthrown by military coups. By the late 1980s, they were shedding what had remained of 'distributive socialism', 'social contracts' and populism. The Palestinian liberation struggle remained perhaps the last of the nationalist movements yet to overturn the occupation of Palestine.

Marxists-Leninist currents were perhaps the most significant revolutionary movements in the Cold War era. Some of these global currents inspired guerrilla-type strategy of revolution in developing countries, including the Middle East. And in the West, sympathy with the idea of revolution continued among the radical left, notably Trotskyist organisations, with all holding elaborate theories of revolution and blueprints of state takeover. They even inspired non-Marxist political movements rooted in religion, notably revolutionary Islam and Catholicism. Even though Euro-Communism opted to follow a reformist strategy and some trends within Marxism-Leninism in the Third World pursued a gradualist 'non-capitalist road to socialism', significant forces within Marxism-Leninism remained committed to the idea of revolution.

But all these changed dramatically after the collapse of the USSR and the Eastern bloc in 1989. The anti-Communist revolutions in Eastern Europe, and the end of the Cold War, diminished the idea of revolution. The idea of 'revolution' was so integral to socialism that the end of actually existing socialism meant the end of revolution as a rapid and radical change. 'Revolution' lost its appeal and attraction, identified now with 'failed' Marxism, authoritarian states and the enemy of freedom. The state-centred policies and perspectives, so deeply associated with socialism, were equated with centralism, repression, inefficiency, and the erosion of individual autonomy and initiative. Thus, instead of socialism, state and revolution, there developed an explosion in the ideas of the individual, civil society, public sphere, rational dialogue, non-violence and 'reform'. The spread of neo-liberalism beginning with Ronald Reagan in the United States and Margaret Thatcher in Britain vastly aided this shift in discourse through state policies, think tanks, aid agencies and the international NGOs and the like. In the end, 'liberal reform' came to occupy the central place in the strategy of change globally.

In the Muslim world, Marxism-Leninism and its idea of revolution had declined, but it had left its imprint on its ideological rival, Islamism. Since the 1970s, militant Islamist movements drew on the revolutionary ideas of the Egyptian Sayid Qutb to fight against the secular ideas and the states in the Muslim world. Qutb had been influenced by the Indian Islamist leader Abul Alaa Maududi, who himself shared aspects of the organisational and political strategy of the Indian Communist Party. Qutb's book *Ma'alin fi al-Tariq* (*Signposts*) became the Islamist equivalent of Lenin's *What is to be Done.* Qutb's ideas furnished the ground for a vanguard of Muslim militants to forcefully overturn the Jahili state to establish an Islamic order. This guided the strategy of the militant Islamist organisations such as Jiahd, Gama'a Islamiyya, Hizbual-Tahrir and Lashjar Jjhad. The intellectual baggage of the Iranian Revolution of 1979 was informed by both Marxist ideas of revolution as well as political Islam, including Qutb's *Signposts*. But more important were the ideas of Ali Shariati who, trained under French Marxist George Gorwitch, had advocated revolution in a mix of Marxist and Islamic idioms, such as class struggle and the establishment of a 'divine classless society'. In short, 'revolution' had become central to the politics of militant Islamism, even though not the reformist trends like the Muslim Brotherhood.

But by the early 2000s, Islamism also began to lose its revolutionary appeal and fervour. With the crisis of Islamism both as a state form (in Iran, Pakistan, Saudi Arabia, Sudan) and as movements, religious polity shifted towards a post-Islamist polity that advocated a non-religious state but a religious society.[16] 'Post-Islamism' expressed a critical departure from the Islamist discourse on violence, militancy and revolutionary rhetoric into a non-violent, gradualist and reformist path towards political and social change. While Islamism and its revolutionism had a foot in Cold War politics, post-Islamism is greatly linked to and informed by the political language of the post-Cold War period – the language of the individual, civil society, accountability, non-violence and reform.

[16] For details, see Asef Bayat, *Post-Islamism: The Changing Faces of Political Islam* (New York: Oxford University Press, 2013).

Thus, the Arab revolutions occurred at a time in the global political stage when the idea of revolution had been dissipated. The decline of the key post-colonial ideologies – anti-colonial nationalism, Marxism-Leninism and Islamism – had delegitimised the notion of 'revolution' as a rapid, radical and forcible change. No wonder few Arab protagonists had really thought, strategised and prepared for the unfolding of revolution, even though many might have dreamt about it. Theirs seemed to be a desire for 'reform', or meaningful change within the existing political arrangement – a desire for political openness, bettering regional disparity, and attending to unemployment and exclusion, but not necessarily a revolution. In Tunisia under the Ben Ali's police state, the intelligentsia had suffered a 'political death',[17] even though provincial working classes had waged angry protests and young civil society activists became more dynamic in the few years prior to the uprisings. In Egypt, the Kefaya and later the 6 April movements, notwithstanding their political innovations, were essentially reformist in orientation; they were lacking a strategy to completely overhaul the state.[18] Even though some of the 6 April activists reportedly received political training in the United States, Qatar and Serbia, the training was largely in the areas of election monitoring, tactics of non-violent protests or building networks.[19] Consequently, what transpired when the uprisings spread were not revolutions *per se*, which begin with a radical shift in state power, but 'refo-lutions', that is, revolutionary mobilisation that wished to compel the incumbent regimes to carry out meaningful reforms.

Implications for the Transition

What did the refo-lutionary trajectory mean for the transition? How did it unfold after the downfall of the dictators in Tunisia, Egypt and Yemen? The 'transition' debates are preoccupied primarily with the process of the

[17] For political apathy under Ben Ali, see Beatrice Hibou, *The Force of Obedience* (London: Polity, 2011).

[18] See Bassem Nabil Hafez, 'New Social Movements and the Egyptian Spring: A Comparative Analysis between the April 6 Movement and the Revolutionary Socialists', *Perspectives on Global Development and Technology* 12(1/2) (2013): 98–113.

[19] See Ron Nixon, 'US Groups Helped Nurture Arab Uprisings', *New York Times*, 14 April 2011.

shift from authoritarian rule to democracy, focusing predominantly on non-violent and non-revolutionary experiences – such as those in the early phase of Huntington's 'third wave' of democratisation in Latin America or the more recent political change in Burma.[20] Revolutionary transitions, when addressed, are often examined within the same conceptual frame as the non-revolutionary shift.[21] In this model, transitions are carried out largely from the top by political elites through 'political pacts' between the authoritarian regimes and democratic opposition. Brinton's *Anatomy of Revolution*, examining the English, French, American and Russian experiences, remains perhaps the only classic work to explore the logic of revolutionary transition after the seizure of power – which may not necessarily entail democratisation. Brinton examines the stages through which the revolutionary mobilisation unfolds leading to regime change, and how power continues to shift in the aftermath. Immediately following the regime change, the dominant groups that were poised naturally to inherit power from the old government are pushed aside by rivals on the left. The power is taken away again, this time by the 'extreme radicals' or 'lunatic left', who then begin to centralise their rule – in particular in times of war – unleashing a 'reign of terror' and 'asceticism'. This period of crisis would shift by the very nature of the society, the network of interactions, into the phase of effervescence, anti-asceticism and joy, eventually ending up in equilibrium, where the revolution comes to an end.

Thus, whereas the transition studies focus largely on the non-revolutionary change from the old into new regimes mainly through political pacts, Brinton's exploration centres mostly on the struggles, negotiations and change within the new revolutionary regimes after the collapse of the old order. How do we account for the dynamics of transition – in Tunisia, Egypt or Yemen – that lay somewhere in between, where powerful revolutionary

[20] The classic work on this includes Guillermo O'Donnell, Philippe Schmitter and Lawrence Whitehead (eds), *Transitions from Authoritarian Rule: Comparative Perspectives* (Baltimore, MD: Johns Hopkins University Press, 1986).

[21] See, e.g., Isobel Coleman and Terra Lawson-Remer, 'A User's Guide to Democratic Transitions', *Foreign Policy*, 18 June 2013; Juan Linz and Alfred Stepan, *Problems of Democratic Transition and Consolidation: Southern Europe, South Africa, and Post-Communist Europe* (Baltimore, MD: Johns Hopkins University Press, 1996); Samuel Huntington, *The Third Wave: Democratization in the Late Twentieth Century* (Norman, OK: Oklahoma University Press, 1991).

mobilisation forced dictators to abdicate, but failed to capture governmental power, thus leaving the interests and institutions of the old order largely unaltered? How to read the logic of transition in such political upheavals that were both revolutionary and non-revolutionary, reflecting both a transition to democracy, and revolutionary desires for economic distribution, social inclusion and cultural recognition?

The refo-lutionary trajectories in Tunisia, Egypt and Yemen proved to be highly paradoxical. While they were less disruptive and less violent, little changed in the structure of the old order; they were far less repressive and more favourable to pluralist polity, but proved to be much more perilous and vulnerable to counter-revolutionary restoration. It is true that Arab refo-lutions suffered interruptions in the economy, state administration and normal operations of life; but the loss of life and general disorder were far more severe in Syria and Libya than in Tunisia and Egypt, where for the most part, salaries were paid, water and electricity ran, shops remained open and supplies available.[22] Beyond avoiding severe disorder, refo-lutions also allowed for a more open and less repressive outcome with real potential for a pluralist social and political order. Indeed, the Arab revolutions remained largely free from the kind of detentions, summary trials and elimination of old and new opposition members that the revolutionary regimes in Russia, China or Islamist Iran espoused. Refo-lutions, in other words, possess the advantage of ensuring orderly transitions, avoiding violence, destruction and chaos – the evils that dramatically increase the cost of change, where revolutionary excesses and a 'reign of terror' can be averted. Unlike revolutionary Iran where summary trials and executions of agents of the shah's regime as well as the oppositional Leftist revolutionaries became the order of the day, a GCC-sponsored 'transitional justice' in Yemen vindicated President Ali Saleh in 2014, despite his atrocities and manipulation of power for some forty years. In Tunisia, a belated Truth and Dignity Commission was established to investigate the previous government's repression; but all of the twenty or so senior officials of Ben Ali's regime (including the interior minister and head of the presidential security service) were set free from detention

[22] The Tunisian activist Rasha was emphatic on this; interview by author, Tunisia, 26 July 2011.

before long.[23] And in Egypt only a few top officials, including President Mubarak and his sons, were tried in controversial hearings only to be acquitted in December 2014. In sum, few officials of the old regimes were purged or placed behind bars.

But precisely because refo-lutions fail to substantially change the old state personnel and institutions, the danger of restoration always lingers. In Egypt, where the ex-President Mubarak, whose thirty-year rule caused an uprising, could escape persecution, points precisely to the perilous potential of refo-lutions for counter-revolutionary restoration. The Egyptian counter-revolution, led by the military, struck back not only because it had remained vocal and vigilant within the un-reformed state, but also because it could skilfully surf on the massive wave of popular opposition against President Mohammad Morsi – an Islamist ruler they deemed to be busy building an electoral theocracy and serving the 'Muslim Brotherhood clan' rather than the interests of all Egyptians. Already despised by the sizeable number of Mubarak supporters, the Brotherhood began rapidly to lose the sympathy of many who had supported Morsi's presidency. By the end of his first year, President Morsi and his patrons were seen as an obstacle to deepening of the revolution. Thus, opposition to the Brotherhood's rule in practice 'allied' the anti-Mubarak revolutionaries with the counter-revolutionary Mubarakists, who together with millions of disenchanted ordinary Egyptians created the monumental 30 June rebellion that called for early presidential elections. The Tamarrod ('rebellion') movement served as a catalyst to mediate the 'alliance' of these strange bedfellows.

This stage in Egypt's revolutionary drama reflected precisely the limits of the refo-lutions – where the protagonists lacked a coercive power to do what they saw the army doing on their behalf. It was the unfortunate predicament of a 'revolution' that enjoyed an enormous popular constituency, but painfully lacked administrative power, with the consequence that it had to rest on the institutions of the incumbent state – such as the military – to change things. From the revolutionaries' prism, Morsi's forceful ouster served as a catalyst to remove the barriers that had prevented a stalled revolution from

[23] Carlotta Gall, 'Release of Ousted Leaders Raises Questions in Tunisia', *International New York Times*, 18 July 2014, p. 5.

moving forward. It served as a desperate midwife for a pregnant nation that was enduring agonizing labour to give birth to a new social order; it needed a dramatic push: revolutionary coercion. But that turned out to be a midwife poised to take the life of the unborn, that is to say, to terminate the very revolution it claimed to want to save.

Highly likely yes, but restoration is not an inevitable outcome of refo-lutions. An inclusive post-revolution government, capable of negotiating a political pact with competing constituencies, could build enough legitimacy and support to neutralise counter-revolution intrigues. In Tunisia, the ruling Islamic al-Nahda, moved by its own wisdom and the lessons from Egypt, forged a successful pact with the labour, liberal and secular forces, including a sympathiser of the old regime, the Nedaa Tounes. In this bid, al-Nahda dissolved its own majority government in favour of a national technocratic alternative, and reached a settlement with all parties for what transpired as a democratic constitution. This successful accord was due not simply to the neutrality of Tunisia's military, but especially to the strong secular sensibilities and organisation in Tunisian society of which the Islamic al-Nahda took account. Unlike the exclusivism of Islamist Muslim Brothers in Egypt, who were fixated on their majoritarian dogma and the fantasy of establishing Islamist rule, al-Nahda's post-Islamism allowed it to embrace the idea of an inclusive and secular state while insisting on promoting a pious society.

The truth is even if the ruling groups such as al-Nahda and the Muslim Brothers wanted to monopolise power and establish a majoritarian rule (as the Islamist rulers did in the Iranian Revolution), they would not have been able to succeed precisely because of the de facto pluralism that refo-lutions tend to engender. In contrast to most twentieth-century revolutions where the new revolutionary regimes, such as those in Cuba or Iran, could, once they seized the government, monopolise power wiping out the old and new opposition in the name of 'saving the revolution', in refo-lutions they find themselves surrounded by multiple power centres, including those sheltered in the institutions of the old state, supporters of previous regimes, diverse oppositional media outlets and a new insurgent civil society. In other words, refo-lutions are by default pluralist. This de facto diffusion of power can potentially pave the way for an electoral democracy, provided that sufficient legal, institutional and social mechanisms are set to block the possible monopolisation of power through coercion or election by the new rulers, and the restoration of counter-revolution. And this may be possible through the incessant mobilisation and organisation of the citizenry, the revolutionary opposition not simply in the streets, but in the key domains of political and social life where contestation for hegemony takes place. But this is what the secular revolutionaries in Egypt and to a lesser degree in Tunisia avoided, leaving the ground for the rise of the free-riders.

Losing to Free-riders

Political contestation and the struggle for hegemony in a society take place in multiple domains. These include the domain of the *state* in the sense of the government, bureaucracy, the military, the state media and the like; the *political society* embodied in political parties, parliament or municipality and local governance; the *civil society* as in associational life, NGOs, the syndicates and collectives at the places of work; the domain of the *street* in the sense of hegemony over public space, public order and public opinion expressed in day-to-day idioms and acts; and, finally, the *private realm*, the realm of the individual, family, taste and life-style. In reality these domains are not separated; they are connected and may overlap, with class, gender and social clustering running through them. Different modes of state–society relations determine where the contestation occurs most.

In times of revolution/insurrection, the fiercest battles take place in the streets, the locus where revolutionary breakthrough is achieved. Street politics, then, become the most critical battle-frame in the exceptional episode of the revolution's life-course. This exceptional episode is marked by a swift transformation of consciousness, utopia and euphoria. It is these extraordinary moments – with their unique spatial, temporal and cognitive elements – that espouse awe, inspiration and the promise of a novel social order. Revolutionaries become the master of the streets at these transitory times; their unremitting initiatives, bravery and sacrifice appear as if they herald the birth of a new historical epoch. This represents the street politics of the revolutionary times.

But revolution as insurrection is different from 'post-revolution' – the day after the dictators abdicate. Whereas the 'street' matters most in times of revolution/insurrection, it is political society and the state that rule the day in 'post-revolution'. While the 'exceptional episode', the insurrection, echoes the mastery of revolutionaries, 'post-revolution' times become the occasion of the free-riders – those non-participants, the well-wishers, the benign and the watchers of events if not opportunists who assume immediate power the day after the dictators relinquish power. They come out, get visible and vocal, and make claims. Most crucially, they become the target of intense mobilisation by the already organised and equally free-riding groups and movements.

A paradox of the 'post-revolution' period is that either the revolutionaries (banking on their political capital) impose their agenda through exclusionary populism (as in revolutions in Iran, Russia, China or Ethiopia) without much regard for the will of the majority by such claims as 'We did the revolution, so we have the right to rule'. Or, if electoral democracy did matter, they might lose political society to the free-rider majority whose votes can bring non-revolutionaries to the centres of power. The fact is that revolutionaries are always in a minority; and revolutions are always carried out by a minority (in Egypt only 11 per cent), albeit a spectacular minority, exceptional and extraordinary players who master the art of insurrection.[24] Revolutions are won not because the majority of people fight the regimes, but because only a tiny minority remains to resist.

But the street politics of revolutionary times shows its limitations when it is deployed in an electoral democracy. The protests in Cairo's Tahrir Square, Madrid's Puerta del Sol or New York's Liberty Square were truly the most extraordinary expression of street politics in recent memory. But they were precisely that, *extraordinary*, which in ordinary times reveal their limitations;

[24] An Abu Dhabi Gallup organisation conducting face-to-face interviews with 1,000 Egyptians in April 2011 showed that only 11 per cent of Egyptians participated in the uprising (which is rather high comparatively), and the 83 per cent supported it; see 'New Poll Gives Insight into Post-Uprising Public Opinion', *Al-Masry al-Youm*, 5 June 2011. During the Cuban revolution, while a handful of Castro's group took over the mountains of Sierra Mystera, Che Guevara began to conquer the rest of the country with 148 men; see Eric Hobsbawm, *The Age of Extremes: The Short Twentieth Century, 1914–1991* (London: Michael Joseph, 1996), p. 438. John Adams famously stated that only a third of the population supported the revolutionaries; just imagine how many were revolutionaries themselves. Adams also believed that another third supported the British, and the remaining third were neutral; see George S. Fisher, *The True History of the American Revolution* (Chestnut Hill, MA: Adamant Media Corp., 2003).

they cannot be sustained for a long span of time because of high resource cost, while their routinisation would diminish their clout and efficacy. Moreover, these *extraordinary* struggles are likely to be short-lived, because they are by definition divorced from the business of everyday life. For instance, whereas the mobilisation of Zapatistas in Chiapas or *horizontalidad* in Argentina were effectively part of the daily struggle for sustenance (campaign for land, worker's self-management for securing jobs, neighbourhood self-rule for ensuring services), the extraordinary street politics of the Occupy Movement or Tahrir was divorced from the daily business of ordinary lives, and, therefore, could not go on for long. Consequently, in post-revolution moments winners are not those who once created the wonders of Tahrir and its magical power, but those who skilfully mobilise the mass of ordinary people, including the free-riders, in their small towns, farms, factories, unions and at the ballot box.

Thus, whereas revolutionaries continued with the motto 'the street is our way', thinking that 'we can always come and sit-in [in Tahrir] if we find that our revolution is being hijacked', the religious parties in Tunisia and Egypt began to mobilise the free-riders as soon as the dictators fell. Al-Nahda, along with its leader Rachid al-Ghanoushi, travelled to the provinces, urban neighbourhoods and villages to hold meetings, establish branches and build networks. Thousands attended these meetings.[25] In Egypt, groups like Gama'a al-Islamiyya, banned and banished under Mubarak, as well as the unassuming Salafis, emerged out of seclusion and began to mobilise in earnest. The Muslim Brothers already had a well-established organisation and a vast network of cells, cadres and local leaders throughout the country. They revitalised those networks in a more aggressive fashion in mosques, villages and neighbourhoods, often deploying their messages along with typical populist dispensations – hand-outs, food and fuel. When the Gama'a al-Islamiyya held its first free rally in Masjid Adam in Ain al-Shams of Cairo, some 4,000 attended.[26] Through such relentless work far away from Tahrir or Bourqiba Boulevard, the religious parties managed to score impressive victories in the constituent assemblies and parliamentary elections in 2011. They dominated political society through side-lining the left, liberal and post-Islamist

[25] Marc Lynch, 'Tunisia's New al-Nahda', *Foreign Policy*, 29 June 2011.

[26] As reported in *'al-Masry 'al-Yawm* (*Egypt Independent*), 16 April 2011.

revolutionaries, not to mention women whose mass presence in the revolutions notwithstanding, ended up being excluded from the centres of power.[27]

It is true, democratic practice is not limited to the ballot box, and recent times have shown how liberal 'democratic' institutions in many countries, including the West, have failed to represent the true wishes of large numbers of their citizens. But this should not be a cause to over-celebrate street politics or to romanticise extra-legal acts. On the contrary, these acts are precisely the inescapable corollary of exclusion from, mistrust in and failure of institutional politics in a volatile revolutionary mode – a tendency increasingly on display in many societies that have experienced popular protests in recent years. In post-revolution times, such institutions as political parties, genuine civil society, voting, parliament and, above all, the rule of law do matter – in fact they are the indispensable, but by no means sufficient, ingredients of building an inclusive polity to which the revolutions seemed to aspire.

Conclusions

The Arab Spring unfolded in such an astonishing manner that it caught observers and protagonists alike by surprise. Most considered them novel. But what precisely was new about these political happenings beyond their youthful, tech-savvy activists who traversed between the online and offline worlds? How did their newness reflect in their transition trajectories? I have suggested that the revolutions in Tunisia, Egypt and Yemen were different from the prevailing trajectories of reform, revolution or implosion. Rather they seem to be a new breed, what I have called Refo-lution, or some kind of 'reformist revolutions'. A product of the post-Cold War era, they emerged at an ideological time in the globe when the very idea of revolution had been disappearing. The refo-lutionary character of the revolutions in Egypt, Tunisia and Yemen in turn produced a contradictory transition path. While the revolutions proved to be less violent and less repressive, they remained vulnerable to counter-revolution restoration. Whereas the post-revolution

[27] Only eight women managed to enter Egypt's parliament with 480 members in the 2011 elections: Hania Sholkamy, 'Why Women Are at the Heart of Egypt's Political Triads and Tribulations?' *Open Democracy*, 24 January 2012. In Tunisia, however, thanks to a quota system, the Tunisian assembly accommodates a more reasonable number of women deputies.

governance embraced political pluralism, including political forces of the old regimes, it caused little meaningful change in state power, and fundamentally ignored social and economic transformation. Thus, Egypt experienced a counter-revolution restoration; Yemen fell into a civil and proxy war; and Tunisia moved towards an electoral democracy – thanks largely to negotiations between the Islamic, labour and secular forces – but its continuing neo-liberal policies left the desire for inclusion, equity and social justice unfulfilled. In the end, the revolutions found their deepest legacies at the grassroots, where the new awareness and imagination among the subaltern marked the post-revolutionary trajectories with unknown possibilities.

5

REVOLUTIONS AND THE COLONIAL QUESTION

Hamid Dabashi

It's not just simply a matter of capturing people and holding them accountable, but removing the sanctuaries, removing the support systems, ending states who sponsor terrorism. It will be a campaign, not a single action.[1]

Paul Wolfowitz, US Deputy Secretary of Defense, 13 September 2001

Are Arab nation-states forever condemned to tyranny at home and colonial/imperial domination from abroad? Were the revolutions that swept the Arab World from one end to another between 2010 and 2012 all in vain – much ado about nothing, were we dreaming, hallucinating or did they actually happen? How can we account for those euphoric uprisings and such dismal collapse into exacerbated tyranny as usual, now epitomised in the ruling junta in Egypt, in clannish tribalism in Saudi Arabia, in its inter-clannish alliances with the United Arab Emirates and Bahrain, in murderous tyranny in Syria, in factional disintegration in Libya? Let us add the rule of Shia clerics in Iran and the belated sultanism in Turkey, and ask the same question not just about the Arab but indeed the Muslim World at large. Is Islam the issue, is Arab patrimonialism, Oriental despotism or Third World tyranny? How come we do not have a single successful state anywhere in the Arab and Muslim World to show the world as a sign of salvation?

[1] Cited in James Bovard, *Terrorism and Tyranny: Trampling Freedom, Justice, and Peace to Rid the World of Evil* (New York: Palgrave Macmillan, 2004), p. 298.

None of these hitherto standard, now entirely cliché, questions or answers they might solicit will any longer suffice. In the aftermath of the Arab revolutions, we need to ask far more basic, far more fundamental questions – questions indeed upstream from all these tired and tiring goose chases. To come to a fresh understanding of the revolutionary uprisings code-named 'the Arab Spring', we need actively to disabuse ourselves of the received illusions and mythologies we have inherited from previous generations – of both the colonial and the post-colonial vintages.

Chief among such illusions is the notion of 'transition to democracy'. The very notion of a 'democratic transition' is *ipso facto* predicated on a teleological trajectory that begins and ends with Europe – with Europe as its origin and destination at one and the same time. All other societies dwell, by definition, on a 'transitional' state – a transition to an unattainable democracy. The objective of history, Hegelian in its very trajectory, is therefore to get to Europe, though 'Europe' as a metaphor not as a physical destination to which darker nations may always aspire but will never actually reach, for to transition to democracy completely they have to become white. Democracy therefore sports an affectively white history. The very notion of 'transition' is therefore a strategy, a stratagem, to keep them subordinate with an abiding sense of defective birth and arrested growth – calling them 'developing' or 'in transition' or 'Third World', all varied forms of pejorative euphemisms. Any such notion of 'transition to democracy', or dwelling fully in neo-liberal capitalism, requires varied forms of dictatorship to speed up the move to democracy, which is of course a ridiculous paradox. In this paradox 'the West' will always remain the epicentre, the objective, the promised land, cast upon the Hegelian telos – by birth and upbringing militantly Eurocentric.

To disabuse ourselves of such abusive ideas we will need to go back to points of fractures in European history itself. In his exquisite posthumous work, *The Myth of the State* (1946), the eminent German philosopher Ernst Cassirer believed the events between the two world wars had cast the entire field of political thought into disarray:

> In the last thirty years we have not only passed through a severe crisis of our political and social life, but we have also been confronted with quite new theoretical problems . . . Problems that had been unknown to the political

> thinkers of the eighteenth and nineteenth centuries came suddenly to the fore.[2]

Cassirer believed 'perhaps the most important and the most alarming feature in this development of modern political thought is the appearance of a new power: the power of mythical thought'.[3] In the aftermath of the Arab revolutions, we are facing no less dramatic transitions. We are in fact in a hiatus we scarce know what legitimate questions to ask, let alone offer what possible answers to offer them. However, Cassirer's uncanny but timely turn to 'mythical thought', right in the grip of Nazism and fascism in Europe, may point us to the right direction.

Whence and Wherefore the 'Arab Spring?'

The Arab Spring took the academic world by surprise, in and out of the Arab World, within or without the discipline of political science. It in fact challenged our very regime of knowledge production – colonial or post-colonial. No one was expecting these revolutions, none of our theories anticipated them, no one was ready even to account for them when they actually happened. In the aftermath of what actually did happen, and the impossibility of reading both the events and their aftermath, none of the existing 'transition theories' holds any water. Indeed, the very idea of 'democracy' (and with it *a fortiori* 'democratisation') required critical rethinking not just in the Arab/Muslim World, but around the globe. The question is no longer limited to the Arab and Muslim World – the very question of 'transition' has become suspect. 'Transition' from what to what? If the crowning achievement of 'Western democracies' is the election of Donald Trump in the United States, the dramatic nativism evident in Brexit, and the rise of right-wing neo-fascism in the rest of Europe, then much more than the proverbial Orientalist assumptions of the Arab culture and Islamic faith being obstacles to democracy are at stake. This is even more if indeed 'the only democracy in the Middle East', is a racist apartheid settler colony created by British colonialism. Would the Arab/Muslim World be truly lucky to reach a point to elect a Donald Trump as their president, or to harbour a meeting between

[2] Ernst Cassirer, *The Myth of the State* (New Haven, CT: Yale University Press, 1946), p. 3.
[3] Ibid.

their own Steve Bannon and Marine Le Pen? If 'Western democracy' was a chimeric construct, a colonial ruse, then how do we 'transition' – and transition from what to what?

The presence of Israel as a settler colony that loudly considers itself 'the only democracy in the Middle East' is particularly sobering and the prime evidence of this chimeric concoction called 'Western democracy'. If it is a democracy, then what is it doing on the stolen homeland of another people? If it is a settler colony, as it is, then how could it be a democracy – unless the mother of all settler colonies the United States is to thrive on repressing its own original sin? The paradox of a settler colony calling itself a 'democracy' and indeed 'the only democracy in the Middle East' is the epicentre of a link between the overwhelming power of the myth of 'Western' democracy and the fact of colonialism contradicting its primary claim to political truth.

Conceptual thrusts like 'uncertainty' or 'transitional periods' are quick to suggest themselves to political scientists still thinking within the trappings of their discipline – but they are no longer convincing. Suppose we stopped looking at the Arab/Muslim World as an aberration from the normative course of democracy and democratisation. Suppose we went to the very core of the assumption of capitalist modernity, turning the gaze towards the Arab/Muslim World, and asking questions far more upstream that include, but is not limited to, this world; watch the watchers, so to speak? What then? Is not the world at large, from the oldest (United States), to the largest (India), to the very epicentre of the colonial conquest of the globe (Europe) right now at the forefront of the crisis of democracy? What exactly is the measure of 'democracy'? The people who are the *demos* or the rulers who claim *kratia* – or cutting it so deeply would dismantle the very systemic apparatus of 'political science'?

Let us look inward: there are two classical studies of the predicament of the Arab/Muslim World we might consider together. One is Gharbzadeghi/Westoxication (1962) by the leading Iranian public intellectual Jalal Al-e Ahmad (1923–69), and the other *Al-Naqd al-Dhati Ba'da al-Hazima* (*Self-Criticism After the Defeat*, 1968) by perhaps his Arab counterpart Sadiq Jalal El-Azm (1934–2016), one an Iranian critic reflecting on the predicament of his homeland after the CIA-sponsored coup of 1953; the other by a Syrian critic in the aftermath of the humiliating 1967 defeat of Arab armies by

Israel. They both target their own political culture for criticism. They both consider a malaise that they believe to be prevalent in their own midst. But Al-e Ahmad considers 'the West' as the source of this malaise, while El-Azm completely abandons 'the West' and goes deeply into what he considers to be the internal ailment of his own people. But what they share is the trigger for their self-criticism, which is the collapse of any hope in the potent and legitimate state apparatus to defend the national sovereignty of their homelands. Suppose we combine them together and go upstream from both these self- and other-criticism? What both Al-e Ahmad in 1962 and El-Azm in 1968 diagnose is the normative impediment of their respective political cultures: one is placing their national and regional domains into a larger colonial context, while the other laser beams on his own people's predicament. Suppose we thank them both, Al-e Ahmad and El-Azm, and bid them farewell as we consider the possibilities of a frame of political reference that is no longer in the domain of blaming, but in the realm of epistemic rupture and emancipatory transcendence.

Suppose we transcended the study of the Arab/Muslim World as 'Area Studies' laboratories, and thus began to look at the very foundations of Eurocentric political science, sociology and anthropology as in fact area studies of a more dogged sort, what then? To what extent is the 'colonial question' still relevant in the Arab World? Is the colonial question only a subterfuge for irresponsible conspiracy theories or is there something historically and theoretically legitimate about the truth of coloniality – and, if so, in what particular way? Is the Arab and Muslim World particularly vulnerable to coloniality or is there something more globally at work here? Partially at fault here is the fixated binary between 'the Arab and the West', now so pathologically fetishised as to impair an epistemic connection to a larger continental frame of reference from Asia and Africa to Latin America and Oceania.

The condition of coloniality was, and its consequences remain, global; it includes the Arab/Muslim World but is not peculiar or limited to it. The framing of the world by European colonialism began with the global conquest of capitalist modernity on every continent. The colonial conquest of the world was transformed, as it became no longer economically viable, into what Hardt and Negri term empire, and particularly into an amorphous empire as

I have discussed elsewhere in detail.[4] From colonial to post-colonial to the Empire – the world has been at the mercy of the whimsical vicissitude of capital and the changing cultures it conditions.

Under these circumstances what is 'political science' to us – or us to 'political science'? If, indeed, as Cassirer's parting wisdom with us had it, myth not reason, was the way politics moved, then what has political 'science' to teach us? Was not 'political science' an academic branch of US State Department normalisation of imperial stability in the world? From fascism to totalitarianism to Nazism, and now to 'democracy', Europe and its American extension have ruled the world (or sought to rule the world) with their successive mythologies – as political scientists have sought to 'study' and normalise the terror of those mythologies. Our realities have run ahead of our scholarly limitations. What we have known as 'political science' was the epistemic foregrounding of sustaining the myth of the state.

On Pure Violence

The point of departure for us must remain the leviathan we recognise and call the 'state'. Max Weber understood the state as the *modus operandi* of a polity predicated on the monopoly of the use of (presumably) legitimate violence. The passage in his seminal essay 'Politics as a Vocation' (1919) regarding his definition of state is crucial here:

> What is a 'state'? Sociologically, the state cannot be defined in terms of its ends. There is scarcely any task that some political association has not taken in hand, and there is no task that one could say has always been exclusive and peculiar to those associations which are designated as political ones: today the state, or historically, those associations which have been the predecessors of the modern state. Ultimately, one can define the modern state sociologically only in terms of the specific means peculiar to it, as to every political association, namely, the use of physical force. 'Every state is founded on force', said Trotsky at Brest-Litovsk. That is indeed right. If no social institutions existed which knew the use of violence, then the concept of 'state' would be eliminated, and a condition would emerge that could be

[4] Hamid Dabashi, *Europe and Its Shadows: Coloniality after Empire* (London: Pluto, 2019).

> designated as 'anarchy', in the specific sense of this word. Of course, force is certainly not the normal or the only means of the state – nobody says that – but force is a means specific to the state. Today the relation between the state and violence is an especially intimate one. In the past, the most varied institutions – beginning with the sib – have known the use of physical force as quite normal. Today, however, we have to say that a state is a human community that (successfully) claims the monopoly of the legitimate use of physical force within a given territory. Note that 'territory' is one of the characteristics of the state. Specifically, at the present time, the right to use physical force is ascribed to other institutions or to individuals only to the extent to which the state permits it. The state is considered the sole source of the 'right' to use violence. Hence, 'politics' for us means striving to share power or striving to influence the distribution of power, either among states or among groups within a state.[5]

State, therefore, as the political organisation claiming a monopoly of (legitimate) violence has been at the epicentre of European capitalist (and by extension colonial modernity. The legitimacy of state is always subject to collective interrogation – particularly on the colonial edges of political modernity. The post-colonial state is therefore doubly violent – and perforce doubly claims but fails to secure legitimacy for its monopoly of violence. We on the colonial edges of European modernity received the modern state as a monopoly of violence inherited from colonialism and imposed on the condition of post-coloniality we call our nationhood.

Weber's reading of violence as definitive to our understanding of state must be linked to later theorists who reflected on the nature and function of violence – chief among them Walter Benjamin and Georgio Agamben. In *Zur Kritik der Gewalt* (*Towards the Critique of Violence*, 1921), Benjamin famously made a distinction between 'law-making violence/Rechtsetzend Gewalt' and 'law-preserving violence/Rechtserhaltende Gewalt'.[6] Law, therefore, is insti-

[5] Max Weber, 'Politics as a Vocation', in H. H. Gerth and C. Wright Mills (eds), *From Max Weber: Essays in Sociology*, trans. H. H. Gerth and C. Wright Mills (New York: Oxford University Press, 1946), pp. 77–8.

[6] See Walter Benjamin, 'Critique of Violence', in Walter Benjamin, *Reflections: Essays, Aphorisms, Autobiographical Writings* (New York: Schocken, 1986), pp. 277–300.

tutionalised violence, in both making and sustaining violence legalised. This legality of violence Max Weber before Benjamin identified as the nucleus of legitimacy, or perceived legitimacy, for state violence. If the state has a monopoly of violence, as Weber proposed, then violence is definitive to the very idea of state and its exclusive ability to make laws, as Benjamin would say, laws that sustain the power of its exclusive violence. Legalised violence is therefore the exclusive prerogative of the state, if we were to put Weber and Benjamin together. The post-colonial state, we might add here, has more claim to violence as foregrounding of legality. Legalisation of violence in European or Eurocentric state formations is a more abstract institutionalisation of violence – where the legal system seeks to camouflage the naked violence of the state and its exclusive right to make laws. As the cases of the United States and Israel clearly show, states have more legal constraints when operating vis-à-vis their own citizens than when they invade (Iraq and Afghanistan) or occupy (Palestine) other countries. For its own exclusively Zionist 'citizens', Israel has a whole judiciary system. But when facing Palestinians under its occupying force it shoots to kill them without any legal compunctions. The same holds true for the United States in Afghanistan or Iraq.

In an essay Agamben wrote in 1970, 'Sui limiti della violenza', and sent to Hannah Arendt in a letter by way of introducing himself to the great patroness of Benjamin readership in English, the Italian philosopher moved forward the thinking of the German-Jewish theorist of violence. In this letter, Agamben wrote, 'Fifty years after the publication of Walter Benjamin's *Critique of Violence*, and more than sixty years after Georges Sorel's *Reflections on Violence*, a reconsideration of the limits and the meaning of violence stands little risk of appearing untimely.'[7] The principal point of departure for Agamben's reflections on violence in 1970 and after was the enormity of the very idea of violence beyond anything that either Sorel or Benjamin could have imagined. Early in his essay, Agamben points to a basic contradiction in the relationship between violence and politics:

> At first glance, the relation between violence and politics appears a contradiction in terms: European history itself is predicated on the notion that

[7] Giorgio Agamben, 'On the Limits of Violence', trans. Elisabeth Fay, *Diacritics* 39(4) (2009): 103–11.

> violence and politics are mutually exclusive. The Greeks, who invented most of the concepts we use to articulate our experience of politics today, used the term *polis* to describe a way of life founded on the word, and not on violence. To be political (to live in the polis) was to accept the principle that everything should be decided by the word and by persuasion, rather than by force or by violence. The essential characteristic of political life was thus *peitharkhia*, the power of persuasion; it was a power so revered that even those citizens condemned to death were persuaded to die by their own hand.[8]

There is, of course, a long distance between what the Greeks fancied as politics and what 'European history itself' did, which is precisely the opposite of what Agamben imagines as 'predicated on the notion that violence and politics are mutually exclusive'. If Agamben were kindly to consider leaving the Greeks of the city-state of Athens in his study room and walk into the horrors of imperial and colonial European history where violence (as Weber clearly saw) has been definitive to politics. Be that as it may, from here, Agamben moves to show how in our own times in fact language itself has become embedded with violence. Then through Sade and Marx, he comes to the point where he identifies violence as 'the midwife of history'. This is what he says:

> Within this framework, identifying just violence is no problem at all: if violence is the midwife of history, it need only hasten and facilitate the (inevitable) discovery of History's necessary laws. Violence that serves this end is just; violence that resists this end is unjust. To appreciate just how clumsy this interpretation is, we need only consider that it paints the revolutionary as a naturalist who discovers a plant species destined for extinction and then uses everything in his power to hasten its demise so that he may realize the laws of evolution. This was precisely the model adopted by totalitarian movements in the twentieth century, whose self-proclaimed exclusive right to revolutionary violence fostered involutional processes within authentic revolutionary movements. This was exactly what happened in Nazi Germany with the deportation of the Jews, and what happened in

[8] Ibid., p. 104.

> Russia with the great purges of 1935, when whole Soviet populations were deported – the only difference being that Hitler sought to 'hasten' the realization of a natural law (the superiority of the Aryan race), while Stalin believed he was 'hastening' the institution of an equally necessary historical law.[9]

Here, Agamben is much closer to the very logic of political violence, when his analysis reaches Nazi Germany and he must face the horrors of European history – but only when perpetrated upon Europeans themselves. At this point, as Agamben realises, violence has assumed cosmic proportions and necessity, 'Violence in nature may only be called just by those who believe in cosmic plans and divine providence; human violence may only be called just by those who believe that history is a steady advancement along the predetermined route of linear time …' (the vision of vulgar progressivism).[10] His conclusion: 'At the dawn of every history aimed at ensuring security and making peace with death, it shall be written: "In the beginning, there was the word". At the dawn of every new temporal order, however, it shall be written: "In the beginning, there was violence".'[11]

What Agamben typically ignores (typically for a European thinker) is the horrors of the self-same logic of violence around the globe, when perpetrated by the self-same Europeans. Evidently unbeknownst to Agamben, from Weber to Agamben's thoughts on the nature and function of violence is historically interrupted by the work of Frantz Fanon on the same subject. What would happen to the link among Weber, Benjamin and Agamben if we interject Fanon? What if we brought Algeria and the rest of the Arab and colonial world to bear on Fanon co-thinking violence with Weber, Benjamin and Agamben? In between Benjamin's 'Zur Kritik der Gewalt' (1921) and Agamben's 'Sui limiti della violenza' (1970), Frantz Fanon had published his *Wretched of the Earth* (1961), in which he begins with a classical reflection on colonial and anti-colonial violence.[12] Why was Agamben unaware of Fanon a decade after the publication of that seminal text on colonialism? How come

[9] Ibid., p. 106.
[10] Ibid., p. 106.
[11] Ibid., p. 109.
[12] Frantz Fanon, *Wretched of the Earth*, trans. Richard Philcox (New York: Grove Press, 2004).

when Mussolini and Italian fascism went on a conquest, Italians know where Libya and North Africa are, but when an eminent Italian philosopher thinks philosophically he cannot see beyond his own nose? Why were Europeans before and after Agamben so blinded to the domain of colonial violence? How would an awareness and/or attention to that colonial violence have affected their legitimate fixation with European violence only when perpetrated on other Europeans? That is a question worth considering.

The trouble is not just with Agamben or other European philosophers. In a recent volume, *Towards the Critique of Violence: Walter Benjamin and Giorgio Agamben* (2015), Brendan Moran and Carlo Salzani have brought together pioneering essays addressing the link between the two seminal European theorists of violence. The invisibility of colonial violence in the European genealogy of critical reflections on violence is a mode of collective Freudian repression that is yet to return to full historical consciousness. That racialised historiography of critical thinking is where the 'West' disregards the rest.

More to the point, what if we interject Fanon (or Césaire) in the refracted navel-gazing of European thinkers? If we take the Jewish Holocaust, from which Benjamin ran to his death, as the epitome of the systemic violence Europeans perpetrated on themselves, then the barbarity of the act exposes the hidden caesura of European colonialism to a theoretically uncomfortable degree. It was Aimé Césaire who in his *Discourse sur le colonialism* (*Discourse on Colonialism*, 1955) argued that the Jewish Holocaust was not an aberration in European history. Rather, Europeans perpetrated similar crimes against humanity on the colonised world at large:

> Yes, it would be worthwhile to study clinically, in detail, the steps taken by Hitler and Hitlerism and to reveal to the very distinguished, very humanistic, very Christian bourgeois of the twentieth century that without his being aware of it, he has a Hitler inside him, that Hitler inhabits him, that Hitler is his demon, that if he rails against him, he is being inconsistent and that, at bottom, what he cannot forgive Hitler for is not crime in itself, the crime against man, it is not the humiliation of man as such, it is the crime against the white man, the humiliation of the white man, and the fact that he applied to Europe colonialist procedures which until then had been

> reserved exclusively for the Arabs of Algeria, the coolies of India, and the niggers of Africa.[13]

What this passage by Aimé Césaire and later Fanon's chapter on violence in the *Wretched of the Earth* demand is not a vindictive dismissal of critical European thinkers like Weber, Benjamin or Agamben. Quite to the contrary: a de-racialised genealogy of critical thinking will open a whole new archaeology of knowledge in which Europe will once and for all recognise itself as the sublime allegory of violence, a mobile army of metaphors inherently violent in its colonial disposition. Only in that recognition will Europe be delivered from its own genealogy of violence and join the world at large in a collective reading of state as the monopoly of violence. The colonial and post-colonial state carried the germs of that violence into the four corners of the world.

Cassirer's work on the mythological dimensions of state is predicated on his own predicament as a German scholar who fled Nazi Germany, where he used to teach philosophy at the University of Hamburg until the fateful year of 1933. He left for Oxford, from which he eventually moved to the University of Göteborg in Sweden, and finally to the United States. There, he taught at Yale, where he was working on his *The Myth of the State* at the time of his passing in 1945. On the colonial edges of European modernity violence has always been naked, pure, undiluted, uncamouflaged by philosophical speculation. It is the naked and exposed truth of that colonial violence that must be the measure of our reading of violence as the cornerstone of the myth of the (post-colonial) state today.

The Global Crisis of Liberal Democracy

On the afternoon of 26 May 2017, two teenage girls board a commuter train in Portland, Oregon, in the United States – one is wearing a hijab. A loud, overweight, violent, angry and abusive man boards the same train, sees the two young girls and starts yelling and screaming anti-Muslim racist slurs at them. The girls get frightened and move away. Three brave souls walk towards the terrorising man to restrain him and calm him down, but the monster pulls a knife and cuts the throats of the three protecting angels, killing two

[13] Aimé Césaire, *Discourse on Colonialism*, trans. Joan Pinkham (New York: Monthly Review Press, 1972), p. 3.

of them, Ricky John Best, 53, and Taliesin Myrddin Namkai Meche, 23. The third, Micah David-Cole Fletcher, 21, is subsequently hospitalised in a serious condition.

We can see the gruesome Portland atrocity (with the many other shocking incidents of mass violence before and after it) as symptomatic of the campaign of domestic terror and intimidation the presidency of Donald Trump unleased on the oldest democracy in the world. The threat to US democratic institutions is far more serious than that of murderous thugs like ISIS, the gravest since the rise of Nazism and fascism in Europe. With the election of Donald Trump, liberal democracies have actually emerged as existential threats to world peace.

A particularly pernicious aspect of Trump's campaign was the targeting of Mexican guest labourers and Muslim refugees. What we are therefore witnessing in tighter border control and construction of walls is in fact the rise of *total states* exposing their *naked violence* as they turn their own citizens inside out into bare lives. The draconian measures targeting foreigners are, in effect, weakening protection for civil liberties inside the borders.

The rise of such wholesale machinations of total states ruling over bare lives through naked violence is in part due to the catalytic impact of ISIS on the very idea of the state as the Weberian monopoly of 'legitimate' violence. There is an 'ISIS' inside each and every state, and the emergence of ISIS has effectively exposed that fact. Today movements like Black Lives Matter, Women's March on Washington DC, Dakota Access Pipe, the Climate Rallies, the global BDS in support of Palestinian national liberation, or the collective defiance of state power as in the Zapatistas, or even far more global uprisings like the Arab Spring, the episodic electoral movements in Iran, the anti-austerity uprisings in Europe, or the Occupy Wall Street movement in the United States are all signs of the global reaction to such tendencies.

The election of Donald Trump in the United States was not an aberration. It is the symptom of a crisis much deeper and more pervasive than just a phenomenon now globally abhorred as 'Donald Trump'. Liberal democracies are in deep crisis, and that crisis is integral and structural to its own deficiencies and contradictions. The very idea of 'the West' as the cornerstone of liberal democracy is today a questionable proposition, as indeed are the very assumptions of democratic institutions, when a president can, with the stroke of a pen, issue an 'executive order' and send the whole judicial and legislative bodies of a democracy spinning around themselves. Wars can be launched, incitement to violence can be on full display, extrajudicial executions and drone attacks with massive civilian casualties can be ordered, and the legislative and judiciary branches can be sidestepped – without much consequence.

Corruption at the state level exposes monumental dislocation of nations. Prolonged mass migration, now exacerbated by waves of refugees running from war-torn countries, is the most immediate index of a global crisis now manifested in xenophobic nationalism and violent polarisation that now mars the visage of liberal democracies from one end of Europe to another. The cherished capacity to encourage and sustain democratic deliberations and critical debates is now severely compromised. The very veracity of news is now in question, as we are told we live in an age of post-truth.

The massive labour migration and waves of refugees are in and of themselves a by-product of the neo-liberal globalisation that produces wealth for a small minority and leaves the overwhelming majority of the global population impoverished and vulnerable to nativist ideologies. Political charlatans put these grievances to electoral use. However, it is false to see these surges as a politics of racist populism appealing to people's basest racialised instincts. Multiple factors are at work here. People are as much aghast at the corruption of the Democratic Party in the United States as they are with the Republicans.

We need, therefore, to make a categorical distinction between the failures of globalised neo-liberal economics that have created deep cleavages manifested in social anomie and political nihilism, and the very marginal xenophobic sentiments in isolationist rhetoric. Brexit was not the result of the British suddenly becoming more xenophobic isolationists than before, although like any other country the British have their share of racist isolationists. The election if Trump in the United States was not the result of a sudden rise in racist white supremacists winning over their cosmopolitan counterparts, though, of course, there is a prolonged history of racism in the United States. Although Macron ultimately won in France, Marine Le Pen came a strong second, representing not just the xenophobic forces in France but also those segments of society disenfranchised by neo-liberal economics.

A key conceptual malfunction domestic to the vagaries of liberal democracies is the term 'populism', which is used against anything positive or negative that disturbs its normative equilibrium. The false equivalency of Donald Trump with Bernie Sanders is an example of a fundamental failure to acknowledge the trouble with neo-liberalism. Trump took full advantage of the structural deficiencies of neo-liberalism to push it towards barbarism, while Sanders was moving towards the very possibility of addressing its enduring ailments. But the term 'populism' concealed this fact in the interest of pushing Hillary Clinton as the natural choice.

In Europe, from Greek austerity measures to Brexit, from the popularity of far-right parties in France, Germany and Holland, to the more endemic Eurozone crisis are equally significant signs of the failures of neo-liberal policies. The rise of xenophobic nationalism in Europe is an indication that the sustained failures of neo-liberalism are the fertile conditions of the rise of right-wing politics of despair and fanaticism, exacerbated by the waves of Syrian and other refugees and migrants into Europe. But between European isolationism evident in its xenophobic nationalism and fanatical neo-liberalism dwells the prospect of an alternative politics that, indeed, as President Macron has said, builds bridges instead of walls. However, over those bridges is the consciousness of the necessity of sustaining a civic life that generates its own pluralistic culture rather than continuing with the false promises of Euro-universalism.

In the Arab and Muslim world, the rise of democratic revolutions was met with counter-revolutionary mobilisation from Syria to Saudi Arabia to Egypt – and in time resulted in the concomitant rise of the monstrous ISIS. The tail end of ISIS has now reached Europe and the United States too, their primary targets are still the Arab and Muslim world. The increasing signs of authoritarianism in Turkey, the limited tolerance of dissent in Iran, the bloodbath of Bashar Assad in Syria, the false binary the Saudis and Iranians have constructed between Sunnis and Shiis, the incessant militarisation of Saudi Arabia to the tune of $110 billion in its most recent deal; with Donald Trump, the slaughter of innocent people in Yemen, the ultra-nationalist right-wing of Zionist takeover of Israeli politics of land theft, are all indications of the maladies facing the Arab and Muslim world.

The result of this confounding scene is the bizarre fact that the oldest existing democracy, namely the United States, is now in fact an existential threat to the cause of democracy in the world, and with it the peace and justice it was meant to produce in the world. European liberal democracies too are exposed for their fundamental lack of tolerance, of pluralism, of moral, imaginative and normative diversity. In the United States, the cause and course of democracy has in fact paradoxically given birth to its own dialectical negation, its inner contradiction. Contrary to common wisdom, the battle is not between liberal progress and illiberal backwardness. The far more serious problem is the inability of neo-liberalism to see its own fundamental contradictions and to acknowledge the systemic rise of inequality nationally and transnationally. Liberal democracies are under threat from their own structural fault lines, and their obliviousness to the trail of death, destruction and destitution they leave behind.

The fall of the Berlin Wall and the collapse of Soviet Union prompted Francis Fukuyama to declare the end of history by the final triumph of liberalism. However, all around Europe miles of other walls are rising, while the United States proposes a 'wall of Trump' on the Mexican border. Or look at the apartheid wall of Israel in Palestine, to see the history never ended, that Hegelian Geist is deeply perturbed. The self-fulfilling prophecy of Huntington about the clash of civilisations has anticipated the intense xenophobia, Islamophobia and claustrophobia in the United States and even in Europe. As the end of history was predicated on the false premise of the ultimate victory of liberalism, its troubled unfolding is in fact conditioned by its sustained failures.

The rise of total states corresponds to pure violence perpetrated on naked lives trapped inside militarised urban spaces that increasingly look like camps – camps that have become the extension of the securitised state best on display in airports, in-between locations where we have all become digitised humanity, bereft of the totality and infinity of who and what we are and what we might be, reduced to a level of atomised sub-individuality scarce experienced, or even imaginable during Nazi Germany. Here what we have learned from Cassirer regarding the Romanisation of the idea of state since the Napoleonic War needs serious upgrading. He proposed, and rightly so, that we have inherited the idea of the nation-state from that Napoleonic era, which was brought to a closure by Hitler, Mussolini and Franco when the myth of history was finally fulfilled far beyond its Romantic origins. With Goethe, Ranke and Schleiermacher, the ideas of 'World Literature',

'World History' and 'World Religion' assumed currency among European Romantics. But these bourgeois romanticisms all paled in comparison with the rise of jingoistic ethnic nationalism in Europe.

ISIS as Total State and Pure Violence

Yemen, Kazakhstan, Orlando, Istanbul, Bangladesh, Baghdad, Medina, Nice . . . try to draw even the most recent map of the vicious, premeditated crimes perpetrated or claimed by ISIS, all targeting innocent, defenceless civilians – the map is spreading but the doctrine is constant: 'shock and awe' – generate fear and loathing by choosing public spaces and symbolic dates: an airport in Istanbul, a busy market in Baghdad, a crowded promenade in Nice, Eid al-Fitr in Muslim countries, Bastille Day in France. This is not blind hatred. This is calculated criminality seeking to dismantle the ruling states it targets: show them to be inept in their protection of civilians. Whether they actually perpetrate the crime (Istanbul and Baghdad) or claim they did when performed by patently deranged individuals (Orlando and Nice), they tally such barbarities towards very specific purpose.

The origin of this malignant disease called ISIS was and remains in powerful states targeting weak states with massive civilian casualties – hundreds of thousands in Afghanistan and Iraq. The result of it is a phantom, abstracted, delusional and fake state (ISIS) waging an asymmetric war against powerful states by deliberately targeting innocent civilians as their primary victims. Common and constant to both its point of origin and its consequences, ISIS is symptomatic of a disease that keeps exacerbating the state monopoly of violence (as German sociologist Max Weber aptly defined it in his seminal essay, 'Politics as a Vocation', 1919) by targeting innocent and vulnerable civilians at moments and in places where their respective states are unable to protect them.

ISIS and all its state nemesis in and out of the Muslim world today come together to form the amorphous shape of a *total state* sustained via *pure violence* perpetrated upon innocent civilians: whether by US and NATO forces in Iraq or Libya, or by ISIS in Istanbul, Baghdad, Medina, Nice or San Bernardino. ISIS is the return of the barely repressed origin of all states, for which all innocent civilians have become what the eminent Italian philosopher Georgio Agamben has aptly called *homo sacer* (the accursed person, the bare life). Unable to protect their citizens, as ISIS intends to show all states to be, all states they target effectively lose their basis of legitimacy and become like ISIS, a state without a nation (supporting it). ISIS is targeting the hyphen holding the very idea of a 'nation-state' together.

ISIS is the basest denominator of all state violence and innocent civilians are the sacrificial sites of exposing that violence. In the aftermath of the Paris attack the French government banned all public demonstrations and increased its systematic surveillance of its citizens, as did the United Kingdom after the 7 July 2005 bombing, or Spain after the 11 March 2004 Madrid railroad attack, and so have Egypt, Saudi Arabia or any other Arab country from Morocco to Jordan. The ruling Syrian state apparatus is today almost identical with ISIS in its brutish disregard for civilian lives and liberties. ISIS is a malignant cell that exposes the naked violence of all other states it touches.

The consistent codification of ISIS as an 'Islamic' phenomenon by both the criminal thugs themselves and by the Islamophobia industry conceals and distorts a far simpler and far more urgent explanation: ISIS is the combined consequence of two deadly compositions: US/EU imperial militarism and Arab/Muslim nativist tyranny. Any assessment that disregards any one of these two complimentary components will misread ISIS. ISIS is the aggressive transmutation of twentieth-century state violence catapulted onto the digital revolution of twenty-first-century spectacle violence. There is therefore a direct structural link among the narco-state, the deep state, the security state, the garrison state and now in the case of ISIS the total state predicated on the pure spectacle of violence.

After each and every ISIS or ISIS-inspired or ISIS-claimed atrocities anywhere in the world – in the Arab and Muslim world, in Europe, or in the United States – the innocent civilian targets are the immediate casualties of their savagery. After each such attack, they will not weaken but in fact strengthen the resolve of their state nemesis to chase after their shadow. With each cycle of violence powerful states that are posing to fight ISIS in fact become more like ISIS and repressive of civil liberties, more intolerant of democratic criticism, more prone to securitisation and surveillance technologies. In Turkey now even criticising the state policies is considered an act of 'terrorism'. Opposing this systematic securitisation of the state, of the expansive surveillance state that Hillary Clinton promised or xenophobic fascism that a Trump presidency unleashed, citizens of a free and democratic nation have no choice but organise to protect their civil liberties. Acts of mourning from Nice and Orlando to Baghdad and Istanbul and beyond must also be acts of civic solidarity, of feeling the palpitations of a collective social consciousness, not just in defiance of those savages who have sought to puncture it, but also against any and all state moves to deny it.

Ending the Myth of the Post-colonial State

The degeneration of the ruling regimes across the Arab and Muslim world and well into the rest of Asia, Africa and Latin America into pure violence is the final desolation of the myth of the post-colonial state. As Ernst Cassirer fully realised and systematically theorised the culmination of state violence in his own time, there is a mythological dimension to all states, not just the fascist state. As the oldest claim on the myth of 'democracy', the contemporary American claim on the classic argument rests on the most widely mystified foregrounding of sanctity invested in their flag, sung in their national anthem, staged in their love for gun ownership, and their mesmerised fixation with the myth of the Wild West, which has never been a geographical but always a mystical allegory.

As nations rise to reconfigure alternative myths for their sense of polity and political purpose, states that laid false claim on them have categorically failed and degenerated into pure violence minus any legitimising claim to their name. The bloody thrones upon which a plurality of autocrats currently sit are prime examples of the defunct and dysfunctional myth of 'nation-state' in the Arab/Muslim world. This final farewell to the myth of the post-colonial state is a liberating moment for nations without states. The urgent moral, imaginative and intellectual crisis in the Arab World is precisely due to the fact that the end of the condition of post-coloniality has denied and finally delivered them from the myth of the state, to which the European Enlightenment modernity they received through colonialism allows them no access.

The very notion of the 'nation-state' has always been and will always remain a troubled colonial legacy and a cruel post-colonial myth. It has never worked. For 200 years of anti-colonial struggles and post-colonial state formation we have not a single solid case of a successful nation-state – a legitimate democratic state ruling over a fully recognised citizenry. At its most successful (Egypt, Iran and Turkey), the illusion has conditioned consistently fertile ground for revolt and created unremitting subnational categories of resentment and supranational geo-politics of aggression and violence. The result is the transformation of the illusion of a legitimate state into the reality of a total state predicated on pure illegitimate violence. The perfect model, and in fact the blueprint of this reality, is the last enduring vestige of European colonialism in the region, the settler colonial garrison state of Israel, a total state with an ideologically engineered nation, built on the broken back of Palestinians – an organic nation with no real state. That the idea of a 'nation-state' is a manufactured colonial concoction is best evident in the case of Israel – a garrison state with no nation, occupying the homeland of a nation without a state.

In the context of fake and dysfunctional 'nation-states', the anodyne politics has moved in two opposite directions: the meta-narrative of geo-strategic alliances of the region and micro-politics of domestic constituencies – such as labour, gender or environment. This also means the end of nation-states for at this moment the hand of every state is in another country's pocket. At the height of European imperialism, the decline of Muslim empires resulted in the rise of fragmented nations and their post-colonial state formations. The Arab and Muslim worlds, like all other worlds in Asia Africa and Latin America, imploded in multiple nation-states from this confrontation between European empires and their colonial conquests of other continents. Muslims were by and large divided into the last three Muslim empires of the Mughals, the Safavids/Qajars and the Ottomans, and subsequently collapsed into myriads of artificial colonial divides and post-colonial states. The process of so-called modernisation was in effect the sustained political legacy of colonialism in post-colonial terms.

It is imperative for us to be absolutely clear: the failure of the category of 'nation-state' in the Arab and Muslim World is not a cultural, or religious or racial proposition. Neither the United States nor the EU has ever offered any legitimate model to be emulated– nor indeed has their propagation of 'modernisation' (aka colonialism) resulted in anything but misery for people around the globe. Picking up from where Europe left off, the United States is an empire not an exemplary democracy. It has been coterminous with the condition of coloniality definitive to tyranny and despotism around the globe.

On a vast spectrum of the Earth from the Indian subcontinent to the Mediterranean Sea, Muslim empires collapsed and yielded first to European and now American imperial domination of their material resources and dysfunctional political orders. Right now, we are all nations without legitimate states – we are all Palestinians ruled by Israeli settler colony garrison states – or states made total by virtue of their friendship or animosity to the Euro-American settlement. There are three imperial designs competing with each other over our fragmented nations: the Chinese business model; the Russian mafia model; and the US military model – all of them lack any semblance of moral, ethical, normative or democratic legitimacy. In between atomised and digitised humanity, on one side, and the total cyber-states, on the other, stand the spectrum of nations and their narrations. The congenital European racism has now metastasised into jingoistic nationalism from one end to another – dismantling the illusion that European democracies were ever a model for anyone. As nations are liberated from the delusion of their post-colonial states they fall into the trap of the false consciousness of self-congratulatory nationalism as an ideology of false pride not in what they are but what they fancy they must have been. In the course of the anti-colonial struggles the power of the European imperial hegemonies were opposed and ended and the myth of the post-colonial state was born – and then with a deferred defiance now the post-colonial state is once and for all dismantled.

The chronic rise and fall of European fascism is not an aberration but in fact integral to their liberal democracy – a fact Cassirer saw and theorised but bashfully limited to Nazism and left his host democracy aside. As early as in his pioneering essay *Dictatorship* (1921), the Nazi political theorist Karl Schmitt paid close attention to the office of presidency precisely because of its proclivity towards dictatorship, which he legally stipulated as 'the state of exception' – which he considered a legal necessity and not a political aberration, and therefore he effectively sought to exonerate the notion of 'dictatorship'. The idea of *Ausnahmezustand* ('state of exception') frees the executive power from any legal restraints to its power, thus freeing the political realm for the rise of a Hitler or a Mussolini within the framework of a liberal democracy. In his later book, *Political Theology* (1922), Schmitt brought the idea of 'free will' into his theory allowing for the sovereign to decide on 'the state of exception' – to rule outside the realm of law and yet as a 'legal' stipulation. In his *Concept of the Political* (1932), Schmitt developed the theory of 'the political' predicated on the distinction between *friend* and *enemy*. This distinction, he proposed, is to be determined 'existentially', which is to say that 'the enemy' is something quintessentially different:

> The political enemy need not be morally evil or aesthetically ugly; he need not appear as an economic competitor, and it may even be advantageous to engage with him in business transactions. But he is, nevertheless, the other, the stranger; and it is sufficient for his nature that he is, in an especially intense way, existentially something different and alien, so that in the extreme case conflicts with him are possible. These can neither be decided by a previously determined general norm nor by the judgment of a disinterested and therefore neutral third party.[14]

Now read Bernard Lewis and Samuel Huntington's notion of a 'clash of civilizations' and see the fascist roots of their ideas and irreconcilable otherness of Muslims qua Muslims in them. If for Schmitt and other Nazis the figure of 'the Jew' was that absolute Other, for Bernard Lewis and Samuel Huntington it has been the Muslim and then the Chinese. The 'Islam' that Bernard Lewis and his entire Orientalist ancestry and progeny had manufactured, and it was the Islam that mattered in the political apparatus of power in the world, is the absolute other of 'the West', the enemy of who is the friend of 'the West'. The issue here is not just who the friend is and who the foe of 'the West'. The question dwells within the Euro-universalised domesticity of what they call 'democracy' in which a Muslim as a Muslim, or a Chinese as a Chinese, can ever be a democrat. The old Orientalist cliché, 'Is Islam compatible with democracy?' conceals a much harsher racist impediment. No civilised human being can be compatible with a democracy with the Janus face of vicious colonialism, on one side, and fragile republican imperialism, on the other. That is the impossibility. The answer to the racist

[14] Carl Schmitt, *The Concept of the Political* (Chicago, IL: University of Chicago Press, 2007), p. 27.

Orientalist question, 'Is Islam compatible with Democracy?' is a categorical 'No!' – no civilised Muslim can ever have anything to do with the rooted barbarism of that question, and this 'No!' has nothing to do with who Muslims are and what are their democratic aspirations. But the always already scripted place of this Muslim as the absolute Other of the Euro-universality in which the very idea of 'democracy' is articulated. Muslims as Muslims, or Blacks as Blacks, or Asians as Asians, Africans as Africans, etc., cannot be democratic so far as they are made in the dark and diabolic mirror of this 'West'. If Muslims were to form a democracy in this global calculus of power, 'the West' as an allegory of globalised hubris would collapse – conceptually, categorically and as an allegory. Muslims and Blacks, one in faith and the other in racialised colour of skin, are these absolute Others of this 'West' in precisely the same way that Jews were the internal Other of the self-same 'West' until the rise of Zionism and the appropriation of the Jewish experience into the extended colonial shadow of Europe as a thorn in the side of Asia. The impossibility of the 'West' as a racialised category is nowhere expressed more succinctly than in these immortal words of James Baldwin in 1969 in London:

> You are formed by what you see and the choices you have to make as you discover what it means to be black in New York. I know how, as you grow older, you watch in the richest city in the world, in the richest freest nation in the world, the corpses of your brothers and your sisters pile up around you! What one realizes is that when you try to stand up and look the world in the face like you had a right to be here, when you do that . . . you have attacked the entire power structure of the western world. If one fine day I discover that I have been lied to all years of my life and my mother and my father have been lied to . . . then by one's presence, simply, by attempt to walk from here to there, you begin to frighten the white world.[15]

Neither the Orientalist readings of Islam is the issue, nor is Arab patrimonialism a meaningful category, nor indeed the old-fashioned cliché of Oriental despotism or Third World dictatorship. The failure of democracy in the Arab and Muslim World is the failure of democracy as it has been articu-

[15] See James Baldwin's speech 'James Baldwin and America's "Racial Problem"', 28 August 2014, available at: https://bit.ly/2xnXq1v, minutes 4:15, last accessed 29 May 2018.

lated in the colonial context of political modernity the world has experienced. In the largest democracy in the world, in India, an Islamophobic Hindu fanatic is the end result of all its democratic institutions. In the oldest democracy in the world, the United States, an avowedly racist white supremacist banked on bizarre conspiracy theories to remain in power. The long and short histories of European democracies are punctuated with a Hitler in Germany, a Mussolini in Italy, a Franco in Spain, a Philippe Pétain in France, a Leopold II of Belgium in Congo, and an unrepentant racist mass murderer Churchill of England in India. Continents from Asia to Africa to Latin America are left in ruins by these 'Western democracies' to which a latter-day evangelical Zionist crusader like Mike Pompeo is today its crowning achievement. Arab and Muslim revolutionary aspirations and democratic intuitions are not meant or destined as transitions to these sham 'Western democracies'. They are integral to a global *intifada* to reimagine the world and our entire fragile humanities on it.

6

AUTHORITARIAN REGIME TYPES AS AN ALTERNATIVE TO THE TRANSITION PARADIGM: A CRITICAL ASSESSMENT

Luai Ali

The publication of Dankwart Rustow's 'Transition to Democracy: Toward a Dynamic Model' ushered in the era of transitology studies in many ways.[1] His call to shift from a functional to a genetic explanation of how 'democracy comes into being in the first place' was to serve as an inspiration to the plethora of studies which began to surface as the democratic transitions in Southern Europe started to unfold.[2] His introduction of this approach to democracy, coupled with his focus on actors and contingent choices, was mirrored in the works of authors like O'Donnell and Schmitter.[3] Later as the Soviet collapse gave birth to some new democracies, and authoritarian regimes too for that matter, the genetic approach to democracy situated within the context of actors and choices served as a basis for works like Przeworski's influential book *Democracy and the Market*, which essentially formalised the approach through game theoretic models.[4] Linz and Stepan enriched this approach by bringing multiple factors that influence the context

[1] Dankwart A. Rustow, 'Transitions to Democracy: Toward a Dynamic Model', *Comparative Politics* 2(3) (1970): 337.

[2] Ibid., p. 340

[3] Larry Jay Diamond, 'Thinking about Hybrid Regimes', *Journal of Democracy* 13(2) (2002): 21–35.

[4] Adam Przeworski, *Democracy and the Market: Political and Economic Reforms in Eastern Europe and Latin America* (Cambridge: Cambridge University Press, 2003).

within which the actors make their choices into the fold (i.e., prior regime types, state-ness and international factors).[5]

However, the euphoria over the new states in Eastern and Central Europe started to wane in the late 1990s, and it became clear that democracy was not the only outcome of the Soviet breakdown. In fact, it became clear that many of the cases of supposed stalled transition to democracy were in fact new forms of authoritarian regimes. As a result, the focus shifted from transitology to studying the resilience of authoritarian regimes types, mainly inspired by Geddes' (GWF henceforth) tripartite typology of authoritarian regimes, and Levitsky and Diamond's innovative articles on hybrid regimes (authoritarian regimes with electoral institutions).[6]

For instance, authors like Gandhi and Przeworski studied how institutions in authoritarian regimes facilitate the survival of autocrats, arguing that a higher-level institutionalisation (and even over-institutionalisation) is associated with higher likelihood of regime survival.[7] Furthermore, Gandhi in collaboration with Lust-Okar gives an overview of how the study of elections under authoritarianism is a particularly promising field.[8] This tendency to study institutions under authoritarian regimes has shifted the focus from understanding how they contribute/hinder transition to democracy, to simply understanding their effect on varying political and economic outcomes, that is, economic growth and regime survival.[9]

5 Juan J. Linz and Alfred Stepan, *Problems of Democratic Transition and Consolidation: Southern Europe, South America, and Post-Communist Europe* (Baltimore, MD: Johns Hopkins University Press, 1996).

6 Diamond, 'Thinking about Hybrid Regimes'; Steven Levitsky and Lucan A. Way, *Competitive Authoritarianism: Hybrid Regimes after the Cold War* (Cambridge: Cambridge University Press, 2010); Barbara Geddes, 'What Do We Know about Democratization after Twenty Years?' *Annual Review of Political Science* 2(1) (1999): 115–44; I refer to Geddes' typology and dataset which was first introduced in the aforementioned article. However, it has since become an expanded dataset co-authored with Joseph Wright and Erica Frantz, which is why I refer to it as GWF throughout the chapter. See Barbara Geddes, Joseph Wright and Erica Frantz, 'Autocratic Breakdown and Regime Transitions: A New Data Set', *Perspectives on Politics* 12(2) (2014): 313–31.

7 Jennifer Gandhi and Adam Przeworski, 'Authoritarian Institutions and the Survival of Autocrats', *Comparative Political Studies* 40(11) (2007): 1279–301.

8 Jennifer Gandhi and Ellen Lust-Okar, 'Elections under Authoritarianism', *Annual Review of Political Science* 12(1) (2009): 403–22.

9 Joseph Wright, 'Do Authoritarian Institutions Constrain? How Legislatures Affect

These type of theories began to replace democratisation studies, a trend that continued until the outbreak of the Arab uprisings in 2011, when the transitology paradigm saw a brief revival. Yet as the pendulum of the Arab uprisings began to swing towards authoritarian revival, and state breakdown in some cases, it is worth asking if the rush to abandon theories of authoritarian regimes in favour of the transition paradigm to explain the Arab uprisings was wise.[10]

This chapter will examine the typological theories of authoritarian regimes and the extent to which they provide a viable alternative to the transition paradigm in terms of explaining the outcomes of the Arab Spring. The assessment will focus on the trajectory (and outcomes) of the Arab uprisings as it pertains to the mode of breakdown of Arab regimes. The chapter has four sections. First, I will give an overview of the different typological theories of authoritarian regimes. Second, I will assess how Arab regimes were classified according to these typological theories. Third, I will assess how useful these theories were for understanding the outcomes of Arab uprisings. Finally, I will explain how and why these theories failed in some sense to predict certain outcomes.

Typologies of Authoritarian Regimes: An Overview

In discussing typologies, it is important to distinguish between descriptive typologies or simply typology and typological theory.[11] The former only specify why and how a specific constellation of variables produces a theoretical type.[12] On the other hand, the latter delineates the causal mechanisms which link each theoretical type, or the independent variables within each type, and

Economic Growth and Investment', *American Journal of Political Science* 52(2) (2008): 322–43.

[10] As this chapter was being written another wave of uprisings shook the Arab world for the first time in eight years, as evidenced by the important changes in Sudan (December 2018), and Algeria, Iraq and Lebanon (2019). If anything the waves suggest that neither transitology nor studies of authoritarian regimes should be abandoned, and that the focus should be on finding a symbiotic relationship between both fields of study.

[11] David Collier, Jody Laporte and Jason Seawright, 'Putting Typologies to Work', *Political Research Quarterly* 65(1) (2012): 217–32; Alexander L. George and Andrew Bennett, *Case Studies and Theory Development in the Social Sciences* (Cambridge, MA: MIT Press, 2005).

[12] Ibid.

the outcome with which it is associated.[13] For our particular purpose in this chapter, we are only interested in the latter.

The typological theories discussed in this chapter can be classified depending on the nature of the causal link between each type and the outcomes to which they lead. Amongst the typological theories of authoritarian regimes, two main kinds can be distinguished: typologies based on syntactic relationships, and typologies based on semantic relationships.[14] In the first kind, the outcomes each theoretical type yield are based on the interactions within each regime type. In the second, the outcomes each type yield are based on the interaction between elements within the regime type, and between these elements and components outside the 'black box' of the regime.

In addition to classifications based on the type of relationship that characterises each typological theory, theories are also distinguished by their scope: some are cross-national, while others are region-specific. Through sheer coincidence, the semantic typologies happen to be based on theories that are geographically bound in regions outside the Arab World. Thus, much of the focus of this chapter will be on the syntactic typological theories (i.e., the theories that focus on internal regime dynamics), except for Svolik's typology, which aims to combine elements of both syntactic and semantic theories. To be more precise, the focus will be on three typological theories: Geddes' or GWF's tripartite classification; Hadenius, Teorrel and Wahman's (HTW henceforth) classification; and Svolik's classification.[15]

[13] Ibid.

[14] According to Andrew Abbott, Morris lists three aspects of symbolic systems: syntactic, semantic and pragmatic. A syntactic relationship is one between the elements of the system. A semantic relationship is one between the elements of the system and the things to which they refer. Based on this we can use Morris' modes of language to classify typological theories depending on the nature of the causal link between each type and the outcomes to which they lead. For more details on Morris' symbolic and language systems, see Andrew Abbott, *Methods of Discovery: Heuristics for the Social Sciences* (New York: W. W. Norton, 2004), p. 48.

[15] Milan W. Svolik, *The Politics of Authoritarian Rule* (New York: Cambridge University Press, 2013); Barbara Geddes, *Paradigms and Sand Castles: Theory Building and Research Design in Comparative Politics* (Ann Arbor: University of Michigan Press, 2003); Geddes, 'What Do We Know about Democratization?' pp. 115–44; Axel Hadenius and Jan. Teorell, 'Pathways from Authoritarianism', *Journal of Democracy* 18(1) (2007): 143–57; Michael Wahman, Jan Teorell and Axel Hadenius, 'Authoritarian Regime Types Revisited: Updated Data in Comparative Perspective', *Contemporary Politics* 19(1) (2013): pp. 19–34.

In this section I will provide a brief overview of these typological theories before evaluating them in the next section.

Geddes' Tripartite Typology

The typology constructed by Barbara Geddes is undoubtedly amongst the most important typologies of authoritarian regimes. Indeed, it is one of the very few efforts aimed at creating a cross-national typological theory of authoritarian regimes. One unique and important aspect of Geddes' typology is that it does not seek to explicate the entire process of regime breakdown and transition. Rather, her approach specifically aims at breaking down or disaggregating the question of regime transition and democratisation into 'more researchable questions about mechanisms'.[16] Geddes' theory, therefore, simply investigates intra-elite competition within authoritarian regimes, or the incentives to liberalise and/or transition to democracy facing leaders in different regimes types. Her theory explains 'why some forms of authoritarianism are more vulnerable than others to exogenous shocks and popular opposition'.[17] However, the theory does not seek to explain the deeper reasons for these exogenous shocks, which may be the result of deeper socio-economic revolts, especially exogenous shocks like popular uprisings. The theory also establishes a connection between societal groups and how the regime affects them.

As such, Geddes' classification of authoritarian regimes reflects this focus on regime intra-elite competition. Indeed, the main basis for Geddes' classification of regimes is the 'the identity of the group from which leaders can be chosen', and how this identity affects the leaders' incentives for maintaining power.[18] Accordingly, she classifies authoritarian regimes into military, single party and personalistic regimes. Military regimes are motivated by a corporatist interest that prizes the maintenance of the military's hierarchy, cohesion and survival.[19] Party cadres in single-party regimes are mostly interested in remaining in office.[20] Within personalistic regimes, the focus of the regime is

[16] Geddes, *Paradigms and Sand Castles*, p. 40.

[17] Ibid., p. 50.

[18] Ibid.

[19] Ibid., p. 54.

[20] Ibid., p. 58.

a personalist dictator, and so the fate of the group most tied to the personalistic regime is intertwined with the dictator's own fate.[21]

The interaction between the actors within each regime type, in the form of rivalries and relationships, is what leads to the outcomes: regime breakdown or survival, and democratisation or re-establishment of authoritarianism. Two examples are necessary to clarify how this interaction leads to specific outcomes. First, since the fate of the clique surrounding the leader is most tied to the dictator in personalist regimes, splits within the regime are not likely, which means that personalist regimes are particularly resilient to internal divisions.[22] This resilience means that the members of the clique surrounding the leader in this kind of regime cling on to power to the bitter end, and their grip on power is only likely to end through some form of violence.[23] It is often the case that the violent overthrow of a regime allows the group that overthrew the regime to consolidate power, leading to a renewal of authoritarianism.[24] Second, military regimes are more amenable to internal divisions. However, because of the military's corporatist interest, it is often the case that a regime transition is often carried out before these internal divisions threaten the cohesion and survival of the military, or before any rebellion against the regime develops.[25] Furthermore, given that military regimes often negotiate their way out of power by setting election dates and rules, they are likely to be followed by competitive regimes.[26]

We can therefore list the hypotheses set by Geddes' typological theory as follows:

H1: Military regimes have the lowest shortest survival time.
H2: Personalistic and single-party regimes last longer than military regimes, but single-party regimes last the longest.
H3: Military regimes are more likely to end in negotiation.

[21] Ibid., p. 60.
[22] Ibid., p. 67.
[23] Ibid., pp. 66–8.
[24] Ibid., p. 68.
[25] Ibid., p. 66.
[26] Ibid., p. 68.

H4: Military regimes are more likely to be followed by competitive forms of government.
H5: Personalist regimes are more likely to end when the dictator dies.
H6: Personalist regimes are more likely to end in popular uprisings, rebellions, armed insurgency, invasion or other kinds of violence compared with military and single-party regimes.
H7: Personalist regimes are more likely to be followed by new forms of authoritarianism compared with military and single party regimes.

HTW

HTW try to expand and improve Geddes' typology by adding several types of non-democratic regimes to her original list, and by treating personalism as a continuous trait rather than as a distinct regime type. The main criteria for classifying the regimes in HTW's typology is the mode of maintaining political power. The authors identify three main modes of maintaining political power: hereditary or lineage-based succession; actual or potential use of military force; and popular election. The three modes correspond to three main types of regime: monarchy, military regimes and electoral regimes. Within each main type of regime, several subtypes can be identified. For example, the electoral regime category is broken down into one-party regimes and limited multiparty regimes. Finally, the authors add a key element: conceiving of personalism as an attribute common to all authoritarian regime types and measured on a continuum rather than a unique regime type.[27]

Theoretically, HTW argue that some modes of political power maintenance lead to more stability for authoritarian regimes, while others have an inbuilt capacity for renewed tensions.[28] As such, the fact that power is more concentrated in the hands of the leader in monarchies and one-party dictatorships, while being more diffuse in military and limited multiparty regimes, leads the former to be less vulnerable to breakdown than the latter.[29] HTW's classifications also argue that some authoritarian regime types are more likely to be followed with a democratic regime than other types. The

[27] Hadenius and Teorell, 'Pathways from Authoritarianism'.
[28] Ibid., p. 151.
[29] Ibid.

clearest example is the limited multi-party regime, which was the most likely type to transition to a democracy.[30] The rationale for this trend is twofold. First, the authors posit that 'a direct path to democracy is highly unlikely'.[31] Yet, because limited multi-party regimes 'normally occupy the middle range in terms of level of democracy', they are both more fragile than regimes that are either fully democratic or fully authoritarian and more amenable to 'stepwise improvements' in the degree of political openness, contestation and civil liberties.[32]

Svolik

Svolik's classification departs from both typological theories based on the logic that neither are 'mutually exclusive nor collectively exhaustive'. As a result, he does not classify these regimes into ideal types or based on their prominent descriptive features.[33] Instead, he first classifies regimes as dictatorships if they fail to (1) hold free and competitive legislative elections; (2) do not feature an executive that is elected either directly in free and competitive presidential elections, or indirectly by a legislature in parliamentary systems. He then identifies four key conceptual dimensions that he considers to be pivotal to the political organisation of dictatorships: military involvement in politics; restrictions on political parties; legislative selections; and executive selection. He identifies four different levels of military involvement: none, indirect, personal and corporate. While restrictions on political parties are based on three levels: parties are fully banned; a single party is allowed; multiple parties are allowed. For the legislative selection dimension five different types are listed: no legislative selection; an unelected or appointed legislature; a one party or candidate per seat legislature; a legislature where the largest party controls more than 75 per cent of seats; a legislature where the largest party controls less than 75 per cent of seats; and a non-partisan

[30] Ibid., p. 152.

[31] Axel Hadenius and Jan Teorell, 'Authoritarian Regimes: Stability, Change, and Pathways to Democracy, 1972–2003', Helen Kellogg Institute for International Studies, Working Paper, No. 331 (2006), pp. 22–3, available at: https://bit.ly/2AmKVVj, last accessed 11 May 2020.

[32] Ibid.

[33] Svolik, *The Politics of Authoritarian Rule*, p. 32.

legislature. Finally, for the executive selection dimension four categories are identified: an unelected executive; an executive elected with one party or candidate; an executive selected by a small unelected body; an executive elected in competitive election with more than 75 per cent of the vote; an executive elected in competitive election with less than 75 per cent of the vote.[34] The advantage of Svolik's classification in comparison with GWF and HTW is that it does not use rigid exclusive criteria for classifying authoritarian regime, a point I will discuss in more detail in the next section. This allows for a better understanding of how the different institutions within authoritarian regimes (e.g., the military or the single party) can interact, rather than assuming the predominance of one institution in explaining political outcomes.[35]

Svolik argues that there are two problems that authoritarian regimes face: authoritarian power-sharing and authoritarian control. The former, relates to the choice the regimes face between the dictator consolidating and maintaining his power, or attempting to balance a ruling coalition that could credibly threaten him and curtail his power. In short, the choice to personalise power as opposed to share power with a ruling coalition. The latter relates to the conflict between 'the authoritarian elites in power and the masses that are excluded from power', and control of the masses requires a combination of repression and co-optation.[36] Using his classification of authoritarian regimes, Svolik attempts to explain when and why they succeed or fail in resolving the two dilemmas. In terms of authoritarian power-sharing, he argues that authoritarian regimes become 'established autocracies' when the 'dictator succeeds in consolidating enough power that he can no longer be credibly threatened by the ruling coalition'.[37] This is what is often called a personalistic dictatorship, and the most important implication of Svolik's argument is that it becomes more difficult for dictators to lose power, and more importantly *if* they lose power, it would be through a process that does not involve the interaction between the dictator and the ruling coalition.[38] However, under circumstances where the balance of power between the dic-

[34] Ibid.

[35] Ibid.

[36] Ibid., p. 9.

[37] Ibid., p. 61.

[38] Ibid., p. 63.

tator and the ruling coalition is fluid, the dictator will be forced to enter into a power-sharing agreement with them.[39] These agreements are usually cemented through the establishment of institutional rules for power-sharing. What is critical about these institutions is that they resolve commitment and monitoring problems in authoritarian regimes, thus avoiding intra-elite conflicts and thereby contributing to regime durability.[40] Moreover, dictators in these regimes often have a higher probability of avoiding removal and collapse through non-constitutional means.[41]

When an authoritarian regime faces the choice of utilising repression to control the masses, it often relies on the military, which is tricky for the dictator. For empowering the military creates a political hazard, whereby the very military that aids the dictator in repressing the masses is now empowered to the extent that it can threaten the dictator.[42] To complicate matters more, if the dictator systematically weakens the military, then its capacity to repress the masses would be limited and could not be utilised to confront popular uprisings.[43] Thus, it becomes essentially a trade-off between threats from the masses or the military, the state's very own arm of repression. The interaction between the military and the masses takes the form of three scenarios: minimal levels of protest from masses leading to limited military empowerment and 'perfect political control' by the dictator; a very high threat from the masses leading to the full empowerment of the military, resulting in a 'military tutelage' and overpowering of the dictator by the military; and, finally, a situation of 'brinksmanship bargaining', where the threat of masses is moderate.[44] 'Brinksmanship bargaining' is considered the most dangerous situation by Svolik, because the military under this scenario has 'resources that are large enough that it is tempted to use the threat of intervention to extract concessions from the regime, yet the threat alone is not sufficient to deter the government from questioning the military's resolve to intervene'.[45]

[39] ibid., p. 96.
[40] Ibid., p. 110.
[41] Ibid., p. 112.
[42] Ibid., p. 125.
[43] Ibid., p. 125.
[44] Ibid., pp. 134–5.
[45] Ibid., p. 135.

The danger occurs when the government underestimates the military's capability and tests the 'military's resolve to intervene' by opposing its demands, thus provoking an overt military intervention and military dictatorship.[46]

Finally, Svolik examines the flip side of repression, co-optation, through an examination of the role of political parties in authoritarian regimes. He argues that parties are effective at facilitating regime survival because of three organisational features: hierarchal assignment of service benefits; political control of appointments; and selective recruitment and repression.[47] Crucially, he examines the empirical connection between regime survival and restrictions on political parties/maintenance of a regime party. He finds that ruling coalitions in regimes that maintain single parties survive two to three times longer than those without parties, or those that allow the existence of multiple parties.[48] Interestingly, he also finds that within regimes that allow for multiple parties, legislative seat-sharing is detrimental for the survival of ruling coalitions. To be more precise, he argues that an increase in the legislative seat-share for a regime party in dictatorships that allow multiple parties reduces the risk that a ruling coalition loses power.[49] Not only this, but he finds that authoritarian regimes with dominant parties within the context of multiple party competition last almost as along as regimes where only a single party is allowed.[50]

Typological Theories of Authoritarian Regimes and the Arab Spring

In this section I will aim to answer three crucial questions: (1) how were the regimes in the Arab World classified based on the typological theories discussed above;[51] (2) to what extent do the Arab regimes conform to the hypotheses set forth in these typological theories; and (3) how much did these theories predict or successfully explain the Arab Spring?

Starting with Geddes' typology the authoritarian regimes that were hit by the Arab Spring were classified as Table 6.1 demonstrates. It can be noted

[46] Ibid., p. 136.
[47] Ibid., p. 163.
[48] Ibid., p. 187.
[49] Ibid., p. 190.
[50] Ibid., p. 191
[51] Arab Spring regimes only.

Table 6.1 Authoritarian regime classification

Regime	Start	End	Classification	Duration (years)
Egypt	1953	2011	Party–personal–military	58
Tunisia	1957	2011	Party	54
Yemen	1979	2011	Personal	32
Libya	1970	2011	Personal	41
Syria	1964	Ongoing	Party–personal–military	54
Bahrain	1971	Ongoing	Excluded from classification	NA

from the outset that there are coding issues, for example, Egypt and Syria are classified as a residual category where the ruling coalition is from all the three (the military, the party and personalist dictator's clique) institutions jointly, while Bahrain is simply dropped from the sample because it's a small country.[52] I will get back to why this coding is problematic later in this section, but for the moment I will focus on the pure type regimes. Tunisia was classified as a party-based authoritarian regime, while both Yemen and Libya were classified as personalist regimes. This classification should aid us in answering four questions regarding these authoritarian regimes: how long did they survive relative to one another; how they ended (i.e., the main source of fragility for the regime); and the mode of transition (violent overthrow as opposed to negotiated transition).

Geddes argues, as we noted in the previous section, that single-party regimes are the most resilient and are the most likely to last longest. We find that indeed the authoritarian regime in Tunisia lasted longer than both the regimes of Yemen under Ali Abdullah Saleh and Libya under Muammar Gaddafi.[53] Since Geddes argues that single-party regimes and personalist regimes are more likely to collapse as a result of external shocks (e.g., uprisings), all three regimes in question appear to comport with Geddes' theory given that they collapsed following a popular uprising. Finally, in line with Geddes' theory the Tunisian regime as a single-party regime ended through negotiations without the violent ouster of the leader.[54]

[52] See p. 22 of the code book for Geddes, Wright and Frantz, 'Autocratic Breakdown and Regime Transitions: A New Data Set', pp. 313–31.

[53] This is based on Geddes' coding which counts Habib Bourguiba (1957–1987) and Zine El Abidine Ben Ali's (1987–2011) period as one regime.

[54] It should be noted that the term 'negotiations' should be qualified especially given that the

Moreover, based on Geddes' theory, we expect that as personalist regimes Libya and Yemen would be more likely to be violently overthrown than military and single-party regimes. Yet Geddes' theory only panned out in the case of Libya, where the regime was indeed violently overthrown following an intervention by NATO on the side of the anti-Gaddafi rebels. However, the removal of Ali Abdullah Saleh in Yemen in fact took place following a popular uprising and with very limited violence. Not only this, but Saleh's own party, the General People's Congress (GPC), was essentially the party that negotiated the end of the regime through the vice president of the GPC, Abdrabbuh Mansour Hadi, who became the president of Yemen following the GCC initiative, and was elected in 2012 with the support of the GPC and many opposition groups.[55] The violence and civil war that ensued afterwards did not result from the violent overthrow of the regime, but rather from a mutiny by a non-state actor (the Houthis) in spite of an initiative by the Gulf Cooperation Council to usher in a peaceful regime transition.[56]

ruling *Rassemblement Constitutionnel Démocratique* party (RCD) was not involved in the negotiation process. When Ben Ali eventually fled the country on 14 January 2014, the prime minister of the government and an RCD party member since 1999, Mohammed Channoushi assumed the position of the president of the country for six months. His tenure was not smooth by any means and there was considerable controversy over him assuming power based on Article 59 of the constitution. He eventually left this position under the weight of protests on 27 February 2011. During his tenure, all ministers who were members of the RCD party had to rescind their membership in that party. Eventually, anyone involved in the RCD party aside from Ghannoushi was removed from the cabinet. Note that despite that fact that this did not necessarily happen through negotiation with the RCD, the entire process did not involve any considerable violence. For more details, see Azmi Bishara, *'Al- Thawra 'Al- Tunisiyya 'Al- Majīda* (*The Glorious Tunisian Revolution*) (Beirut: Arab Centre for Research and Policy Studies, 2012), pp. 293–316.

55 Adil Sharajbi, '*'Al- Taḥawwul 'Al- Dīmuqratī Fī 'Al-Yaman*' ('Democratic Transition in Yemen'), in Idris Lakrini (ed.), *'Atwār 'Al-tārīkh 'Al-intiqālī: Ma'āl 'Al-thawrāt 'Al-'arabiyya* (*Phases of Historical Transition: The Fate of Arab Revolutions*) (Beirut: Arab Centre for Research and Policy Studies, 2015), pp. 339–52.

56 For detailed reports on the developments in Yemen from the uprising in 2001 until the Houthi coup, including a very crucial chronology of events, see the following analysis and reports Aleksandar Mitreski, 'Civil War in Yemen: A Complex Conflict with Multiple Futures', Arab Center for Research and Policy Studies, Case Analysis, August 2015, available at: https://bit.ly/35Xy8UY; Mohamed Jamih, 'Yemen After the Fall of Sanaa', Arab Center for Research and Policy Studies, Policy Analysis, November 2014, available at: https://bit.ly/2yNSXpt; 'The Houthis Seize Sanaa: Implications', Arab Center for Research and Policy

Moving on to the two regimes that are classified as hybrid regimes, Syria and Egypt, we find that Geddes describes these regimes as the most resilient of all regime types. Yet aside from their expected long duration, she does not elaborate on the sources of breakdown for these regimes or their mode of transition. The omission is concomitant with her theory's lack of discussion of the dynamic interaction between the three institutions from which the regime's ruling elite is drawn: the military; the ruling party; the clique around the personalist leader. We do know, for example, to whom the balance of power within the schema of this hybrid regime tilts. If we examine the cases of Syria, we can hypothesise based on the outcome of the uprising that shook the country in 2011 (a violent civil war), that the balance leaned towards the personalist leader and his clique. In the Egyptian case, the army played the principal role in controlling the transition phase opting for elections. This in spite of the fact that it was largely a dormant political player since Mubarak removed his powerful defence minister, Abd al-Halim Abu-Ghazala, in 1989, relying since on the ruling National Democratic Party and his own personalist clique at the helm.[57] Yet these are mere conjectures based on knowledge of the cases examined, since Geddes' theory does provide any insight into understanding the dynamic interaction between the three institutions that make up hybrid authoritarian regimes beyond telling us that they are the most resilient of all regime types.

Moving on to HTW's typology, we find that the Arab regimes that experienced uprisings were classified as per Table 6.2. In terms of duration, all the regimes are above the average duration of their regime type. This is significant in the case of Syria, which is classified as a military regime, yet has

Studies, Assessment Report, September 2014, available at: https://bit.ly/2yNTfN5; 'After Capturing Amran, Will the Houthis Aim for Sanaa?' Arab Center for Research and Policy Studies, Assessment Report, July 2014, available at: https://bit.ly/3dDVL7k; 'Outcomes of Yemen's National Dialogue Conference: A Step Toward Conflict Resolution and State Building?' Arab Center for Research and Policy Studies, Assessment Report, February 2014, available at: https://www.dohainstitute.org/en/PoliticalStudies/Pages/Outcomes_of_Yemens_National_Dialogue_Conference_A_Step_toward_Conflict_Resolution_and_State_Building.aspx; all above last accessed 11 May 2020.

57 Azmi Bishara, *Thawrat Masr 2: Min al Thawra Ilā al- inqilāb* (*The Egyptian Revolution, Vol. II: From Revolution to Coup d'Etat*) (Beirut and Doha: Arab Centre for Research and Policy Studies, 2016).

Table 6.2 Classification of Arab regimes that experienced uprisings

Regime	Start	End	Classification	Level of competition	Duration (years)	Average duration of similar regime
Egypt	1976	2010	Multi-party	Limited multi-party	34	9.97
Tunisia	1994	2010	Multi-party	Limited multi-party	16	9.97
Yemen	1993	2011	Multi-party	Limited multi-party	18	9.97
Libya	1977	2011	Other	Other	34	–
Syria	1972	2011	Military	Military one-party	39	11.1
Bahrain	2002	2011	Monarchy	No-party monarchy	9	25.4

a duration that far exceeds the duration of the average military regime. Yet what is notable is that HTW's main finding that limited multi-party regimes have a higher probability of transitioning to a democracy did not pan out. Of the regimes classified as limited multi-party regimes only Tunisia successfully transitioned to a democratic regime.

Finally, we examine Svolik's typology and the extent to which its theoretical implications are vindicated by the Arab Spring. We focus on the last part of Svolik's theory, dealing with control through co-optation in authoritarian regimes, because the first two parts of his theory (authoritarian power-sharing and authoritarian control through repression) mainly utilise game theory and do not rely on classification of authoritarian regimes. As noted previously, Svolik argues that the level of authoritarian control can be classified using the regime's maintenance of single-party and through ruling party legislative seat-share in regimes that allow for multiple parties. Moreover, he argues that the maintenance of a ruling single party and high legislative seat-share for the ruling party with the context of a limited multi-party system leads to a higher probability of survival. Table 6.3 details how Svolik classified Arab regimes that experienced uprisings, based on the two authoritarian regime control measures.

Thus, we note that these regimes were classified amongst the category of regimes that are likely to have comparatively longer durations due to the utilisation of a single ruling party or their capacity to maintain an advantage of more than 75 per cent of the legislature's seats within the context of a limited multi-party system. Yet beyond authoritarian regime duration, Svolik's theory does not explain when and how these regimes are likely to collapse.

Table 6.3 Svolik classification of Arab regimes that experienced uprisings

Regime	Year	First classification	Year	Second classification
Bahrain	1999–2008	Non-Partisan	–	–
Egypt	1981–2008	Largest party controls more than 75% of seats	–	–
Libya	1969–1976	None	1977–2008	Unelected or appointed
Syria	2000–2008	One party or candidate	–	–
Tunisia	1954–1993	One party or candidate	1994–2008	Largest party controls more than 75% of seats
Yemen	1994–2008	Largest party controls more than 75% of seats	–	–

His theory, however, as I will explain in the next section may be useful for other purposes.

A Critique of Typological Theories

The typologies of authoritarian regimes assessed in the previous section have had limited success in explaining the events of the Arab Spring (even when it comes to their main aim which is to explain the initial stage which explains the dynamics under which authoritarian regimes collapse). Even when these typologies are successful, the findings are very general, limited and moot when it comes to the internal dynamics of these regimes. This is not to say that these typologies are not without value, but, rather, that much work needs to be done to build on and deconstruct their main findings.

First, we note that the inability to chart a trajectory consistent with Geddes' typology in the cases of Egypt, Syria and Yemen is a consequence of two interrelated factors: errors in coding these regimes; and the insistence on a mutually exclusive regime classification that imposes the dominance of one political institution (the military, the dominant party or the personalistic leader and his ruling clique) and vague residual classifications, where regimes are classified as hybrid because it is assumed that all three institutions predominate equally. In the case of all three criticisms, the main issue is that the dynamic interaction between the three ruling institutions Geddes emphasises is concealed. This is an issue that seems to afflict authoritarian typologies that emphasise institutional configurations, and what often happens is what Pepinsky describes as the failure to account for both the origins

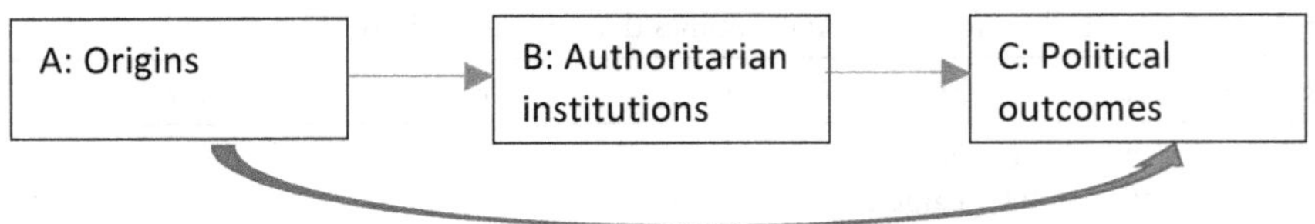

Figure 6.1 Pepinsky's causal argument

of authoritarian institutions and the political outcomes that these authoritarian institutions lead to. He summarises his argument in the causal graph in Figure 6.1 where he argues that: 'To study the effects of institutions under authoritarianism on authoritarian political outcomes (Path B), regardless of the causal mechanisms invoked, researchers need an account of both the processes through which political institutions form and change (Path A), on the one hand, and the consequences of those processes for the outcomes that untitled institutions are thought to explain, on the other (Path C).'

To be more precise, 'absent a research design that can do this, it is impossible to distinguish the effects of institutions on outcomes from the effects of structural variables or elite preferences that shape both'.[58]

It would be instructive to use the cases of Egypt and Syria to demonstrate this issue in Geddes' classification, and how it affects utilising her typology to understand the outcome of regime breakdown during the Arab Spring. More precisely, the coding conceals variation over time with the regimes, and does not properly illuminate the dynamic interaction between the different ruling institutions within the regime.

If we take the case of Syria, we find that Geddes classified the regimes from 1964 to the present as one hybrid party–personal–military. This coding ignores two crucial coups: the 1966 coup against Amin Al-Hafiz and the 1970 'Correctional Movement' by Hafiz Al-Assad. Both were transformative moves reflecting the struggle between the military and civilian wings of the party.[59] Hafiz Al-Assad's was decisive in as much as it ended the struggle

[58] Thomas Pepinsky, 'The Institutional Turn in Comparative Authoritarianism', *British Journal of Political Science* 44(3) (2013): 631–2.

[59] Shams al-Din Kilani, *Madkhal fi 'Al-Ḥayā 'Al-siyāsiyyah 'Al-Sūriyya: Min ta'sīs 'Al-kayān ilā 'Al-Thawra* (*An Introduction to Syrian Political Life: From the Establishment of the State to Independence*) (Beirut: Arab Centre for Research and Policy Studies, 2017), pp. 89–113; Azmi Bisharah, *'Al-Jaysh Wa 'Al-siyāsa: Ishkāliyāt Naẓariyya Wa Namādhij 'Arabiyya* (*The

within the Baath Party and reined in its military wing.[60] This did not mean the end of the Baath Party or its transformation into a provincial player, but rather it meant that increasingly the party was in many ways subservient to a strong personalistic leader, even as it played a crucial and critical political role. The party began to seriously decline from the 1990s onwards, with Syria increasingly becoming a personalistic regime and the regime essentially side-lined the party, which if anything became a mere mechanism to renew Hafiz Al-Assad's leadership or set the stage for the succession of his son Bashar Al-Assad.[61] Not only this, but with the succession of Bashar Al-Assad in 2000 the military was also gradually side-lined and weakened politically. So much so that by 2010 it had become a military that closely resembles that of a personalistic authoritarian regime.[62] These dynamics are important because they reveal in the personalisation of authoritarian rule a variable that explains the outcomes of the uprisings in Syria: an uprising from outside the regime's ranks, few if any defections from the regime's ranks and a brutal civil war. These outcomes would have been hard to understand based on Geddes' hybrid tripartite classification of the Syrian regime, which does not explain the proper balance between the three ruling institutions within her classification.

The Egyptian case is also instructive in this regard. Like the Syrian regime, Geddes classifies Egypt as a hybrid regime since 1953, again ignoring crucial changes in the dynamic relationship between the military, the ruling party, and the personalistic leader and his clique. Under this classification, it is assumed that the relationship between the three ruling institutions is static and did not vary under Nasser, Sadat or Mubarak. Not only this, but even with the context of each of these separate presidencies there was a constant struggle between the military, the presidency and to a lesser extent the party. Thus, we see an internal military struggle following the 1967 Egyptian defeat in the Six Day War with Israel, a struggle that was the culmination of tensions between Gamal Nasser and his minister of defence, Abdul Hakim

Army and Politics: Theoretical Issues and Arab Models) (Beirut: Arab Centre for Research and Policy Studies, 2017), p. 119.

60 Ibid.

61 Ibid., p. 133.

62 Ibid., p. 135.

Amer. The struggle resulted in 1968 in a rebalancing of the relationship such that the military became more closely controlled by the presidency under Nasser.[63] Sadat's period in power would also see the further removal of the military from the public sphere during what is often described as Sadat's battle against the 'centres of power'. Sadat also entrenched his position as commander-in-chief and strengthened internal security further as a counter-balance to the military.[64] Mubarak's period, especially from 1983 onwards, continued Sadat's trend of pushing the military outside the political arena, with this eventually culminating in what is often described as the historic deal between the presidency and the military in Egypt, whereby the military would refrain from interfering in politics in exchange for wide-ranging freedom and control in the economic sphere. Mubarak's period also saw the rise of the NDP which retained reasonable power before being eventually sidelined and becoming a clique for Mubarak and his cronies.[65]

It is clear from both cases that Geddes' classification has left out some crucial aspects of the interaction between the three ruling institutions, which would have explained the different trajectories that Syria and Egypt went through despite both being classified under the same hybrid category. The model would predict similar outcomes for both regimes in the event of an external shock. Yet, in the case of Syria, the dynamic interaction and bargaining eventually led to the personalisation of the regime and the complete subservience of the party and military to the president. In Egypt, this interaction led to the army being pushed away from the political arena, mainly in terms of governance, while retaining considerable independence in other spheres, namely, the economic sphere. This would certainly explain why when uprisings in Syria and Egypt erupted, the former regime managed to remain intact with both the military and party fully on the president's side (save for minor, mostly lower rank defections) much like in a personalistic regime, leading to a long violent struggle against the rebels. While in the latter regime, the army abandoned the leader because the personalisation of the regime was cutting close to its economic independence.

[63] Ibid., pp. 170–2.

[64] Ibid., pp. 173–4.

[65] Ibid.

If we move on to HTW's typology (similar to Diamond's hybrid regimes category, i.e., authoritarian regimes with electoral institutions), we find that the most important aspect of the theory that could potentially be useful to understanding the Arab Spring is the connection between the classification limited multi-party regimes and the likelihood of democratic transition as mentioned in the previous section. The category is similar to what is often described as a hybrid regime, that is, an authoritarian regime that integrates electoral institutions within its structure.[66] HTW classify three of the regimes that underwent the Arab Spring as limited multi-party regimes: Tunisia, Yemen and Egypt. Only Tunisia managed to successfully become a democracy, while Egypt slid back into an even more repressive authoritarian mode. The Yemeni state collapsed into a civil war. Moreover, even if it is argued that in all these limited multi-party regimes, the regime's breakdown was followed initially by successful elections, the classification still misses two crucial factors: who controlled the interim process prior to elections and why? In other words, the classification does not explain why, in the cases of Yemen and Tunisia, members of the ruling party (even if as former members of the party) were still involved in the interim process, while in the case of Egypt the ruling party simply faded away, with the military taking over the process.[67] The classification is neither useful in explaining who is likely to control the interim process, nor the likelihood that this interim process will lead to a successful democratic transition.

Even we were to assume that HTW's classification of limited multi-party regime is useful in predicting the likelihood that it would be followed by a democratic government, the mechanism through which this particular transformation takes places is not specified.[68] Instead, it is summed up in a

[66] See Levitsky and Way, *Competitive Authoritarianism*, pp. 21–35.

[67] See n. 54 for more details on Tunisia, and n. 55 for more details on Yemen.

[68] It is interesting to note that this is a common issue with cross national literature on hybrid regimes. So, for example, Larry Diamond's foundation piece Thinking About Hybrid Regimes cited above only classifies regimes based on their levels of electoral competition but does not connect his classification with any particular outcomes, and as such he only puts forth a typology, not a typological theory. Another example is Levitsky and Way's influential book *Competitive Authoritarianism: Hybrid Regimes after the Cold War*. The book explicitly uses the hybrid regime typology, yet when it comes to the variables that ultimately explain the likelihood of democratic transition, they specify state capacity and linkages to

vague claim that 'a direct path to democracy is highly unlikely' and that these regimes 'normally occupy the middle range in terms of level of democracy'. That is, they would be both more fragile than regimes that are either fully democratic or fully authoritarian, and more amenable to 'stepwise improvements' in the degree of political openness, contestation and civil liberties.[69]

Finally, we turn to Svolik's typology. Svolik's typology in many ways avoids the shortcomings of the two other typologies because it does not rely on 'mutually exclusive and collectively exhaustive' categories. But because it mainly deals with the dilemma's authoritarian regimes face, namely, authoritarian power-sharing and authoritarian control, the typological theory is limited in terms of explaining the Arab Spring, especially as it pertains to regime breakdown. However, Svolik's theory does provide some very useful insights into the resurgence of authoritarian regimes. For example, his theory provides a game theoretic foundation for how and why authoritarian regimes personalise power. This is particularly useful given that, in some countries affected by the Arab Spring (and even in countries that were not directly affected by it), the personalisation of power appears to be rapidly taking place. The cases of Egypt under Abelfattah El-Sisi after the coup in 2013 and Saudi Arabia under the crown prince of Saudi Arabia Mohammed Bin Salman (MBS) are instructive. For example, under Sisi's regime, most of the military figures who helped him with the 2013 coup have been removed, and the regime has to rely on an incredibly narrow coalition which mainly consists of the General Intelligence Service, the Administrative Control Authority and specific members of the Military Intelligence and Reconnaissance Administration.[70] In a similar vein, MBS created two key bodies that lumped all the ministries and bureaucracies under the authority of the Council of Political and Security

the West. In other words, two variables that do not have anything to do with the classification of an authoritarian regime.

[69] Hadenius and Teorell, 'Authoritarian Regimes'.

[70] '*Wuzara' wa Siyāsiyyūn Li 'al Sharq: 'Al Sīsī Ya 'zil 'al Qiyādāt 'al 'askariyya li Yu'assisa li Ḥukm Jadīd*', ('Ministers and Politicians to AlSharq: Sisi Isolates Military Leaders to Establish New Rule'), *al-sharq*, 25 December 2018, available at: https://bit.ly/2LgfEFE, last accessed 11 May 2020; '*6 Sanawāt Ba'd 'al-Thawra: 'al- Inqisāmāt fī Ajhizat al-Niẓām wa Mu'assasātih*' ('Six Years after the Revolution: Divisions in the Organs and Institutions of the Regime'), *The New Arab*, 25 January 2017.

Affairs and the Council of Economic and Development Affairs.[71] Both councils are headed by MBS and have considerable authority. While Svolik only examines why and how authoritarian regimes personalise power, personalisation in and of itself can be a critical independent variable that accounts for many key outcomes. For instance, personalisation of power, as we see not only from Geddes' theory but also other scholars, often leads to regime collapse via external shocks, often with a violent transition, and possibly the resurgence of authoritarianism. Not only this, but there is evidence to suggest that the personalisation of power and personalistic regimes tend to generate poor economic performance and disastrous foreign policy choices.[72]

Conclusion: The Future of Typological Theories of Authoritarian Regimes

In this chapter I have attempted to examine typological theories of authoritarian regimes, and the extent to which they provide a viable alternative to the transition paradigm in terms of explaining the outcomes of the Arab Spring. I focused on the mode of the breakdown of Arab regimes as well as the outcomes of these breakdowns. After giving an overview of these typological theories, the chapter examined two main questions: to what extent does the structure and fate of the Arab regimes conform to the hypotheses set forth in three typological theories?; and how much did these theories predict or successfully explain the Arab Spring?

In answer in these questions, it was noted that the typological theories discussed were generally modest at best in their capacity to explain and predict the outcomes of the Arab Spring. To be more precise, the regimes classified by Geddes as pure types (Libya, personalist; Yemen, personalist; Tunisia, single party), appear to conform to the hypotheses she put forth when it comes to the theory in terms of tenure and sources of breakdown. This is also

[71] '*I'ādat Tashkīl Majlis 'al Wuzara' wa Insha' Majlisay 'al Shu'ūn 'al- Siyāsiyya wa al-'Amniyya wa 'al- Iqtiṣādiyya*' ('Restructuring the Council of Ministers and Establishing the Council of Political and Security Affairs, and the Council of Economic Affairs'), *AlYoum Newspaper*, 30 January 2015, available at: https://bit.ly/2SYj0RX, last accessed 12 May 2020.

[72] See, e.g., Erica M. Frantz and Natasha M. Ezrow, 'Yes, Men and the Likelihood of Foreign Policy Mistakes across Dictatorships', *APSA* (2009), available at: https://bit.ly/2WQ3AQV, last accessed 12 May 2020.

true for the mode of transition, except for Yemen which experienced a trajectory not predicted by Geddes' theory. The serious omission in Geddes' theory was the category of hybrid regimes (Egypt and Syria based on her classification), where her theory only discusses the tenure of this regime type, ignoring any discussion of other variables. The result is that theory tells us very little about the Syrian and Egyptian regimes during the Arab Spring.

The predictions of Hadenius, Teorrel and Wahman's theory are even more limited when considering the failure of their main finding regarding democratic transition (that limited party authoritarian regimes have a high probability of transitioning to democracy once they collapse) to hold when applied to Arab Spring countries. To reiterate, of all the regimes classified as limited multi-party by HTW, only one transitioned to a democracy: Tunisia.

The limited success of the aforementioned typologies is due in large part to the insistence on mutually exclusive authoritarian regime classifications, as in the case of Geddes' typology, or as a result of coding errors. Not to mention the fact that HTW contains an unwieldy number of authoritarian regime classifications, making it redundant.

Finally, while Svolik's authoritarian regime classification skilfully avoids the pitfalls of that of Geddes and HTW, his focus is not on how his typology pertains to democratic transition, but on survival mechanisms for authoritarian regimes faced with popular challenges to their rule. His theory, while limited for understanding the transition phase of the Arab Spring, can nevertheless be useful for understanding the renewal of authoritarianism and especially the phenomenon of the personalisation of power by autocratic leaders like Sisi and MBS.

But going beyond criticising the internal logic of these typological theories, we note that these (mainly syntactic) theories largely ignore the relationship and effect of authoritarian regime on society. One important issue they ignore is that of state-ness, specified by Linz and Stepan as the problem of 'profound differences about the territorial boundaries of the political community's state and profound differences as to who has the right of citizenship in that state'.[73] Accordingly, 'when the population of the territory of the state is composed of plural, lingual, religious, or cultural societies, the more

[73] Linz and Stepan, *Problems of Democratic Transition and Consolidation*, p. 16.

complex politics becomes', and the more acute the state-ness problem also becomes.[74] The issue of state-ness is key in the context of the Arab Spring, because it can and did in fact complicate the transition process. It is a crucial question that the typologies missed the extent to which each regime type had affected the state-ness issue, whether through purposive social engineering, or inadvertently. We see, for example, the clear effects of lack of state coherence and consensus around its form and parameters on complicating the transition process in Yemen and Libya, both of which faced state collapse and a civil war between warring factions over control of the state. Thus, the theories need to be refined to understand if there is any potential relationship between regime type and the state-ness issue.

This conclusion does not advocate the abandonment of the typological theories. Rather, it urges the following amendments to build on these theories and refine them. First, closer attention should be paid to coding the authoritarian Arab regimes; this cannot be done without a careful and judicious reading of the vast literature now being produced in Arabic about these states.

[74] Ibid., p. 29.

7

VISIBLE AND INVISIBLE POLITICAL ACTORS AND THEIR STRATEGIES DURING THE ARAB SPRING TRANSITIONS

Abdel-Fattah Mady

This chapter examines two main questions: what were the strategies of key political actors during the transitional periods of the 2011 Arab uprisings; and how did these strategies affect the fate of democratic transitions? Related questions will also be considered, such as the identity, core interests of the main political actors, and whether they were linked to other concealed forces in the background. Also what factors, internal and external, influenced the choices of these actors? Finally, what can Arab cases add to our understanding of democratic transition?

The research approach combines two types of analysis. The first analyses the attitudes and decisions of the main actors during the democratic transition process and examines the impact of these choices on democratisation. The second investigates the contexts and structural factors that elucidate the motives and interests. Contexts and motives do not engender a specific pattern of choices, so elite choices are not taken in isolation from internal and external influences. The main focus is on Tunisia and Egypt, which witnessed peaceful attempts to transition to democracy after 2011, with different outcomes: relative success in Tunisia and failure in Egypt. To determine the validity of the concepts and assumptions on democratic transitions, the chapter utilises a comparative approach to identify the similarities and differences between the Arab and non-Arab cases.

The chapter consists of two sections and a conclusion. The first section briefly examines the literature on democratisation in general, with a focus on Arab countries. The second deals with the strategies of the main internal actors during the transitional periods. It explores three issues: the mode of transition triggered by the popular mobilisation and protest movements; the strategies of the forces that managed the transitional periods; and the impact of external factors on these strategies. The conclusion summarises the principal findings.

Democratic Transition Literature and the Arab Region

Democracy studies, later defined as the structural or requisites approach, which preceded the literature of the democratic transition of the 1970s and 1980s, focused on macro sociological analysis and the assumptions of modernisation theory. In the last two decades of the twentieth century, attention shifted to the so-called 'transition' or 'agency-based' approach.[1] Successful democratic transition requires the consensus of the elites regarding the democratic system, and the elites' ability to reach agreements that provide each party with a portion of what they are seeking.[2] In Sartori's terms, it is 'politics as a bargaining' rather than 'politics as war' or politics as zero-sum game.[3] This approach assumes that the process of transition has a final product, 'procedural democracy'. Although similarities can be traced in different cases, no general theory or single explanation for successful transition exists.[4]

Prior to 2011, the field of democratic transition did not focus on Arab cases, and not only for the dearth of successful transitions. Based on the structural approach, research was conducted on tribalism, sectarianism and rentier economy as impediments to regime change.[5] Islam was also considered an

[1] Dankwart A. Rustow, 'Transitions to Democracy: Toward a Dynamic Model', *Comparative Politics* 2(3) (1970): 337–63.

[2] Michael Bratton and Nicholas Van de Walle, *Democratic Experiments in Africa: Regime Transitions in Comparative Perspective* (Cambridge: Cambridge University Press, 1997), pp. 24–6.

[3] Giovanni Sartori, *The Theory of Democracy Revisited* (Chatham, NJ: Chatham House, 1987), pp. 224–6.

[4] Bratton and Van de Walle, *Democratic Experiments in Africa*, pp. 26–7.

[5] Nazih N. Ayubi, *Over-stating the Arab State: Politics and Society in the Middle East* (London: I. B. Tauris, 1996); Roger Owen, *State Power and Politics in the Making of the Modern*

obstacle, being 'incompatible with democracy'.[6] Conversely, Alfred Stepan wrote that the 'democracy gap' was Arab, not Islamic, and, therefore, cannot be blamed on Islam.[7] For Stepan, there is no strong attachment between peoples in Arab countries and their nation-states, established after the First World War, and 'many contemporary Arab states have relatively new and arbitrary boundaries because they were cut out of the Ottoman Empire, and were afterward occupied and often reconfigured as European colonies'.[8] Asef Bayat considers it contingent whether social groups use Islam to support authoritarianism or democracy.[9] On the other hand, some research has concluded that the liberalisation policies announced by some Arab regimes ended with more entrenched despotisms, due to lessons the ruling elites learned from the experiences of the third wave, and because of the divided opposition.[10] In fact, the Arab governments modernised their authoritarian systems,[11] undertaking cosmetic measures, including multi-party systems and elections to enhance their image and ease internal and external pressures for reform.[12]

These arguments faced criticism for focusing on internal factors at the expense of external ones. Moreover, only a few studies examine the impact of

Middle East (Abingdon: Routledge, 2002); Giacomo Luciani (ed.), *The Arab State* (Berkeley: University of California Press, 1990).

6 Samuel P. Huntington, *The Clash of Civilizations and the Remaking of World Order* (New Delhi: Penguin, 1997); Steven M. Fish, *Are Muslims Distinctive? A Look at the Evidence* (Oxford: Oxford University Press, 2011).

7 Alfred Stepan and Graeme B. Robertson, 'An "Arab" More than a "Muslim" Democracy Gap', *Journal of Democracy* 14(3) (2003): 30–44.

8 Ibid., p. 41.

9 Asef Bayat, *Making Islam Democratic: Social Movements and the Post-Islamist Turn* (Stanford: Stanford University Press, 2007).

10 Abdel-Fattah Mady, '*'aqabāt al-'intiqāl 'ila Niẓam Ḥukm Dīmuqrātī fi Misr*' ('Obstacles to Transition to a Democratic System in Egypt') in Ali Khalifa Al Kuwari and Abdel-Fattah Mady, *Why Have Others Transitioned to Democracy While Arabs Lagged Behind?* (Beirut: Centre for Arab Unity Studies, 2009).

11 Steven Heydemann, 'Upgrading Authoritarianism in the Arab World', Saban Center for Middle East Policy at the Brookings Institution, Analysis Paper, No. 13, October 2007; Daniel Brumberg, 'Democratization in the Arab World? The Trap of Liberalized Autocracy', *Journal of Democracy* 13(4) (2002): 56–68; Raymond Hinnebusch, 'Liberalization without Democratization in "Post-Populist" Authoritarian States', in N Butenschon, U. Davis and M. Hassassian (eds), *Citizenship and the State in the Middle East* (Syracuse, NY: Syracuse University Press, 2000), pp. 123–44.

12 Mady, "aqabāt al-'intiqāl 'ila Niẓam Ḥukm Dīmuqrātī fi Misr', pp. 202–3.

US support for the longevity of Arab despotisms, as in Egypt where the objective was to preserve the peace treaty with Israel.[13] Stephen Zunes wrote that democracy in the Arab region is not in American interests and that America believes it is easier to deal with authoritarian elites than with elected governments.[14] On the tribalism and sectarianism arguments, Azmi Bishara argues that the problem is not the presence of the sect itself, but the 'formation of sectarianism' as a strategy to stay in power or to achieve other political gains for internal or external actors.[15]

Furthermore, there is a tendency to overlook the impact of regime performance on the possibility of change, that is, the impact of human rights violations and repression on the prospects for the transition. Arab regimes and some opposition elites have ulterior motives, as they regard external pressure for democratisation as interference in internal affairs.[16] Ironically, external pressure is also rejected by some opposition groups as part of attempted 'Westernisation'. A few even believe that the United States orchestrated the uprisings of 2011.[17]

Finally, advocacy of democracy and reform in the Arab World has a long history, refuting the claim that democracy was not an issue of interest before 2011.[18] In addition to the efforts of the pioneers of the 'Arab Renaissance' at the end of the nineteenth century and the beginning of the twentieth century,[19] a group of thinkers developed an extensive literature on

[13] Glenn Perry, 'The Arab Democracy Deficit: The Case of Egypt', *Arab Studies Quarterly* 26(2) (2004): 91–107.

[14] Stephen Zunes, 'Continuing Storm: The US Role in the Middle East', *Foreign Policy in Focus*, 1 April 1999, available at: https://goo.gl/xk4wfe; Stephen Zunes, 'The United States and the Prospects for Democracy in Islamic Countries', *HuffPost*, 27 January 2011, available at:, https://goo.gl/6dtxdt, both last accessed 1 May 2020.

[15] Azmi Bishara, *'al-Tā'ifa, 'al-Tā'ifiyya wa 'al-Tawā'if 'al-Mutakhayyala* (*Sect, Sectarianism and Imagined Sects*) (Beirut: Arab Centre for Research and Policy Studies, 2018).

[16] See Azmi Bishara, *Fi 'Al-mas'ala 'Al-'Arabiyya: Moqaddima li bayān dīmoqrātī 'Arabī* (*The Arab Question: Introduction to an Arab Democratic Statement*) (Beirut: Arab Center for Research and Policy Studies, 2018), ch. I, p. 335.

[17] Among these Arab intellectuals are Tariq Ramadan, Galam Ameen and Asem al-dosouqi.

[18] See, e.g., Lisa Anderson, 'Searching where the Light Shines: Studying Democratization in the Middle East', *Annual Review of Political Science* 9(1) (2006): 205–7.

[19] Such as Jamal al-Din al-Afghani, Muhammad Abdo, Khair al-Din al-Tounsi, Abdul Rahman al-Kawakibi and others.

constitutional reforms and the compatibility of Islam and modernity.[20] Numerous opposition parties and groups advocated political reform and democracy in every Arab country. In Saudi Arabia, a reformist movement called for a constitutional monarchy during the 1990s and again at the beginning of the new millennium. Furthermore, Arab academics and researchers who wrote from within their home countries or in the diaspora have conducted extensive research on democracy and reform.

With the outbreak of the Arab revolutions in 2011, and the subsequent counter-revolutions and civil wars, it was difficult to understand what occurred in the Arab countries through the concepts of the democratic transition approach, or by solely focusing on internal factors. The 2011 Arab uprisings reveal at least three issues that have been neglected in the literature on transition. The first relates to the mode of transition, as the youth movements and civil society activists sparked widespread protests while the traditional political actors mismanaged the transition.[21] The second is the attitude and strategies of the main actors, and the failure to secure elite consensus on a political agenda responding to the demands of the uprisings. This was made worse by the involvement of invisible and external actors. The third issue relates to the outcome of the transition process. The assumption that this process has one end, procedural democracy, led to confusion, as this chapter explains.

Key Internal Actors and their Strategies during Transitional Periods

The Mode of Transition

The literature on democratic transition has focused on modes of transition through elites, that is, reformists within the ruling elite and the moderate democratic opposition. Although many cases had witnessed mobilisation from below, the focus was on elites. When two parties reach a pact

[20] Among these thinkers are Muhammad Selim al-Awa, Tariq al-Bishri, Fathi Othman, Muhammad Mahdi Shams el-Deen, Abdelwahab al-Messeri, Abdelwahab El-Affendi, Muhammad Kamal Abu el-Majd and Fahmui Howedy.

[21] By 'traditional' I mean the opposition parties under authoritarian regimes before the 2011 uprisings as well as former regime loyalists, such as the military in Egypt and remnants of the old ruling parties in Tunisia who joined the Nidaa Tounes party.

that reduces the uncertainty and prevents the domination of hardliners on both sides, democracy becomes possible.[22] In such cases, leaders of opposition movements then become part of the institutions of transitional periods. Examples include the Polish trade union, Solidarity, in Poland, the Congress Party in South Africa, and the Coalition of Parties for Democracy (*Concertación*) in Chile.

The 2011 Arab cases were different, except for Tunisia. There is no doubt that intellectuals and the elites of the traditional opposition parties contributed to the creation of the political climate that facilitated the uprisings. Islamic, liberal, leftist and nationalist currents have converged on cross-ideological initiatives, such as the 'Egyptian Movement for Change' (better known *Kifaya* (Enough!) and the 'National Assembly for Change in Egypt; the 'October 18 Initiative' in Tunisia; or the 'Joint Meeting' in Yemen. However, the popular mobilisation in 2010–2011 was spearheaded by youth protest movements that, to a large extent, were not part of the traditional opposition. In Egypt, days before the uprising of 25 January 2011, leaders of the National Assembly for Change were discussing how to restrain the youth from calling for popular demonstrations at a time when the Assembly's sole objective was to urge Mubarak to amend the constitution to permit free presidential elections. The Assembly leaders did not believe in the possibility of overthrowing the regime. Once popular mobilisation toppled the old system, the old elites resurfaced and dominated the transitional period. What is significant here is to understand how the nature of the old regimes affected the way in which the change transpired, and how the mode of change influenced the establishing the democratic system.

The literature of transition has indicated that the more violent the regime, the more intense will be the conflict between the ruling elites and their adversaries, and the more likely the regime will be transformed by violent or non-consensual means (popular mobilisation, coups, insurrection, etc.).[23] In the Arab region, the 'state' has a distorted origin; its political frame of reference is inconsistent with the society's culture and heritage, and its

[22] See Philippe C. Schmitter, 'Democratization and Political Elites', online version, available at: https://bit.ly/3ce6rtb, pp. 5–6; George Sørensen, *Democracy and Democratization: Process and Prospects in a Changing World* (Boulder, CO: Westview, 2008), pp. 13–15.

[23] Bratton and Van de Walle, *Democratic Experiments in Africa*.

regimes serve parochial interests, relying on alliances with forces hostile to the notion of democracy. In addition, the colonial borders are in contradiction with the logic of the 'nation-state', which presupposes the unity of nations and peoples.[24] Arab regimes also conform to the 'personal rule' (also known as neo-patrimonial or sultanistic) model, where the division is not between the government and the opposition, but between insiders and outsiders. The more intense the conflict over privileges, the more likely the excluded would aim to get rid of the regime so as to access privileges and benefits. The nature of these regimes made any gradual reform near impossible, and, thus, the uprisings, or similar confrontations, unavoidable.[25] Traditional opposition parties were not the main actors in these uprisings; rather, it was non-partisan protesters and activists, that is, youth and protest movements, who initiated and sustained action.[26] As noted earlier, some Middle East research has blamed the 'people' for its anti-modernity culture for the longevity of authoritarianism. However, the 2011 uprisings demonstrated the inaccuracy of these assumptions.

Although revolutions furnish an opportunity for a comprehensive revamp of social and political institutions, they also make democratic transi-

[24] For more details, see Abdel-Fattah Mady, *'Al-'islāmiyyūn wa 'Al-'Almāniyyūn Fī A'qāb 'Al-Thawarāt Al-'Arabiyyiyya, i'ādat 'Al-Naẓar fi Jawhar 'Al-Mushkila* (*Islamists and Secularists in the Wake of the Arab Revolutions: A Review of the Essence of the Problem*) (Cairo: Civilization Center for Studies and Research, 2015/16), pp. 314–47.

[25] See Abdelwahab El-Affendi, 'Political Culture and the Crisis of Democracy in the Arab World', in Ibrahim Elbadawi and Samir Makdisi (eds), *Democracy in the Arab World: Explaining the Deficit* (London: Routledge, 2010), p. 30. In fact, several Arab intellectuals understood this early. In a famous article published in 2004 and re-printed in 2006, Egyptian Islamic thinker Tariq al-Bishri called Egyptians to civil disobedience as Arab regimes would not change gradually. See Tariq al-Bishri, *Misr bayn 'al-Tafakkuk wa 'al-'isyān* (*Egypt between Disobedience and Disintegration*) (Cairo: Dar al-Shorouk, 2006). Moncef Marzouki, human rights activist and the first president in Tunisia after the 2011 uprising wrote in 2004: '[Arab] tyrants act as if they were foreign governors . . . in order to stay in power, they lost national honour . . . they lost what remained of the gestures of independence. Thus, we are now people under guardianship, and the Arab dictatorships are merely the claws of the global guardianship.' See 'Interview with Moncef Marzouki' (in Arabic), *Quds Press*, 2 January 2004, available at: https://bit.ly/2Xgs7MU, last accessed 1 May 2020.

[26] For more details on the role of the opposition in preserving the legitimacy of the Arab regimes before 2011, see Holger Albrecht, 'How Can Opposition Support Authoritarianism? Lessons from Egypt', *Democratization* 12(3) (2005): 378–97.

tions arduous by creating uncertainty, raising expectations and encouraging violence.[27] Classical revolutions usually engendered absolutist regimes, except for a few cases, such as the American one. However, the Arab cases did not follow that pattern, nor did they conform to national liberation revolutionary models, where independence was achieved without establishing democratic systems. The Arab uprisings – except for the Tunisian case thus far – have not attained what colourful revolutions in the post-Cold War period have accomplished. Eastern Europe experienced swift democratic transitions, led by a multiplicity of actors, and strongly supported by the West.[28]

A few developments could be cited in support of Asef Bayat's point about Arab revolutions having erupted at a time 'when the possibility of "revolution as change" –that is, rapid and radical transformation of the state – has been drastically undermined'.[29] These include the reinforcement of elections as the dominant way of change, the supremacy of the global capitalist economy, and the development of new tools of repression and the capabilities of security institutions. Yet absolute monarchies in the West only became democratic republics through major revolutions interspersed with acts of violence in numerous forms. For Hannah Arendt, there is no revolution without violence, because, in its classical sense, a revolution is not just a search for freedom from oppression, but a struggle for political freedom and the establishment of a new political order.[30] Indeed, Western democracy has a long history of violence,[31] and the question is whether this violence did lead to radical change and political freedom or not.[32]

[27] Judith Large and Timothy D. Sisk, *Democracy, Conflict and Human Security* (Stockholm: International Institute for Democracy and Electoral Assistance, 2006), p. 8.

[28] Huntington, *The Clash of Civilizations*, p. 282; Adam Roberts and Timothy Garton Ash (eds), *Civil Resistance and Power Politics* (Oxford: Oxford University Press, 2011), pp. 371–90.

[29] Assef Bayat, 'Revolution in Bad Times', *New Left Review*, No. 80 (2013), pp. 55–6, available at: https://goo.gl/abJMJy, last accessed 1 May 2020.

[30] Hannah Arendt, *On Revolution* (London: Penguin Classics, 1965), pp. 22–58.

[31] Barrington Moore, *Social Origins of Dictatorship and Democracy* (Boston, MA: Beacon Press, 1993), p. 20.

[32] Koenraad Bogaert, 'A Reflection on Violence and Democracy', *Jadalyya*, 3 July 2013, available at: https://goo.gl/Jqip4D, last accessed 1 May 2020.

The critical issue is whether leaders of change can modify the balance of power in their struggle with the old regime and its allies at home and abroad, and thus successfully and decisively form an alternative democratic system. Realising this requires that the actors agree on the alternative system and a clear road map to reach it.[33] Except for Tunisia, due to internal and external reasons, Arab actors fell short of such an agreement, as examined in the following section.

Managing Transitional Periods

The Retreat of the Youth and the Advance of Traditional Forces

The retreat of the youth and protest social movements was the first element of the transition periods, when traditional political parties and some elements of the old regimes began to gain influence. In Egypt, the youth protest forces incited the popular mobilisations using social media, non-violent techniques and decentralised organisation. They were also free from the ideological polarisation that plagued traditional parties. However, the leaders and activists of the protests failed to translate this into leadership during the transitional period, and thus sustain and expand the revolutionary spirit. They were not concerned with forming parties or institutions that represented them, as their focus remained on the 'outputs' of the desired political system, rather than the mechanisms necessary to achieve those outputs. The youth persistently insisted that the 'other' (the military council, political forces and elites) meet their demands, achieve social justice and punish human rights abusers, etc., but remained passively on the sidelines.

The larger political parties, weakened by the legacy of repressive authoritarianism, failed to connect with and mobilise the youth, while the media was able to do so by offering material rewards. Party politics had also been weakened by foreign funding policies aiming at strengthening civil society on specific issues (women, family, the environment, etc.), at the expense of political parties. Furthermore, the Arab uprisings occurred when the parties were declining in favour of ascending social movements.[34] This is in contrast

[33] Ali khalifa al-Kuwari and Abdel-Fattah Mady, '*Mafhūm 'Al-kutla 'Al-Tārīkhiyya 'ala qā'idat 'al-Dīmuqrātiyya*' ('The Concept of the Historical Bloc on the Basis of Democracy'), *Arab Future*, Center for Arab Unity Studies (March 2010).

[34] Phillipe C. Schimtter, 'Ambidextrous Democratization and its Implications for MENA',

to transitions in Southern Europe and Latin America, which witnessed the increasing influence of political parties in democratic transitions.

Nevertheless, by virtue of their control of security, intelligence and information apparatuses, old regime loyalists, including security, commercial and intellectual elites, have managed either to officially remain as part of the political scene (Yemen), or to form new counter-revolutionary alliances that re-entered the political arena (Egypt and Tunisia).[35] The presence or re-emergence of old regime forces is not the problem, but rather it was their anti-democracy stance. In other non-Arab cases, the political actors who led the popular mobilisation either came to power or participated through parties, coalitions or civil society movements. In many Eastern European countries, for example, the Communist parties changed their ideological orientations and programmes and supported democratic change. Moreover, commercial and business elites favoured democratic and pro-free market policies that protected property rights and reduce uncertainty.[36] In the Arab experience, however, the old forces became the predominant threat to democracy. Abdelwahab El-Affendi argues that the mutual fears among the major Arab political trends fed into anti-democratic tendencies.[37] Fears of the liberal and leftist camps, as well as that of major foreign actors, of the rise of the Islamists and the potential establishment of 'theocratic regimes', was translated into hostility to democracy. At the same time, Islamists' fear of a return of the oppressive regimes of which they were victims prevented cooperation with other forces and reaching compromise.

In Egypt, the Supreme Council of the Armed Forces (SCAF) had managed to defuse the uprising in February 2011, and safeguard the rest of the old regime from total collapse by removing its head, but leaving the rest intact.[38] Its subsequent handling of the transitional process vitiated the

European University Institute, September 2015, available at: https://bit.ly/3fqrdbd, last accessed 6 May 2020.

35 See Shana Marshall, *The Egyptian Armed Forces and the Remaking of an Economic Empire* (Washington, DC: Carnegie Endowment for International Peace, 2015).

36 Schimtter, *Democratization and Political Elites*.

37 See Abdelwahab El-Affendi, Chapter 3, this volume.

38 See Azmi Bishara, *'al-Jaysh wa 'al-Siyāsa* (*The Military and Politics*) (Beirut: Arab Center for Research and Policy Studies, 2017), pp. 183–98; Emad El-Din Shaheen, '*Ḥalat Misr*' ('The Case of Egypt'), in Ali al-Kuwari and Abdel-Fattah Mady (eds), *Troubled Democracy:*

democratic transition, making the military the greatest threat to democracy.[39] Bayat also argued that, by imposing strike bans etc., the army had halted the struggle for political freedom. According to Bayat, 'violence' meant the continuation of an endeavour beyond simply restoring the pre-January 2011 patterns of authority.[40] Indeed, several factors have contributed to the military's return as a major player, in particular, the fear of questioning the economic privileges enjoyed by the military establishment.[41] The failure of the Muslim Brotherhood's (MB) appeasement strategy towards the military also failed to balance the civil–military relations. Appeasement is not uncommon as a strategy in transitions. However, in this instance, the policy had major flaws, chief amongst which was lack of expertise among the civilian leaders, and their lack of unity, and the decision by the MB leaders not to involve other pro-democracy forces in its (mostly secretive) negotiations with the military. This led to competition among civilian parties to win over the military, thus strengthening the hand of the latter. The military did not take over in 2013 until they had gained the support of sizeable segments of liberal, leftist, nationalist and even Salafi forces. Similar polarisations had also favoured anti-democracy forces and led to military coups in other Arab countries, including Sudan, Iraq and Syria.[42]

Electoral Revolutions

The preferences of dominant political forces, and specifically the demand for immediate elections to designate new presidents and parliaments, contributed to the failure of Arab transitions. The competition for electoral gains fragmented the ranks of the revolutionaries and intensifying uncertainty gave the counter-revolution forces an advantage. In the literature on democratic transition, the term 'electoral revolution' refers to a set of revolutions or upris-

The Current Arab Movements for Democracy (Beirut: Center for Arab Unity Studies, 2014), pp. 111–63.

39 Bayat, 'Revolution in Bad Times', pp. 55–6.

40 Ibid.; James L. Payne, 'The Prospects for Democracy in High-Violence Societies', *The Independent Review* (2005), available at: https://bit.ly/300NG5S, last accessed 12 April 2018.

41 Yazīd Ṣāyigh, 'Above the State: The Officers' Republic in Egypt', Carnegie Middle East Center, Carnegie Endowment for International Peace, 1 August 2012.

42 Bishara, '*'al-Jaysh wa 'al-Siyāsa*', pp. 37–46.

ings that took place at the turn of the new millennium (mainly in Eastern Europe and Soviet successor states), and involved limiting democracy and revolutionary demands to electing new executive and legislative institutions, rather than tending to other recognised pillars of democracy.[43] Such elections are usually conducted in the absence of consensus on constitutional and legal provisions, often leading to a victory for traditional powers and elites due to their networks, influence and resources. Such outcomes are likely to generate conflict and derail the transition.

In Egypt, the prioritisation of 'electoral legitimacy' began early as political actors espoused partisan agendas immediately after the fall of the regime, feeling an urgency to reap political benefits before it was too late. Accordingly, this 'foundational period' established a precept of 'political contestation' in a zero-sum game among parties that failed to understand the requirements of democratic transition in the wake of a revolution. The road map framed by the SCAF had helped to establish this tendency as the March 2011 plebiscite on the constitutional amendments provoked fruitless debates over issues irrelevant to building a truly democratic system, such as identity issues.

A similar problem arose as the political elites assumed that holding elections was the solution. The problem did not lie in the principle of holding elections per se, but in the hasty conduct of elections before reaching a broad consensus over the rules of the game (i.e., election legislation and procedures, legal and judicial guarantees, etc.). Moreover, one party, the military junta, along with their allies (especially the Muslim Brotherhood), passed electoral laws and regulations without adequate dialogue with other political actors. In this sense, it was misleading to compare the Egyptian situation (which involved a transitional period and a state of severe political polarisation) to

[43] See Valerie Bunce and Sharon L. Wolchik, 'Favorable Conditions and Electoral Revolutions', *Journal of Democracy* 17(4) (2006): 5–18; Josephine T. Andrews, 'The Democratic Revolution', PhD dissertation, University of California, 2009; Katya Kalandadze and Mitchell A. Orenstein, 'Electoral Protests and Democratization: Beyond the Color Revolutions', *Comparative Political Studies* 1(45) (2012): 312–40; Valerie Bunce and Sharon Wolchik, 'Diffusion and Postcommunist Electoral Revolutions', *Communist and Postcommunist Studies* 39(3) (2006): 283–304; Josh McCrain, 'When do Revolutions Lead to Democracy? The Conflict between Democracy and Governance in Georgia and Tunisia', MA thesis, University of North Carolina, 2013; Vladimir Tismaneanu, 'Electoral Revolutions', *Society* 35(1) (1997): 61–5.

that of established democracies, where a deeply embedded political culture makes it possible to settle controversial issues at the polls. As Robert Dahl noted, democracy is not a matter of elections, which is only one pillar of democracy and one of its last stages.[44] Since 1991, periodic elections in sub-Saharan Africa have ousted more than thirty presidents, yet not many are yet democracies.[45]

Political forces in Tunisia chose to manage the transitional phase based on 'electoral legitimacy'. The proportional representation formula, on which the first elections for transitional institutions (the Constituent National Assembly (CNA), president and a transitional government) were held,[46] had a negative impact on the Tunisian political scene. It prioritised electoral contestation in a transitional phase that required consensus and cooperation. However, electoral legitimacy later declined and lost credibility within the broader political spectrum. The powers of the CNA (the Powers Law was approved on 2 December 2013) were also disputed, as the CNA extended its remit, initially limited to drafting the constitution and managing the interim phase, to encompass all functions of any parliament. The opposition parties rejected this and accused the majority of forcing its will on the minority.[47] Disputes over the constitution escalated further during the rest of transitional phase, with a series of draft constitutions failing to gain support due to deep disagreements over some pivotal issues, such as the establishment of a 'civil state' (read 'secular state'), the state–religion relationship, the separation of powers, women's rights, liberties and what was termed the 'Revolution Protection Law'.[48]

The government–opposition conflict escalated due to weak economic performance and the transitional government's inability to institute crucial reforms or fulfil promises regarding development and security. In addition,

[44] Robert A. Dahl, *Polyarchy: Participation and Opposition* (New Haven, CT: Yale University Press, 1971).

[45] Pauline H. Baker, 'The Dilemma of Democratization in Fragile States', *UN Chronicle* 48(4) (2011), available at: https://bit.ly/2J5ZA96, last accessed 25 June 2018.

[46] Hamadi Redissi, 'The Decline of Political Islam's Legitimacy: The Tunisian Case', *Philosophy Social Criticism* 40 (2014): 384.

[47] Interview with Ahmed Naguib Al-Shamy, *Al-Safeer Newspaper*, 25 February 2013.

[48] Amel Grami, 'The Debate on Religion, Law and Gender in Post-Revolution Tunisia', *Philosophy and Social Criticism* 40(4/5) (2014): 392–4, 396–8.

the government hesitated on transitional justice measures, and was indecisive on the deep split between those favouring gradual reforms and those calling for a clean break with the old regime and the adoption of decisive political and economic measures.[49] Furthermore, the government was criticised for its partisan formation and accused of Islamising bureaucratic institutions.[50] The governing Ennahda Islamist party was also criticised for lacking experience, and failing to stand up to the old regime's significant influence on sectors such as the judiciary and the media. Many doubted whether it was actually ruling.[51] The government–opposition conflict was further exacerbated by the political role of the main Tunisian labour union (Union Générale Tunisienne du Travail, the UGTT), which continued to organise agitated protests, sit-ins and work stoppages. Ennahda accused the UGTT of being the 'labour wing' of the leftist opposition parties. However, in spite of these differences, the UGTT helped to conduct a crucial national dialogue, as discussed later.

In sum, in Egypt and Tunisia, mutual mistrust and fears affecting political actors hindered consensus on the foundations of a democratic system in preparation for holding elections.[52] Misgivings by secular parties (liberal, leftist and nationalist) about electoral arrangements were influenced by fears that Islamic forces had stronger popular support and organisational capacities, so are more likely to win early elections. It was thus necessary to gradually address the polarisation through a set of strategies based on dialogue, compromise, and institutional and constitutional guarantees. However, the rush towards elections thwarted this possibility.

Polarisation: Dialogue or Failure

Several factors have contributed to the deepening polarisation during the transitional stages in Egypt and Tunisia. However, the outcome of democratic transitions diverged in the two cases according to key actors' strategies.

[49] Amna Jablawi, 'Democratic Transition in Tunisia: Where To?' Political Follow-up Papers, Arab Reform Initiative, February 2013.

[50] See Hamada al-Radaisi, 'What is the Role of the National Dialogue in Tunisia Under Mahdi Juma's Government?' Arab Reform Initiative, June 2014.

[51] Kamal Al-Qusayr, 'The Tunisian Political Scene: Calculations of the Political Crisis', Al-Jazeera Center for Studies, 7 January 2014.

[52] For more details, see Abdelwahab El-Affendi, Chapter 3, this volume.

In Egypt, apart from hasty elections, the main actors remained undecided about their commitment to democratisation. They failed to engage in serious dialogue or offer real compromises and guarantees to ensure the success of the process. In other cases, as Larry Diamond explained with regard to Asia, the common thread was elite consensus regarding the legitimacy of the rules of democracy.[53] The Egyptian experience has revealed the tenuous commitment by many forces to democracy. In particular, the Salafi movements that practiced electoral politics for the first time, and used to condemn democracy, quickly sided with the forces of authoritarianism. But so did most liberal and leftist parties and figures, that had been rather vociferous in championing democracy but were quick to sacrifice it in order to exclude their main more popular Islamist competitors.[54]

Contrary to the third wave's more successful democratic transitions, where distinct political forces represented certain interests, strata or social strata, polarisation in Arab cases was often influenced, even manufactured, by secretive actors directing political action from behind the scenes. It has become habitual to refer to state actors involved in this (mainly the military and intelligence agencies, together with sections of the judiciary and the bureaucracy) as the 'deep state'.[55] These actors often cooperated with external powers. Within the opposition, the MB had a dual political structure, with the Freedom and Justice Party, the official political forum, while the broader organisation, controlled by the MB Guidance Office exerted ultimate power. The presence of this duality has serious and multiple consequences, complicating the process of dialogue and reaching agreements, since the visible party giving assurances (whether official government figures or party leaders) may not have the full authority to deliver. The real actors may also evade responsibility for their actions, since they are not visible on the scene to account for them. The problem was less evident in Tunisia, but the influence of actors

[53] Larry Diamond, Juan Linz and Seymour Martin Lipset (eds), *Democracy in Developing Countries, vol. 3: Asia* (Boulder, CO and London: Lynne Rienner and Adamantine Press, 1989), p. 49.

[54] For more details, see Dalia Fahmy and Daanish Faruqi (eds), *Egypt and the Contradictions of Liberalism: Illiberal Intelligentsia and the Future of Egyptian Democracy* (London: Oneworld, 2017).

[55] See Robert Springborg, 'Deep States in MENA', *Middle East Policy* 25(1) (2018): 136–57.

like the security sector and other old regime loyalists, and the trade unions, remained significant.

Polarisation is also related to the varying roles played by Islamists.[56] In Tunisia, the acknowledged moderation of Ennahda under the leadership of Rached Ghannouchi helped to mitigate this polarisation. Ennahda contributed to the national dialogue with leftist forces and former Ben Ali loyalists. Its priority was to establish the rule of law and safeguard freedoms.[57] Unlike the Egyptian MB, Ennahda did not seek political domination during the transition, and made compromises during vital discussions on the constitution.[58] In the Egyptian case, in contrast, the polarisation continued, and consensus on a constitution remained elusive. Two constitutions were rapidly ratified: one by the MB, their Islamist allies and the military; and the other by non-Islamic political actors, also with the military.

Although the Egyptian MB undoubtedly had a sizeable democratic bloc and a discourse that continued to defend democracy, its practical conduct and political discourse did not take into account the precariousness of the emerging democratic order. Its approach to democracy was defined as majority rule, as demonstrated during the formation of parliamentary committees in parliament in 2012. This was also applied to the Constituent Assembly of the Constitution, also dominated by the MB and its Salafi allies, whose presence pushed the MB to the right, thus intensifying the polarisation between Islamists and the rest of the political forces. Other practices, such as a lack the separation between group and party, also raised concerns.[59]

The positions of liberal and left-wing political forces contributed to the polarisation, as their commitment to democracy proved to be fragile. Those parties generally sought to contain the Islamic trend, rather than to strengthen their popular support. Following Mohamed Morsi's November 2012 constitutional decree restricting judicial review of executive decisions, these forces

[56] For more details on Islamic parties, see Khalil Al-Anani, 'Islamist Parties Post-Arab Spring', *Mediterranean Politics* 17(3) (2012): 466–72.

[57] Rashed Ghannouchi, 'Will the National Dialogue Save the Tunisian Spring?' *Al-Jazeera*, 11 November 2013.

[58] Hafez Ghanem, 'Will Tunisia Follow Egypt?' Brookings Institution, 25 July 2013.

[59] For more details, see Khalil Al-Anani, 'Upended Path: The Rise and Fall of Egypt's Muslim Brotherhood', *Middle East Journal* 69(4) (2015): 527–43.

irresponsibly escalated their demands. They insisted on the jettisoning of the constitution despite participating in the referendum that endorsed it, and demanded early presidential elections. Their next escalation was calling on the Army to intervene to depose the elected president.[60]

In Tunisia, civil society actors, led by the UGTT, played a more constructive role, even though some were partisan and hostile to the dominant Ennahda. Mutual confidence was, however, restored as both parties realised the need to look to the future. As a result, the UGTT led a quartet of civil society bodies to undertake mediation to rebuild confidence and pressure all parties into urgently needed dialogue.[61] The resulting compromise balanced 'electoral legitimacy', represented by the Constituent Assembly and Ennahda, on the one hand, and 'consensual legitimacy', represented by dialogue on the other.[62] Ghannouchi and other moderate Islamists realised that democracy should be safeguarded, even if the price was ceding power to an interim consensual government. Several moderate secular parties realised that political Islam had become a social and political reality, and that dialogue and reconciliation were a better alternative to factional disputes and chaos.[63] Furthermore, the instability and serious human rights violations in Egypt pushed the Tunisian parties to moderate their demands to achieve compromise.

The timing and legacy of old regimes also contributed to polarisation. In Tunisia and Egypt, attempts to bar old regime loyalists from seeking political office failed. However, in December 2013, the Constituent Assembly in Tunisia ratified a transitional justice system. In Libya, a ten-year ban on former regime officials became a catalyst for renewed violent zero-sum conflict that divided the country and invited foreign intervention. Other factors complicated the transitions, including disputes over foreign policy issues in Egypt, such as the relationship with United States and the Egyptian–Israeli peace agreement. This strengthened the counter-revolutionary alliance between internal and external actors.

[60] See 'Osama Al-Ghazali Harb's Interview', *Al-Shorouq*, 29 September 2011.

[61] For more details, see Abdel-Fattah Mady, *Dialogue Processes after the 2011 Arab Uprisings* (Geneva: Cordoba Foundation of Geneva, 2016), pp. 26–7.

[62] al-Radaisi, 'What is the Role of the National Dialogue in Tunisia'.

[63] For more details on Islamists and Secularists, see Radwan Masmoudi, 'Political Pluralism in Tunisia', *Reset Dialogues on Civilizations*, 29 December 2012.

In short, the intense polarisation provoked by mutual fears and intolerance among key political actors overshadowed democracy. The exception was Tunisia. This confirmed Adam Przeworski's point that uncertainty can push the parties to negotiations, compromise and adherence to a democratic system that preserves the rights of small groups.[64] The opposite happened in Egypt as Islamists and their rivals failed to reach a compromise. Military intervention then tipped the balance of power in favour of the counter-revolution. In addition, the regional context was hostile to the transition in Egypt as the next section will show.

The Influence of External Actors

Until the 1990s, the literature on democratic transitions did not focus much on international actors, preferring to concentrate on the internal political scene.[65] The 2011 Arab cases dramatically demonstrated the significance of these external factors. The 2011 uprising in Bahrain was quashed with a Saudi-led military. In Syria, Yemen and Libya, regional and international powers transformed the uprisings into civil and regional wars. Without powerful external support, the 2013 Egyptian coup could not have succeeded. This section highlights five issues that negatively affected the strategies of internal actors during transitional periods after the 2011 uprisings.

First, in view of a long-standing Western reluctance to promote or tolerate Arab democracy, the uncertainty associated with the results of any democratic elections in the Arab countries could not remain a domestic issue. International hostility to Arab democracy was evident in the substantial Western military, economic and political support authoritarian Arab regimes continue to receive. According to a US researcher, American support to Egypt since the 1970s has prevented or aborted opportunities for transition

[64] Michael McFaul, 'The Fourth Wave of Democracy and Dictatorship: Noncooperative Transitions in the Postcommunist World', *World Politics* 54(2) (2002): 219; Adam Przeworski, *Democracy and the Market: Political and Economic Reforms in Eastern Europe and Latin America* (Cambridge: Cambridge University Press, 1991), p. 87.

[65] See Philippe C. Schmitter, 'The Influence of the International Context upon the Choice of National Institutions and Policies in Neo-democracies', in Laurence Whitehead (ed.), *The International Dimensions of Democratization: Europe and the Americas* (Oxford: Oxford University Press, 1996), p. 28.

to democracy.[66] Indeed, support of Arab 'allies' was one of three declared Western interests in the region, alongside Israel's security and ensuring the flow of oil, thus instituting a 'red light' against any real democratic transition. As Henry Kissinger made clear in 2012, the rise of democratic governments in the region would threaten American hegemony:

> For over half a century, American policy in the Middle East has been guided by several core security objectives: preventing any power in the region from emerging as a hegemon; ensuring the free flow of energy resources . . . These interests have not been abolished by the Arab Spring; their implementation has grown more urgent. A process that ends with regional governments either too weak or too anti-Western in their orientation to lend support to these outcomes, and in which American partnerships are no longer welcomed, must evoke American strategic concerns – regardless of the electoral mechanisms by which these governments come to power. Within the framework of these general limits, American policy has significant scope for creativity in promoting humanitarian and democratic values.[67]

Western fear of Arab democracy is manifested in another light, 'a green one', directed at the allies and adversaries of Arab governments alike, to continue to suppress dissent or access to power by those deemed hostile to American interests. Previous instances include the massacres of the Muslim Brotherhood in Hama (1982), the suppression of the Shiite and Kurdish uprisings in Iraq (1991), and the destruction of the army rebellion in Libya (1993). Today, the Assad regime receives military backing from its regional and international allies with tacit Western support for massacres committed against civilians. Likewise, little condemnation was voiced when the Egyptian military perpetrated massacres and other gross human rights violations following the July 2013 coup. Atrocities in the Yemen war have passed without international accountability. Eva Beilin was partly right when in 2004 she wrote that the problem in the Middle East was not the absence of preconditions for democracy as in condi-

[66] Jason Brownlee, *Democracy Prevention: The Politics of the US–Egyptian Alliance* (Cambridge: Cambridge University Press, 2012).

[67] Henry A. Kissinger, 'Defining a U.S. Role in the Arab Spring', *International Herald Tribune*, 2 April 2012, available at: https://bit.ly/2D5dO8s, last accessed 15 December 2017.

tions supportive of tyranny, especially the robustness of security apparatuses.[68] Yet it is necessary to take into account the external dimension of that support for tyranny, considering the arms sales and strong military cooperation.

Second, employing the 'war on terror' discourse is a key strategy to block peaceful democratic transitions, as it gives stability and security precedence over democracy promotion.[69] The region has witnessed a 'war on terror' at least three times over the past three decades. Each time, it involved silencing the opposition, restricting political participation and lumping Islamists in one category as an 'internal enemy'. This happened in the late 1980s and early 1990s with the return of the so-called Arab Afghans. The second time was in the wake of the attacks of 11 September 2001, in which the peaceful opposition voices were silenced as security concerns became a priority as many Arab and Islamic countries became the main arena of that war. The third time occurred after the 2011 uprisings and the rise of moderate Islamists through democratic processes. A 'war on terror' was again invoked, shifting the focus in transitional periods democratisation and expanding freedoms towards counter-insurgency/civil conflict. Both the Obama and Trump administrations chose to support the counter-revolutions and authoritarian regimes at the expense of democracy and human rights.

This coincided with a revival in official and research circles of culturalist explanations for the survival of tyranny in the region. For Obama, 'The Middle East is going through a transformation that will play out for a generation, rooted in conflicts that date back millennia.'[70] One of Trump's tactics during his election campaign was to repeat the phrase 'radical Islamic

[68] Eva Bellin, 'The Robustness of Authoritarianism in the Middle East: Exceptionalism in Comparative Perspective', *Comparative Politics* 36(2) (2004): 139–57 at 143.

[69] Some American experts in the Middle East have very different views. For example, in 2005, an American Middle East expert objected to George W. Bush's approach to democratiaation in the Arab world, declaring that democracy would not stop 'terrorism' there. See Gregory F. Gause III, 'Can Democracy Stop Terrorism?' *Foreign Affairs*, 2005, pp. 62–76.

[70] Obama refers here to the Sunni–Shiite divide, see 'President Obama's Final State of the Union Address', NPR, 12 January 2016, available at: https://goo.gl/eBdE7F, last accessed 3 May 2020.

terrorism' to emphasise the culpability of Muslims.[71] Other conservative and liberal writers have similar views.[72]

Third, the Arab uprisings erupted against the background of a worldwide ascendancy of authoritarianism, as well as a democratic decline in the West. Countries like Russia and China presented a pattern of governance that could be simulated in the region, and their propaganda fed anti-democratic attitudes worldwide. Both countries also cooperated and coordinated their anti-democratic policies in international forums and organisations. Russian Defence Minister Sergei Shoigu frankly admitted that the Russian military intervention in Syria was aimed at achieving a geo-political goal, which is to prevent 'colour revolutions' like those of Ukraine and Georgia from spreading to the Middle East and North Africa.[73]

On the other hand, the democratic model of governance is declining in the West, with tensions arising from government failure to address acute economic crises. The rise of populism, political party decline and the repercussions of migration from conflict areas have also weakened democracy. According to a recent report on freedoms in the world:

> Democracy is in crisis. The values it embodies – particularly the right to choose leaders in free and fair elections, freedom of the press, and the rule of law – are under assault and in retreat globally . . . the world's most powerful democracies are mired in seemingly intractable problems at home, including social and economic disparities, partisan fragmentation, terrorist attacks, and an influx of refugees that has strained alliances and increased fears of the 'other'.[74]

The democratic decline includes the United States, Turkey, Mexico, Bolivia, Myanmar, Poland, Hungary and Tanzania.

[71] Donald J. Trump, 'The Inaugural Address', The White House, 20 January 2017, available at: https://goo.gl/iUyabG, last accessed 3 May 2020.

[72] See, e.g., Thomas Friedman, 'Tell Me How This Ends Well', *New York Times*, 1 April 2015, available at: https://goo.gl/9AvyGW, last accessed 3 May 2020.

[73] 'Moscow's Syria Campaign "Breaks Chain of Colour Revolutions" in Mid-East, Africa', *Sputnik*, 21 February 2017, available at: https://bit.ly/307bxkE, last accessed 3 May 2020.

[74] Michael J. Abramowitz, 'Democracy in Crisis', Freedom House, 2018, available at: https://bit.ly/2WzGMEV, p. 1, last accessed 6 May 2020.

Fourth, the Arab transition to democracy is becoming increasingly difficult with strong alliances between the 'deep state' forces in the region and authoritarian regional powers. Indeed, the Arab uprisings of 2011 were perceived as an existential threat to the region's entrenched autocracies. The UAE and Saudi Arabia defended Mubarak and tried to prevent his trial.[75] Later, both regimes backed the military efforts to undermine the democratic experience and eventually quash it, deploying substantial sums of money for this purpose.[76] The outcome of any free elections in Arab capitals also became linked to Israeli security concerns. Israeli leaders regraded the Arab Spring as an existential threat to the legitimacy and historical narrative of the Israeli state as the only democracy in the region. Many Israeli politicians described the 2011 revolutions as 'an earthquake' that threatened to create a new Middle East.[77] In August 2011 the Israeli newspaper *Maariv* published a statement by Israeli PM Benjamin Netanyahu, calling for the establishment of an international fund to support anti-Islamist forces in the Arab World, similar to the Marshall Plan in Europe, to encourage what he called the move towards 'democracy and economic growth'. Danny Ayalon, the then deputy foreign minister, called upon rich Arab countries to endow this fund.[78] Indeed, for decades, Arab rulers have used the phobia of the Islamists to remain in power.

Finally, there is the subject of offering democracy as a ready-made recipe for Arab countries and prioritising procedural democracy. Besides, Western and Arab researchers have linked democracy to liberalism as a frame of reference, while neo-liberal economic reforms have been promoted in many countries as a *sine qua non* for the transition to democracy. This combination has provoked many Arab political forces, as it seemed to deny that

[75] Mustapha Rouis and Olga Shomakhmadova, 'Arab Aid on the Rise 2011–2016', *Quick Notes Series, World Bank,* No. 163, 2/2018, available at: https://goo.gl/umMk1o, last accessed 3 May 2020.

[76] Azmi Bishara, *Thawrat Misr: min 'al-thawra 'ila 'al-'inqilāb* (*The Revolution of Egypt, Part II: From Revolution to Coup*) (Beirut: Arab Center for Research and Policy Studies, 2016), pp. 495–519.

[77] Mahmoud Muhareb, 'Israel and the Egyptian Revolution', Situation Assessment, Arab Center for Research and Policy Studies, 10 May 2011.

[78] 'The Prime Minister's Marshall Plan to Stop Islam', *Maarive,* 3 August 2011, available at: https://goo.gl/ykTFVe, last accessed 3 May 2020.

democracy has roots outside contemporary Western civilisation.[79] Indeed, democracy is not a political doctrine, nor is it inescapable from a specific ideology. While it has been historically linked to Western liberalism, the values and practices of democracy extend beyond the liberal Western system. The spread of democracy following the third and fourth waves of democratic transitions has shown that democracy can coexist with cultures and civilisations not based solely on Western liberal values (India, Japan, South Korea, South Africa, Indonesia and Latin America). Even in the West, several models and versions of democracy coexist (Anglo-Saxon, Scandinavian, consociational, etc.).[80]

Promoting liberal, procedural democracy as a ready-made model for Arab countries has generated strong scepticism towards external democracy and human rights promotion. Western democracy has begun to lose its appeal anyway, in particular due to suspicion of hidden agendas and ulterior motives among Western democracy promotion. This suspicion stems from the colonial past and current Western hegemonic policies supporting Israel and undermining Arab states. In contrast, Eastern European countries welcomed Western political, financial and technical support.[81]

Conclusion

This chapter demonstrated the validity of some assumptions of the democratic transition literature in the Tunisian case. Youth and civil society activists led the popular mobilisation, and then political parties and civil society organisations joined the negotiations with old regime reformers. Political elites managed to reach compromises when they converged, and the army did not intervene in favour of one party against another. At least one group of old regime figures reorganised in a new party that joined the dialogue

[79] See Raul S Manglapus, *Will of the People: Original Democracy in non-Western Societies* (Westport, CT: Greenwood, 1987).

[80] For more details, see Larry Diamond and Marc F. Plattner (eds), *The Global Divergence of Democracies* (Baltimore, MD: Johns Hopkins University Press, 2001), pp. 1–165.

[81] Philippe C. Schmitter, 'Ambidextrous Democratization and its Implications for MENA', manuscript, European University Institute, Florence, available at: http://www. eui.eu/Documents/DepartmentsCentres/SPS/Profiles/Schmitter/AmbidextrousDemocratization.pdf, accessed 14 May 2012.

with the revolutionaries after realising that democracy would not seriously threaten its interests. Islamists have firmly adhered to the democratic system and projected open-mindedness towards other political forces. In addition, favourable external conditions, including limited Western interest due to Tunisia's marginality in Middle East conflicts, and the Tunisian elites' worry about a repeat of the Egyptian 2013 coup, facilitated compromise. Contrary to the Tunisian case, the democratic transition in Egypt principally failed due to the choices of internal and external actors.

In general, this chapter shows some similarities and differences between the pathways of change in the Arab countries and other democratic transitions mentioned in the literature of democratic transition. The six following findings need further research:

1. The problematic founding of Arab states and its impact on the mode of change in 2011. There are at least three reasons why the post-colonial Arab state had abnormal and deformed roots. First, the majority of Arab states were established according to political doctrines inconsistent with their culture and heritage. The states still confront major challenges of nation-building, including contestations over national identity, and over a path of modernisation consistent with the religious and cultural heritage, and accommodating all components of society. The second reason is that although the emblems of the modern state have seemingly been adopted, the brutally tyrannical coercive apparatus on which these states were built serves only the interest of a small minority, and is anathema to the requirements of modernity. Finally, most post-colonial Arab states face a multifaceted challenge to its presumed 'artificiality' in relation to 'proper' nationhood. At one level, they are challenged by ethnic and religious minorities seeking special recognition, autonomy or even secession. This led to continuing conflict and contestations over statehood and national identity, and continues to invite external intervention. At another level, pan-Arabists and pan-Islamists want this state to be incorporated into the wider *umma*, regarding the current state as an illegitimate partition of the Arab nation/Muslim *umma*. Such distorted roots of the post-colonial Arab state have affected the way of change and the course of the uprisings of 2011. The coercive and tyrannical authority led to a zero-sum struggle between the ruling class and its opponents. The level of violence varied according to the levels of exclusion and amount of brutality

deployed by the regimes, with Syria and Libya being the worst, compared with Tunisia and Egypt. Ultimately, however, all these regimes have witnessed popular uprisings, and violently defended themselves. Yet their fates varied according to the choices of the main actors and the levels of regional and international involvement.

2. The gap between the masses, the elite and the youth activists had been quite evident and consequential. The masses were the initiators of action, moving ahead of, and wrong-footing, the elites, who played catch-up but failed to turn the demands of the masses into political programmes. The elites have failed to manage their differences via dialogue and compromise, and transferred these differences to the streets, often deploying divisive 'sectarian' tactics. The 2011 uprisings exposed that gap, contradicting academic narratives that continue to blame the people for tyranny.

Additionally, popular uprisings emanated from a mobilisation process which was not initiated or led by the mainstream parties or civil society organisations, but spearheaded by youth activism transcending habitual political, ideological or even sectarian–religious affiliations. Yet, on the other hand, the Arab cases proved that the youth protest movements failed to change the balance of power between the supporters of the revolution and its opponents. Young protesters only succeeded in bringing down the old regime, but did not effectively participate in transitional periods, leaving it to the traditional political forces to fulfil the demands of the uprisings. Tunisia was the exception here, but in Egypt the discourse of many youth protest movements focused on the outcomes of the desired political system not on how to build the system itself (institutions, mechanisms and procedures), thereby formulating policy and programmes.

3. The political actors mismanaged the transitional periods amidst intense political polarisation and the rush to hold elections before reaching the minimum level of consensus. Tunisia has overcome this obstacle by combining the 'legitimacy of consensus' with the 'legitimacy of the elections'. The leadership of civil society and Ennahda helped greatly with this. The polarisation in Egypt has contributed to undermining the idea of democracy itself. Moreover, the different Islamist forces contributed to the problem in various ways. In Egypt, the problematic input of 'invisible actors' working behind the scene was one of the main contributors to failure. Overall, intense

polarisation and mutual hostility among political forces overshadowed commonalities and impeded consensus. The rush to hold elections contributed to the transformation of the Egyptian revolution – in the first stage – into an 'electoral revolution' and then into a 'counter revolution', culminating in the July 2013 coup.

4. Another obstacle was the re-emergence of old regime loyalists on the political scene, either directly (the military junta in Egypt and the former ruling party in Yemen) or indirectly (the re-formation of new parties with an old agenda, as in Tunisia). This became a major threat to democracy, given the deep divisions between the pro-democracy forces, and the remaining influence of the unreformed coercive state apparatus. The threatened economic interests of influential political and economic actors also brought onto the field powerful allies to the counter-revolution who, with equally significant support from regional and international actors, managed to tip the balance. This contrasted significantly to how the re-grouping of old regime loyalists in successful third wave cases did not seriously undermine democracy, regarding it as an asset that would guarantee their interests.

5. The Arab cases have highlighted the importance of regional and international contexts for the success of transitions to democracy. The Arab uprisings erupted against the background of the ascendancy of authoritarian alternatives in the East, and the retreat of democracy in the West. The 'war on terror' as well as political conditionality prioritised security and commercial goals of powerful international actors, rather than strengthening democracy. A powerful anti-democratic regional alliance exploited the so-called 'red lights' imposed by the major Western powers to limit Arab democracy. Fears that democracy will undermine Western hegemony in the region and perhaps Israeli security, coalesced with the fear of democracy as such among Arab despots to create an overwhelming anti-democracy force, unlike the case in Southern and Eastern Europe. The 2011 uprisings proved Western policies on Arab democracy to be based on a narrow-minded view that sees their interests via a trade and security prism.

6. One of the big gaps in the literature concerns the impact of the promotion of procedural democracy as a model ready for export and implementation. This has contributed to strengthening the polarisation among various political trends, affording old regime loyalists the chance to link democracy

to external interference threatening sovereignty. It has also promoted mistrust – at the level of elites and people in the Arab countries – of any externally originating or supported discourse on democracy.

8

ELITE WOMEN AND DEMOCRATISATION IN MOROCCO, 1998–2016

Tourya Essaoudi

Addressing the subject of women elite political actors in Morocco poses a series of challenges for researchers, primarily due to the scarcity of literature on the issue. However, such an approach is encouraged by the prominence of this category of actors in the public sphere, and its increasing influence on the monarchy, political parties and trade unions. Their role is also rising in importance in other economic, cultural and social fields. The topic is also open to a range of treatments: historical, political, legal and anthropological approaches.

Today, only a small proportion of women participate in the conduct of Morocco's political affairs, in spite of the progressive emergence of prominent women in different fields, be it cultural, economic, political, religious, artistic, sports, etc. This in turn poses one aspect of the paradox underlying elite theory, especially the challenge of specifying a single ruling 'elite' or a plurality of 'elites' present on the public scene – even when their roles are limited or indirect.

Morocco's democratic transition, which could be said to have started with the 1998 accession to power of the so-called 'consensual rotation government', involved the appointment of a government led by the opposition left-wing Socialist Union of Popular Forces (SUPF). This arrangement was inaugurated by King Hassan II in the last year of his reign, and ended in 2002. It was taken further after the constitutional reforms in 2011, and the appointment of a coalition government headed by the Islamist Justice and Development Party which won the elections of that year. It is this period that witnessed the emergence and evolution of formations of elite women, who adopted many forms of struggle. At one point, there were even attempts to form a feminist lobby to press for women's demands.

This study takes as its staring point claims by scholars that vanguards of Moroccan elite women – political ones specifically – significantly contributed to the formulation of the concept of democracy within the parties in which they were active. This they achieved through their struggle to reach the centres of decision-making, which, in the 1980s and 1990s, was exclusively restricted to men.

Interrogating the ramifications of the role of this elite group in society and how they contributed to the experience of democratic transition in Morocco is key precisely because democracy is the goal of this transition in the first place. Democratisation, however, cannot be achieved in the absence of the basic principle of equality, which in turn is the essence of feminist demands, elite or otherwise. The chapter is also concerned with the impact of feminist elite in Morocco, and whether their actions had a positive or negative impact, either on the whole of society or on women sectors exclusively.

The concept of gender frames this study because of its central importance in this field. But we also use other key words which will be clarified as we go along, including 'democratic transition', 'elite women', 'women lobby' and 'silent hidden elite'. By gender we mean the set of social characteristics and roles of men and women defined according to the culture of a given society, and on the basis of which roles, behaviours, values and functions specific to each of the two groups are assigned. These roles and behaviours change within the same society over time and place, and from one society to another. A number of factors determine the nature of these social roles, such as the socialisation, geographical region, educational level, customs, traditions, etc.[1]

In her book *Sexual Politics*, Kate Millett defines gender as the various authoritarian structures that shape women's roles from a societal, political,

[1] Colette Guillaumin, 'Pratique du pouvoir et idée de Nature (1) L'appropriation des femmes', *Questions Féministes* 2 (1978): 5–30.

sexual, historical and cultural perspective.[2] Collette Guillaumin's interpretation follows the same logic when she asserts that nature almost assumes the place of gods: it defines social laws, to the point of programming the genes for those who are to be socially controlled.[3]

Against this backdrop, this study will first discuss the conceptual approach to Morocco's democratisation experience, before moving on to the concept of the elite and its applications to elite women in Morocco. It then provides examples of silent or invisible female elites in Moroccan history. The chapter sheds light on the contributions of elite women during the years of political breakthrough, specifically their roles during Morocco's democratic transition, including the period of transitional justice, the events of the Arab Spring, and the emergence of an Islamist feminist elite looking for a foothold in the Moroccan arena. Some preliminary conclusions are offered at the end.

A Conceptual Approach to Democratisation in the Light of the Moroccan Experience

The concept of democratisation emerged during the second half of the twentieth century as a result of the transformation and gradual transition to democracy that took place in many countries around the world, such as in Greece, Portugal, Latin America, Eastern Europe after the fall of the Berlin Wall, and South Africa. Given the multiplicity of approaches that have advanced this concept, our focus will be on two specific elements because they are closer to the Moroccan experience.

Transition through Negotiation between the Ruling Elite and Opposition Forces

Consensual transitions proceed through negotiations between the ruling elite and opposition forces. They are usually the result of a balance of power between the two sides, and the recognition from the ruling elite that it cannot sustain exclusivist policies and repressive practices when faced with internal and external pressures. As a result, it adopts political openness and transition to some form of democratic system as part of an agreement with the

[2] Kate Millett, *La Politique du mâle*, trans. Elisabeth Gille (Paris: Seuil, 1983), p. 38.

[3] Collette Guillaumin, *Sexe, race et pouvoir: L'idée de nature* (Paris: Côté-femmes, 1992).

opposition. As for the opposition, the sense of its inability to defeat the ruling elite leads it to resort to negotiations with rulers to achieve a democratic transition. Poland, South Africa and El Salvador are models of this option.[4]

In the Moroccan context, proponents of this approach assert that the 1990s were characterised by a softening in the positions of the opposition, the search for understandings with the monarchy, and, in particular, the growing role of new elites within opposition parties that championed reconciliation with the regime and adopted a discourse aimed at creating a new foundation for political action.[5] This culminated in the coming to power of SUPF's Abderrahmane Youssoufi in 1998, who called himself 'the man of the stage of the transition to power'.[6]

Democratisation from Above

Democratisation from above refers to transitions led by the authoritarian regime or any of its reformist factions. It is thus a choice from within the regime. This transition process comes in the context of the existence of objective factors that negatively affect regime legitimacy, pushing the elite to recognise the need for reform to ensure continuity.

Based on the experiences of countries that have undergone this form of transition, it can be said roughly that this process usually contributes to the creation of a gradual transformation of the political system through overlapping and diverse influences. This generally starts with a movement on the path of political openness, which becomes a prelude to democratic transition. Democratic consolidation then follows. In this case, the balance of power is often in favour of the ruling elite, while the opposition forces are weak, and therefore have limited ability to influence the

[4] Gary A. Stradiotto and Sujian Guo, 'Transitional Modes of Democratization and Democratic Outcomes', *International Journal on World Peace* 17(4) (2010): 10.

[5] Khalid Alioua, '*Taḥawwulāt 'al-sirā' 'al-siyāsi fi 'al-maghrib*' ('Transformations of the Political Conflict in Morocco'), in Pierre Salam et al. (eds), *Jadaliyyat 'al-dawla wa al-mujtama' bi al-maghrib* (*The Dialectic of State and Society in Morocco*) (Casablanca: Ifriqiya al-Sharq lil-Nashr wal-Tawzia, 1992), p. 246.

[6] 'Text of TV Programme with the Leftist Leader French TV 5', *al-Ittihad al-Ishtiraki*, 28 February 2001.

management of the transition. Spain and Brazil are examples of such a transition.[7]

This later scenario is closer to the Moroccan experience, given the general context in which Morocco interacted with world events, such as the fall of the Berlin Wall, the collapse of dictatorships in Eastern Europe, and the growing resonance of human rights values. These shifts prompted the Moroccan regime to enter into a form of democratic opening, starting with the foundation of the Advisory Council on Human Rights (1990); the creation of the Ministry of Human Rights (1993); the first change to the Family Code (1993), which had been sacrosanct since 1958; the release of detainees and the return of exiles (1991, 1993, 1994); and the two constitutional amendments (1992, 1996) when the monarchy accepted the opposition's demand for arbitration through the 1992 Constitution – a significant indicator in this context.[8]

Added to these developments was also the appointment of an opposition figure, Habib El Malki, as leader of the Youth and Future Council. No less significant was the Crown Prince's speech to a conference organised by the Abderrahim Bouabid Foundation on democratisation in 1996. Notably, the foundation was affiliated to the party most fiercely opposed to the regime. All of these moves signalled the desire of the monarchy to enter into this kind of transition, and take the initiative in the matter.

As Mohamed El Moussawi put it, 'The monarchy succeeded in imposing itself as a central actor in the Moroccan political space, by insisting on limiting the role of other actors to merely subsidiary, even auxiliary, to it. For the monarchy, there was no difference between member of parliament and minister, or between government and opposition.'[9]

[7] G. L. Munck and Carol Skalnik Leff, 'Modes of Transition and Democratization: South America and Eastern Europe in Comparative Perspective', *Comparative Politics* 29(3) (1997): 347–51.

[8] Mohammed al-Massawi, '*Jadaliyyat 'al-tawafuq fi 'al-faḍa' 'al-siyāssī 'al-maghribī*' ('Dialectic of Agreement and Conflict in the Moroccan Political Space'), in Aamal Hajij et al. (eds), *'Al-Maghrib 'al-'arabī: thuql 'al-mawārīth wa-nidā' 'al-mustaqbal* (*The Arab Maghreb: Weight of the Legacy and Call of the Future*), ed. al-Ilahi Belqaziz (Beirut: Center for Arab Unity Studies, 2013), p. 123.

[9] Ibid., p. 125.

The Concept of the Elite and its Application to Upper-class Women in Morocco

The term elite acquired huge importance at the beginning of the last century, with the emergence of theories by scholars such as Vilfredo Pareto and Gaetano Mosca. Terms like 'vanguard', 'upper class' and 'aristocracy' were used. Pareto defines the elite as:

> a minority of society, excelling over the masses by a high level of abilities, competencies, and qualifications in various fields of social life (economic, social, scientific, religious, political, etc.), in addition to its organizational superiority gained from awareness of its common interests . . . To fulfil its role, that elite depends on intermediate sub-elites. Its membership is renewed, and in some cases the elite may be renewed entirely, meaning that a new elite takes the place of an old elite. This usually occurs when new social forces appear on the social scene.[10]

Pareto makes a distinction between two senses of the elite: a broad sense that applies to the social elite composed of a small number of individuals who, thanks to their own capacities and qualities, are able to occupy the highest ranks in the professional hierarchy; and a narrow sense applying to a small group ('the elite of society') that is characterised by playing, directly or indirectly, an important role in government. Pareto calls this 'the ruling elite'. While a chess grandmaster by virtue of his or her skill and a mistress of a powerful ruler by virtue of her beauty belong to the elite, they nonetheless only belong to 'the ruling elite' to the extent that they have other significant qualities and capacities that enable them to play a role in the government political field. It is that which makes them part of 'the ruling elite'.[11]

In a parallel context, a number of studies have attempted to engage with the composition and roles of the Moroccan elite. With a few exceptions, however, they paid little attention to elite women. John Waterbury's thesis is one of the studies that addressed this subject in the mid-1960s. Despite the

[10] Abdessalam al-Haymar, *'Al-Nukhba 'al-maghribiyya wa-'ishkāliyyat 'al-taḥdīth* (*Moroccan Elites and the Problem of Modernization*) (Casablanca: Al-Najah al-Jadid Press, 2001), p. 124.

[11] Ibid., p. 6. See also Raymond Aron, *Les Etapes de la pensée Sociologique* (Paris: Gallimard, 1967), p. 413.

absence of the direct influence of women leaders at the centres of decision-making, Waterbury emphasised their distinct roles within the family, and hence their contribution to building the horizontal relationships that preserve the social order, such as raising children, choosing a spouse and stoking or calming conflict. Women also mediate openly or in a hidden way.[12] He gives an example of their crucial role in strengthening the relations by marriage within the political elites of the major families, such as Ben Sliman and al-Khatib, and Bujabar and Hisar.[13]

The work of Myriam Catusse here is also relevant. At the end of the 1990s, borrowing Rémy Leveau's term from his book on economic elites, *Le fellah marocain défenseur du trône*, she emphasised the tyranny of the male mentality, and the scarcity of avenues for women's political elites to reach centres of decision-making, despite their presence as economic actors.[14]

Notably, specifically during the period of democratic transition, there was a real crisis facing Moroccan elites. As Ali Sedjari puts it, 'The structure of the Moroccan political elite escapes all the classic designs of political science and organizational sociology. Far from forming a homogeneous and harmonious social group through affiliations and composition, it is multifaceted and occupies diverse positions and assumes unspecified tasks in the political realm.'[15] He continues: 'The [term] elite has lost its connotations, becoming fluid, linked to self-serving anomie.'[16] Turning to the alternative, which in his view is civil society organisations, he states: 'Local associations and social movements in civil society are currently a real lever for the emergence of alternative elites, defending the true values of commitment to local and national public affairs.'[17]

12 John Waterbury and Amir al-muminin, *'al-malikiyya wa 'al-nukhba 'al-siyāsiyya 'al-maghribiyya* (*Commander of the Faithful: The Monarchy and the Moroccan Political Elite*), trans. Abd al-Ghani Abu al-Azm, Abd al-Ahad al-Sibti and Abd al-Latif al-Falaq (Rabat: Muassasat al-Ghani lil-Nashr, 2004), pp. 172–3.

13 Ibid., p. 159.

14 Myriam Catusse, *Le temps des entrepreneures? Politique transformations du capitalisme au Maroc* (Paris: Maisonneuve & Larose, 2008).

15 Ali Sedjari, 'Figure moderne de l'élite marocaine ou la conscience d'être utile', in Ali Sedjari (ed.), *Elites, gouvernance et gestion du changement* (Paris: Éditions l'Harmattan, 2002), p. 79.

16 Ibid.

17 Ibid., p. 99.

Mohammed Berdouzi stresses the problem of internal democracy within the political parties as a major cause of the weakness of the elites and the decline of their role.[18] Women have been victims of this problem, prompting an intensification of their activism within civil society. This was to fight what Mohammed Mouqit called 'the intellectual and ideological orientation opposed to all representations, ideas, values, behaviours, policies, and laws that enshrine the inferiority and inadequacy of women. This feminist perspective also expresses an intellectual vision that seeks to change the social and legal conditions of women in accordance with the principle of gender equality, by which is meant equality in human dignity as well as equality in rights.'[19]

In the context of democratisation, it is worth referring to instances where civil society actors and organisations, including the Catholic Church in some countries, played an important and influential role in the transition process. All of this is connected with the extent to which there is societal demand for democracy, which civil society plays a major role in strengthening and expanding.[20] This is what the former Moroccan Minister of Communications, Khalid Naciri, refers to when he describes the role of the elite in the women's movement at the beginning of the democratic transition period as 'an essential component of the democratic movement in general', adding that the intervention of leading women actors 'had shown boldness and a great deal of responsibility, two characteristics inherent in its makeup and necessary to achieve the profound transformations needed in society'.[21]

In this context, the women's elite activist sector in Morocco is aware of

[18] Mohammed Berdouzi, *Destinées démocratiques* (Montréal: Renouveau, 2000).

[19] Mohammed Mouqit, *'Al-Qadiya 'al-nisa'iyya fī 'idyūlūjiyat 'al-aḥzab 'al-siyasiyya 'al-maghribiyya* (*The Feminist Question in the Ideology of Moroccan Political Parties*), trans. Mohammed al-Saghir Janjar (Rabat: Moroccan Association for Moroccan Women, 2008), p. 13.

[20] Rein Mullerson, 'Democratisation through the Supply–Demand Prism'" *Human Rights Review* 10(4) (2009): 531–67; Suh Doowon, 'Civil Society in Political Democratization: Social Movement Impacts and Institutional Politics', *Development and Society* 35(2) (2006): 173–95.

[21] Khalid Naciri, 'Le mouvement des femmes et la transition démocratique au Maroc', in *La démocratie mutilée: Femmes et pouvoir politique au Maroc* (Casablanca: Association Démocratique des Femmes du Maroc, 2001), pp. 93–4.

connections and interrelationships (economic, cultural, religious and political) between its components, as well as the significance of its presence on two levels: as a visible elite or as silent and concealed elite, with both levels being influential. The main prerequisites for admission into the elite are good education, inherited social origin, marriage, political and civic action, etc. This study aims to explore their development, based on the model of Max Weber, which defines three characteristics of elites: popularity, competence and confidence. What, then, about silent or concealed elites?

The Characteristics of Silent or Invisible Elite Women

Historical circumstances have often been behind determining the presence of elite women in Morocco and elsewhere in the world. Women elites had been confined for long periods to the margins by the masculine mentality, or 'patriarchy', that defines women's roles, often depriving them of access to material returns. Historically, however, women have nonetheless continued to contribute from their position as invisible, but still influential elites. A few of them may break the mould, as happened with the young Corsican woman, 'Marta Franchesini' (1756–1799), who became the 'Sultana of Morocco'. Her father was a slave who served as head of the servants of Sultan Moulay Abdullah, who called her 'Davia' because of her stunning beauty. There are at least two publications that deal with her life and role within the royal court.[22]

Moroccan history exhibits many instances of the role in which affiliation through marriage was a tool to assert sovereignty in distant regions far from the central authority. It also granted women significant power, as was the case with Khnata bint Bakkar, who hailed from the Western Sahara, far from the seat of government. She became the wife of Sultan Moulay Ismail (r. 1672–1727), and later played decisive roles even after his death. As revealed by French documents from the Quai d'Orsay, she managed to restore her son Moulay Abdullah to the throne after he was deposed seven times. This shows her grip on the highest authority in the country.[23]

[22] Marie-José Loverini, *L'interdite: Davia une sultane corse au Maroc* (Ajaccio: Éditions Albiana, 2003); Jacques Caillé, *Une corse sultane du Maroc, Davia Franceshini et sa famille* (Paris: Éditions Pedone, 1968).

[23] Abu al-Abbas Ahmad bin Khalid al-Nasiri, *'Al-'istiqsā' li-'akhbār duwal 'al-maghrib 'al-aqsā*

This is also the case in conflict resolution and alliance formation, such as in the case of the strategy of Madani El Glaoui, who, like his brother Thami, married three women from the Ait Haddou tribes in Wadi el-Mallah, overlooking Ouarzazate, to ease the conflict with them.[24] Other alliances were formed in this way, such as that linking Thami El Glaoui to the daughter of Haj el-Menebhi el-Mahdi, vizier of Moulay Abdelhafid, whose influence continued until around 1918. Also, the marriage of Lalla Khadouj, daughter of Thami El Glaoui, to Abdussalam al-Muqri, son of the minister of finance.[25]

The queen mother may play a decisive role in the installation of the new sultan, as was the case of the Circassian Lalla Ruqaya (d. 1902), wife of Hassan I, described as the 'Sultan who carries his throne on the back of his horse' (r. 1873–94). She was with him during his last journey, and was behind a plot, with the help of the grand vizier Ba Ahmed, to conceal his death from the riders accompanying him until his arrival at his palace, so as to secure the transfer of power to her son Moulay Abdelaziz (r. 1894–1908).[26]

Marital alliances were also crucial in obtaining guarantees, such as in the case of Moulay Abdelhafid (r. 1908–12), who married four women from influential families in one night to secure his political base and ensure the loyalty of influential people in Marrakech, He did this as he declared himself the sultan of jihad, and led his movement towards the capital, Fez, to challenge his brother Moulay Abdelaziz over power at the behest of his mother, whose family and tribe came under French occupation in 1907 as part of France's policy to gradually colonise the whole of Morocco.[27]

These relationships often contributed to the circulation of elites and the coming of new factions to power. Even with the availability of other avenues

(*The Investigation of the News of the Far Maghrib, vol. 8: The Alawite State*), ed. Jaafar al-Nasiri and Mohammed al-Nasiri (Casablanca: Dar al-Kitab, 1956), part 1.

24 Pascon Paul, *Le Haouz de Marrakech*, vol. 1 (Rabat and Paris: CURS, Inav/CNRS, 1977), p. 313.

25 Ibid., p. 317.

26 '*Zawjāt Moulāy 'al-Hassan 'al-'Awwal: 'al-shirkasiyya Lallā Ruqayya …*' ('Wife of Moulay Hassan I: The Circassian Lalla Ruqaia …'), *Al-Ayyam al-Usbuiyya*, No. 716, 9 June 2015, p. 16.

27 Edmund Burke, *'Al-'Iḥtijāj wal-muqāwama fī 'al-maghrib mā qabl 'al-isti'mār (1860–1912)* (*Prelude to Protectorate in Morocco: Pre-Colonial Protest and Resistance, 1860–1912*), trans. Mohammed Aafif (Rabat: Faculty of Literature and Human Sciences, 2013), p. 198.

for the production of elites, such as universities, higher institutes, etc., during the last century and early this century, this method is still very much present on the Moroccan political scene.[28] Such was the case with Ahmed Osman, son-in-law of the late King Hassan II, who became first minister at a crucial period of history immediately after the two failed coups in 1972. Also with Moroccan Prime Minister Abdellatif Filali, whose son was married to Princess Lalla Meryem, daughter of King Hassan II, and who was one of the trump cards in the political hand of the late monarch.[29]

During the period of Moroccan democratic transition, there was joint coordination and cooperation between a group of women who were at the centre of decision-making, but who were concealed away from direct political action. On this basis, elite women were active on the political scene in many of the main battles they fought and where they achieved significant results.[30]

Contributions of Elite Women during the Years of Political Easing, 1990–9

The women's movement was one of the founding components of the democratic transition process in the early 1990s. This started with the launch of the 1-million signature petition (1992) by intensely politicised women activists. They hailed from the left-wing Organization for Popular Democratic Action, the founders of the newspaper, *March 8*, the first dedicated women's media platform in independent Morocco, and the founders of the Action Union. This group was, in the opinion of observers, the spearhead of the Moroccan feminist movement, which gave a real jolt to Moroccan society. It left a deep impact on the left-wing parties, which had felt that feminist issues should be invoked only after the achievement of democracy. This opinion was expressed by Abdullah bin Ibrahim in his statement to journalist Zaki Daoud on the

[28] Ali Benhaddou, *Maroc: Les élites du Royaume, essai dur l'organisation du pouvoir au Maroc* (Paris: Éditions l'Harmattan, 1997).

[29] Yahia H. Zoubir and Haizam Amirah-Fernandez, *North Africa: Politics, Region, and the Limits of Transformation* (London: Routledge, 2008).

[30] Fatema Mernissi, oral testimony (the house of the late Madame Mernissi, Harhoura, Rabat: June 2015) stating: 'Zoulikha Nasri, adviser to King Mohamed VI forged strong ties with a number of pioneers in the Moroccan feminist movement, who told her their demands, which she in turn would pass on to the highest authority in the country.' There are other examples which are not mentioned for reasons of space.

issue, when he said: 'There are two ways to deal with women's issues: the first is progressive, by putting it in the context of the general struggle for the overall progress of society as a whole; and the second is the activity of a small bourgeois faction that aims to prioritise feminist concerns over the struggle of society as a whole, and this weakens the first option.'[31]

The Istiqlal Party and the Socialist Union Party withdrew their women's sectors from the National Coordination Committee for the 1-million signature campaign, citing the change of priorities following the formation of the Democratic Bloc as a political pressure coalition. Meanwhile, the conservative wing (the Islamists) led a fierce campaign against any change or amendment in favour of improving the status of women, which culminated in the issue of a fatwa condemning the signatories of the petition to amend the Family Code as non-believers. The petition managed to exceed its ambitions, surpassing the 1 million signatures by a very large margin.

The regime in Morocco, on the other hand, found itself facing a new kind of demand that forced it to acknowledge that it has failed women. This is shown by the speech of the late King Hassan II:

> When I saw your demands and the list of the grievances of Moroccan women, whether mothers or just married, I found that in fact, we did not apply the basic rule in all legislation that Islam instituted before other legislations.

In another speech, he quoted the Prophet's saying: 'Women are the counterparts (*shaqa'iq*) of men' in legal rulings and otherwise.[32]

The issue was finally settled through the appointment of a committee of religious scholars, taking various sensitivities into account by ensuring the representation of different opinions. The committee was tasked by Hassan II to study the issue and make proposals to solve the problems. The conclusions of this committee did not live up to the expectations of the feminist movement, which had begun to work collectively and pool its efforts. This movement continued its advocacy, succeeding in 1994 in achieving the abrogation

[31] Thawriya al-Saʿudi, *Qadāya wa-'ihtimāmāt 'al-nisā' min khilāl jarīdat 8 Maris* (*Women's Issues and Concerns as in the March 8 Newspaper*) (forthcoming).

[32] Ibid.

of Article 6 of the Commercial Code, which placed businesswomen under the guardianship of their husbands, and removing the requirement for the husband's permission to obtain a passport.

Using the same collective advocacy strategies before different authorities, bodies and institutions, the leading feminist activist Damia Benkhouia[33] coordinated in 1997 between the various bodies and sectors of all political parties active on the ground – thereby bypassing ideological conflicts and the logic of electoral competition – to support women candidates in parliamentary elections, and to conduct training sessions for their benefit. This dynamism pushed political parties and the regime itself to pay attention to the most important component of Moroccan society, that is, women and the family. This resulted in the emergence of an embryonic consciousness that women's issues are inseparable from the civilisational level and democratic climate of society, since each level overlaps with economic, social, political, cultural and emotional factors. Any fragmentation or confinement may negatively impact the whole social structure in the country.

Elite Women and the Moroccan Democratic Transition up to the Arab Spring

A new turning point for Moroccan women elite occurred on 8 March 1999, since it marked the announcement by Prime Minister Abderrahmane Youssoufi of the draft National Plan of Action for the Integration of Women in Development. The plan covered education, literacy, reproductive health, women's economic integration, and the strengthening of their legal and political status. This was to be achieved through numerous proposals and measures to improve the status of women.[34]

The Islamist movement, which began to emerge on the political scene

[33] Damia Benkhouya is a feminist and rights activist, a founder of the *March 8* newspaper, who was invested and charged with many tasks and responsibilities within rights associations and organisations. She has written widely on women's issues and published many literary works.

[34] Damia Benkhouya, 'Le mouvement féminin Marocain au cœur du combat pour la démocratie: La réforme des lois discriminatoires', in Elisabeth Joris and Brigitta Klaas Meilier (eds), *Olympe: Feminitische Arbeitshefte zur Politik, Fokus: Demokratie* (Zürich: Autorinnen Verlag, 2007), p. 21.

in the country, opposed this project, especially everything related to personal status law concerning the family. It led a forceful opposition campaign culminating in the march organised in Casablanca on 10 March 2000, countering the march organised by supporters of this plan in Rabat. The Islamists outnumbered the ranks of the modernists.

Elite women loyal to the plan worked to create the National Network to Support the Plan for Integrating Women in Development, including more than 300 supporting national associations. This was a remarkable achievement, since some parties within the power-sharing government were against the project. In parallel, Islamist feminist organisations (even though there is a trend that rejects this label) formed coalitions and banners of the Islamist political women's elites began to emerge on the Moroccan scene. Nadia Yassin,[35] daughter of the leader of the banned Adl and Ihsane Association, was one of the most prominent faces in this agitation.

In 2000, Moroccan feminist elites participated in the Beijing 5 conference at the UN headquarters in New York, and took part in a protest – even though it was banned by the US authorities – outside the headquarters, denouncing the non-implementation of the proposals in the Plan to Integrate Women in Development.[36]

As the conflict between the two sides intensified, unions and supportive parties withdrew, and the issue was parked in preparation for the 2002 elections. This pushed feminist elites to shift towards the strengthening of women's presence in the political arena once again. This was conducted through the establishment of the 'Group of 20', which aimed for a review of electoral laws and the adoption of a 20 per cent quota for women. This demand was advocated to various parties, bodies and the government. But although only a 10 per cent quota was approved, this permitted many women to enter parliament, which before that had been akin to a men-only club.

After this achievement, the support network for the draft plan went back

[35] She came onto the political scene specifically during the struggle over the draft plan and was the official spokeswoman for the Adl and Ihsane group. She was prosecuted many times for her political activities. Following the death of her father, the group's spiritual leader, her role noticeably declined.

[36] Damia Benkhouya, oral testimony (house of Damia Benkhouya, Yacoub El Mansour, Rabat: 7 June 2016).

to pressing its demands. This time it resorted to royal arbitration, which appointed a commission of twenty men and three women (Rahma Bourquia, Zohour El Hor and Nouzha Ksous).[37] The commission invited all the feminist components involved in the 'Spring of Dignity' to make submissions in this regard. The outcome was the new Family Code of 2003, which included many controversial articles but enjoyed a consensus, thereby confirming that the conflict was not as much religious as it was political and ideological.

A year later, the Labour Code was promulgated. For the first time, it stipulated gender equality in wages, the right to belong to trade unions, maternity rights for working women, and the combating of sexual harassment in the workplace. These developments encouraged the women leaders to mobilise and advocate again for a mother's right to pass on citizenship to her children. King Mohamed VI responded in a speech in 2005, 'As the King – Commander of the Faithful – we have resolved to endow the child of a Moroccan mother with the right to acquire Moroccan citizenship.'

In 2008, the Alliance for the Fight for One-Third Representation for Equity led an advocacy movement directed at political parties, the government, and the monarchy to amend the Electoral Code and the Community Charter in a manner that responded to their demands, which occurred, albeit to a relative extent, by virtue of the King's speech of 10 October 2008.

The results of this feminist mobilisation have been evident on the ground. For example, the presence of female political elites has evolved through the increasing number of women in Moroccan governments, which first saw the appointment of two female secretaries of state (Nezha Chekrouni and Aïcha Belarbi) during the consensual power-sharing government (1998–2002). In the 2002 government, there was a delegate-minister (Nezha Chekrouni) and a secretary of state (Najima Thay Thay Rhozali). In 2007, the number of women ministers jumped to five for the first time in Moroccan history (Amina Benkhadra, Yasmina Baddou, Nawal El Moutawakel, Thuraya

[37] Rahma Bourquia is a university professor, former dean and member of the Academy of the Kingdom of Morocco. She has written important works of sociology. Zohour El Hor is a judge who has held many judicial posts. She has written forcefully on women's issues and produced many reasoned legal rulings with a feminist dimension. Nouzha Ksous is a biologist and a feminist and rights activist who has made many contributions in her field and concerning women.

Djebran and Nouzha Skalli) and two secretaries of state (Latifa Labida and Latifa Akherbach). These changes can be applied to other remaining areas.

Women and the Experience of Transitional Justice in Morocco: The Equity and Reconciliation Commission

The creation of the Equity and Reconciliation Commission came as part of a series of actions since the early 1990s to settle the issue of gross human rights violations in Morocco in the 'years of lead'. The Human Rights Advisory Councils mainly drew their women members from civil society and political parties. This was the case with Aicha Belkaid (1996–2002), and in the following council (2002–6) Mbarka Ouarzazi, Assia Al-Wadie, Najat M'jid, Amina Lemrini El Ouahabi, Latifa Djebabdi, Fatoum Qudama, Aicha Khamlich and Fawzia Akdira; followed by Halima Embark al-Warzazi, Assia Al-Wadie, Najat M'jid, Aicha Khatabi, Amina Lemrini El Ouahabi, Latifa Djebabdi, Fatoum Qudama, Aicha Khamlich and Saadia Belmir in the Council, which sat from 22 January to 20 May 2007, and then on to 2011.

The Equity and Reconciliation Commission was the cornerstone for Moroccans' reconciliation with their past. It was established by Royal Decree on 6 November 2003, and comprised sixteen members, including one woman, Latifa Djebabdi.[38] She says about this experience: 'I had the privilege of attending among the 16 members appointed by His Majesty to shed light on the events of the years of lead, and to reconcile Morocco with its past. I was able to come into contact with the mothers and wives of those abducted, and was deeply touched by their hurt and pain. This was the most moving experience in my career.'[39]

The contribution of women in this process began in the mid-1970s when the mothers and wives of detainees and forcibly disappeared persons started to demand remedies. Halima Zine El Abidine[40] is considered one of the most

[38] Feminist, rights and political activist, a former political detainee from the end of the 1970s, she has been active on many local and international levels. She is described as the 'godmother of Moroccan feminist movement' for the vital role she has played and her service to and sacrifice for the issues of Moroccan women.

[39] Farid Alilat and Juliette Basti, 'Paroles de femmes', *Jeune Afrique*, No. 2408, 5 March 2007, p. 3.

[40] She is considered part of the cultural elite because of her many publications that have

important actors who ensured the coordination of this effort. The experience also acted as a 'nursery' that produced a significant number of prominent human rights activists, including Amina Bouayach. This movement went through three phases: the first, from its initiation until the end of the 1980s, when it was known as the 'families of political prisoners and unaccounted for abductees'; the second, throughout the 1990s, when the scope of coordination expanded to include the previous category as well as the families of survivors and victims of Tazmamart prison; the third, beginning in 2000, when relatives of victims and groups of those released were organised under the 'Coordination Committee for the Families of the Unaccounted for and the Disappeared'.[41]

Their movement played a major role in improving the conditions of political prisoners, raising awareness about them, and contributing to detainees' voices being heard at the national and international level. It allowed many of their demands to be met during the period of their detention, and gave them a voice on their release.[42]

The Equity and Reconciliation Commission therefore also took into account the suffering of women. It attempted to reconsider the specificity of women's sacrifices and roles based on a gender approach as a long-term systematic choice. This is evidenced by the recommendations of the Commission, which stipulated the importance of the education and empowerment of women, and the development of their capacities to participate in public life. The need to establish a national mechanism for the advancement of women's rights, and to follow up the implementation of public policies in this field, was also stressed.[43]

enriched the literary field. She has also played important roles at key moments for the Moroccan feminist movement since its inception.

41 *'Al-Taqrīr 'al-khitāmī li hay'at 'al-'insāf wa 'almusālaha* (*Final Report of the Equity and Reconciliation Commission*), Book 2, special edition in honour of the late Driss Benzekri (Rabat: Advisory Commission for Human Rights, 2006), p. 30.

42 Amina Daoud, '*Amina Bou'ayach 'al- 'imra'a 'al- munāsiba fi 'al- makān 'al- munāsib*' ('Amina Bouayach, the Right Woman in the Right Place'), *Nisaa min al-maghrib*, February 2007, p. 47

43 *'Al-Taqrīr 'al-khitāmī li hay'at 'al-'insāf wa 'almusālaha*, p. 125.

Elite Women and the Repercussions of the 'Arab Spring'

The Arab Spring 'fever' was transmitted to Morocco, but it was a relatively quiet revolution. Given the gradual process of democratic openings that started from the early 1990s as noted above, the demands were moderate. Feminist activities did not lag behind this action. The presence of women went further than the accustomed accompanying role. Women were present in the front lines of demonstrations, raising the same demands of equality, freedom and social justice.

According to Faten Nourallah:

> Factional slogans were absent from the chants of the February 20 [revolution]. Those were not exclusive to women, but other constituencies also voiced generic demands of interest to wider sectors of society. This is an indication that the feminist movement that became involved on February 20 had become mature enough to adopt societal issues and not just factional issues, despite their importance.[44]

After the king's speech of 9 March 2011, in which he announced major constitutional reforms, Moroccans voted overwhelmingly in support of amendments to the Moroccan Constitution. For the first time, four women participated in writing it: Nadia Bernoussi, a professor of constitutional law; Amina Bouayach, a jurist and professor of economics; Raja Naji Al-Makkawi, a professor at Dar El Hadith El Hassania; and Amina Messaoudi, a professor of public law. Thus, for the first time, feminist action was present and impactful in constitution-making at a delicate stage in Morocco's history. This was influential in including a chapter on equality and strengthening the hopes of Moroccan women in the electoral dispensation that followed the constitutional amendment.

This was viewed by the Feminist Alliance as a 'progressive outcome of the struggles of democratic and modernist forces, and a positive response to the social mood in the context of the social and youth mobilisation

[44] Faten Nour Allah, '*Muntadā Assileḥ 34 yaḥtafi bi-ḍayf sharaf 'al-dawra 'al-ittihād 'al-maghāribī*' ('Assileh Forum 34 Celebrates Guest of Honour the Moroccan Union'), *Nisaa min al-maghrib*, August 2012, p. 45.

witnessed by Morocco and the whole of the Arab region'. The condition for achieving what was required by the epoch depended on making basic rights 'a central element for democratisation, modernisation, social justice and the consolidation of universal values of human rights'.[45] This included three main items:

- Stipulation of positive discrimination in favour of women's access to public office and elected positions.
- Stressing the importance of international conventions and covenants ratified by Morocco, in line with the provisions of the Constitution and the principles of the kingdom and its laws.
- Creating a body for equality and combating all forms of discrimination.

Although the Arab Spring helped to nurture a new generation of young talented women leaders within the feminist movement, such as Karima Nadir, Houda el-Sehli, Ghizlane Ben Omar, Wadad Malhaf, Amina Boughalbi and Sarah Soujar, it has also become clear that radical improvement in the status of women was not easy to achieve. It is an issue concerning 'mentalities' that might take decades to change. Women's demands became stuck in a bottleneck. The transition from the revolutionary moment to ordinary politics has meant the disappearance of women from leadership positions.

The first government under the 2011 Constitution, Chapter 19 of which was hailed by Moroccan women, contained only one female minister (Bassima Hakkaoui of the Justice and Development Party). After the campaign led by feminist alliances, which strongly condemned this decline in representation, the Islamist-led government used the 2013 amendment to add another minister (Fatima Marwan) and four delegated ministers (Mbarka Bouaida, Soumia Benkhaldoun, who was replaced by Jamila Musalla, Charafat Afilal and Hakima El Haite).

Nezha Alaoui[46] noted the hierarchical approach to women rights:

[45] Several authors, *Manshūr dākhilī li 'al-taḥaluf 'al-nisa'i 'al-maghribī li-'ajl taḥqīq 'al-musāwāt fī 'al-dustūr* (Internal publication of the Moroccan Feminist Alliance for Equality in the Constitution) (Rabat: Al-Amniya Press, 2012).

[46] Nezha Alaoui is a lawyer and former member of parliament. She was one of the founders of the Moroccan feminist movement and, with others, led the 1-million signatures petition.

> which can be observed from the very beginning of the formation of the government that appointed a single female minister. Even once this mistake was corrected in a later reshuffle, the appointments persisted in assigning the added female minsters 'women' portfolios, such the ministries of women affairs, solidarity, and traditional and cooperative industry; but not the interior or economy. Women are also habitually assigned directorates within ministries under the name of delegated ministries.[47]

Other issues remained unresolved, such as poor representation of women in centres of decision-making; the failure to pass a law to tackle violence against women; failure to adopt a comprehensive law to combat human trafficking; and failure to create the Equality Commission provided for in the 2011 Constitution. The latter is currently facing an attempt to misrepresent it by voting to turn it into a body that deals with a plethora of issues, such as people with special needs, etc., which will dilute its impact. This is not the first such occasion. The same happened with the quota for women, which has been integrated into the youth category since 2011.

In a parallel context, the status of women reflects the degree to which society has evolved and the level of the transformation of mentalities within it. Many Moroccan women have indeed distinguished themselves in the new era, such as Mohamed VI's appointment of women to positions they had never held before, like Fawzia Imansar (head of a prefecture *(amala)*, 2006), Zeinab El Adaoui (Governor of Gharb-Chrarda-Beni Hssen and then Souss-Massa-Draa, 2015), Miriem Bensalah-Chaqroun (Head of the General Confederation of Moroccan Businesses, 2012),[48] and Nabila Mounib[49] (General Secretary of the Unified Socialist Party). Women were also promi-

She has made many reasoned legal rulings based on religious texts concerning women's issues. She currently remains a powerful presence in feminist militancy.

47 '*'Al-Dukhūl 'al-siyāssī: jam'iyyāt tuqayyim muktasabāt 'al-mar'a fī ḥukūmat Benkirāne*' ('Entering Politics: Associations Assess Women's Gains in the Benkirane Government'), *Nisaa min al-maghrib*, October 2014, p. 33.

48 'Présidence de la CGEM: Le tournant', *L'observateur* 168(4/5) (2012): 20.

49 University professor and activist in the Unified Socialist Party, in 2012 she was able to persuade party members to vote in her favour. She has made many contributions in human rights issues, and despite her leadership of the campaign to boycott the vote on the 2011 Constitution, the state found it necessary to rely on her to resolve tensions with Sweden over the Western Sahara issue.

nent in the fields of scientific research, social work, political action and others both in Morocco and abroad. Many indicators, however, also confirm that there is a decline, and even regression, as pointed out by Hayat Habayli:

> The issue of women is plagued by uncertainty and confusion, and there is a lack of a clear vision among all human rights or feminist actors. In as much as the expressed political discourse or intentions reveals an orientation towards the future . . . we are experiencing setbacks at the level of participation of female and male citizens.[50]

Has the Ascendancy of Islamists Regionally and Locally Produced Islamic Feminist Elites?

The Moroccan arena has witnessed an embryonic emergence of an Islamic women's movement since the mid-1990s. It primarily emerged during the conflict over the plan for the integration of women in development, and it has attracted large popular bases through its religious discourse and charitable work. Its main distinctive feature may be its categorical rejection of the term 'feminist movement' because of its Western origins. Bassima Hakkaoui stands out for her position in rejecting the draft national plan and her leadership of the campaign against it, in addition to Nadia Yassin mentioned above.

The movement soon emerged as a political force. Through its opposition to the provisions of the draft plan for the integration of women in development, and its U-turn to accept and celebrate it once it was adopted by King Mohamed VI, it contributed to a purely ideological struggle. As Hakima el-Naji points out: 'The religious women's movement has entrenched itself within a conservative position against equality, and against its own historical interests for narrow political calculations.'[51]

Only once, in 2002, did this group agree with the rest of the feminist movements, when a joint communiqué by all the female political party activists was issued on the demand for a women's quota in the legislature, a demand that was eventually met. Islamist women continued to hold their ideological

[50] '*'Al-Dukhūl 'al-siyāssī*', p. 32.

[51] Hakima el-Naji, '*'Al-Nisā' fī qalb qadiyyat 'al-'islaḥ 'al-dustūrī wa 'alsiyāsī*' ('Women at the Heart of the Issue of Constitutional and Political Reform), *Nisaa min al-maghrib*, April 2011, p. 35.

line even with the 2011 Constitution through Minister Bassima Hakkaoui's vision of the advancement of women, which was termed 'IKRAM' (an Arabic acronym standing for 'the meeting of all to advance Moroccan women'). This stance represents, according to Atifa Timdjriden, 'a return back to the 1970s approach to improving conditions and not the advancement of rights; that earlier approach has been harmful to equality in societies'.[52]

In recent years, an Islamic feminist movement that does not reject the term has also emerged. Its values combine the principles of Islam and the universal values of human rights. Asma Lamrabet is one of its most prominent faces. She states:

> This feminist movement, which seeks to bear the name of the feminist movement alongside the description Islamic, differs from the radical secularist orientation and from the traditional Islamic orientation. It rejects the first model because it sees it as a model imported from a different culture and therefore does not suit the Islamic reality; and it does not accept the second model because of the ineffectiveness of the proposals it makes in the field of the problem of women in Islam and because of its rejection of any attempt at reform, which the proponents of this tendency see not only as a betrayal of the spiritual message of Islam, but as dangerous westernization.[53]

Many observers believe that the work carried out by Asma Lamrabet is a continuation of the solid groundings left by the late Fatema Mernissi, but from different standpoints, since Lamrabet is a medical doctor and an active member of the *Rabita mohammadia des oulémas* (Mohammadia League of Scholars). The sociologist Mernissi, in contrast, has always refused to associate with state institutions except the university, and preferred to conduct her research with complete independence and away from any pressures.

Mernissi believes that a proper analysis of women's relationship to power in Muslim societies reveals their status in these societies as often subordinate

[52] '*Mā hiya hikāyat ikrām?*' ('What's the Story of IKRAM'), *Nisaa min al-maghrib*, March 2013, p. 46.

[53] *'Al-Ḥaraka 'al-nisā'iyya 'al-'islāmiyya: nahj jadīd wa-manẓur jadīd* (*The Islamic Feminist Movement: New Method and New Perspective*), trans. Bushra Laghzali, Center for Studies and Research on Women's Issues in Islam, available at: https://goo.gl/9PWqT7, last accessed 20 February 2018.

to the ways in which regimes approach modernisation. It is not linked exclusively to the authoritarian or democratic character of these regimes, she adds, as can be seen in the modernisation models of the Shah of Iran, Turkey under Atatürk, or Tunisia in the era of Habib Bourguiba.

In general, what can be observed about this period of democratic transition is the shift of elite women towards the demand for full equality, without any reservations, and working to reach what Alain Touraine calls 'the right to be right in your demands'.[54]

It is difficult to overlook the decisive role of the monarchy's intervention in the various transformations to the situation of Moroccan women, as stated in a feminist media platform: 'The royal initiative was behind the victory for the issue of women's rights, and breaking deadlocks at a number of milestones: via the royal arbitration on the Family Code, the initiative on the citizenship law, the royal message lifting reservations on CEDAW.'[55] There are some who point out that women's issues have become a source of modernist legitimacy for the monarchy.[56] There is still a third view that holds that elite women created alliances that enabled them to exert pressure on political actors, on the one hand, and push the king, on the other hand, to align with them.[57] Thus, they were able to create a real dynamic within Moroccan society. However, one should also not neglect the importance of Morocco's international commitments to achieve the millennium development goals, on which basis it receives international support, especially as it has committed to achieving these goals, including the political empowerment of women by 2015, as well as the implementation of the gender approach.

54 Alain Touraine, *Le Monde des femmes* (Paris: Fayard, 2006).

55 '*'Irāda malikiyya siyāsiyya li 'al-daf'i bi malaf 'al-mar'a nahwa 'al-musāwāt wa 'al-munāsafa*' ('Royal Political Will to Push the Issue of Women towards Equality and Equity'), *Nisaa min al-maghrib*, No. 142, August 2012.

56 Lakrie Mohamed Fadhel, '*'Al-Niẓām 'al-siyāsi 'al-maghribī wa-ishkāliyyat 'al-mashru'iyya 'al-ḥadāthiyya 'alā daw' 'al-tahawwulāt 'al-ijtimā'iyya 'al-mu'āsira: muqāraba sūsyū-siyāsiyya*' ('The Moroccan Political System and the Problem of Modernist Legitimacy in Light of Contemporary Social Transformations: A Socio-political Approach'), doctoral thesis Faculty of Law, Hassan II University, 2006.

57 Larbi Eyesh, '*'Al-Lūbī 'al-nisā'i 'al-maghribī wa-ma'rakat 'al-thulth fi 'ufuq 'al-munāsafa*' ('The Moroccan Feminist Lobby and the Battle for One-Third Representation in the Horizon of Equality'), *Dafatir Wujhat Nazhar*, No. 21 (Casablanca: New Al-Najah Press, 2012).

Preliminary Conclusions

This brief look of the roles of feminist elites during the democratic transition in Morocco over the last two decades allows us to reach the following preliminary conclusions:

- There is a need to interrogate this transition itself, even if it has anchored Moroccans on the shores of political transformation, leading towards the consolidation of democracy. A closer examination of the economic, social and political conditions and indicators in the country may make it difficult to talk about the signs of democratisation in Morocco at the current time. It does not matter which perspective on democratisation or transition you take: the economy-focused modernisation approach of Seymour Lipset, that of a political focus from Charles Adrian, or the transition approach of Walt Rostow, and even the structuralist approach.
- The accession to the throne by a young monarch espousing some of the values of modernity and democracy contributed to grounding the hopes and demands of women elites through the arbitration missions permitted by his status as the 'Commander of the Faithful'.
- Moroccan elite women have been able to mobilise and penetrate into the political hierarchy through many strategies and tactics to present their demands, using media and social media, as well as international leverage to exert pressure on the national level.
- These women's groups intensified their coordination processes among themselves. During the tenure of an Islamist government a large number of them shifted from field work to a focus on advocacy with various higher and even international bodies. This enabled them to realise many of their demands, such as amending the Family Code and obtaining greater political representation. Here, we can speak of the formation of a Moroccan feminist lobby.
- With regard to Islamic women elites, two currents emerged. The first was active within the political parties, and has not been able to develop its own discourse on the issues and problems facing women associated with the challenges of globalisation (domestic servants, underage marriage, etc.). It also tended to reject all initiatives coming from the modernist feminist

elites. Accordingly, it has not been possible to internalise the principle of equality, and its contributions to the Moroccan democratic transition debate remain minimal. The second, and newly emerging, trend, is based on the reconciliation between universal and Islamic rights, and is little by little finding its place within the Moroccan arena.

- Despite the achievements by Moroccan feminist elites, especially ensuring that the constitution should accommodate the demands of human rights activists, feminists and democratic movements, the path to equality is still very long and full of pitfalls. Given the slow transformation of mentalities, which, in Braudel's term, enters 'slow time', this was to be expected.

If the concept of feminism emerged in the early twentieth century, the spark of the Islamic feminist movement was ignited as an intellectual and social movement with the writings published in the Iranian magazine *Zanan* (*Women*) in 1992, a few years before the emergence of a new feminist movement based on Islam as a source of legitimacy. Many middle-class women engaged with it in reaction to the discriminatory laws promulgated by the revolutionary regime, to which women had contributed significantly.

In parallel, Iranian women academics in exile declared their affiliation to it. They were joined by a Muslim Afro-American scholar of religions, Amina Wadud, forming a movement to re-read religious texts thought to diminish the value of women. They were influenced by the writings of Fatema Mernissi, who in her book *The Veil and the Male Elite: A Feminist Interpretation of Islam* questioned the authenticity of the hadiths attributed to the Prophet that disparaged women, such as the hadith 'A people who make a woman their ruler will never be successful.'[58]

The works of Nilüfer Göle on Turkish Islamic feminism, Afriba Adlikha in Iran, Dalal al-Bizri on women activists in the Lebanese Hezbollah movement, or Lara Deeb on Shiite feminism in Beirut provide fertile ground for opening the way for women's Islamist movements to turn towards social mobility and daily practices.[59]

[58] Stephanie Latte Abdallah, 'Le Féminisme islamique: Vingt ans après: économie d'un débat et nouveaux chantage de recherche', *Critique internationale* 46 (2010): 9–23.

[59] Ibid.

While it is also possible to compare the contribution of the Moroccan women's movement to democratisation to the role of activist women groups in other regions, particularly in Latin America, there are important differences. For example, Latin American feminist movements, whether practical or strategic, if we accept Georgina Waylen's classifications, were mainly grassroot movements.[60] In contrast, the Moroccan movements we focused on were mainly 'elite' movements, and their mode of operation was also linked to actors in a top-down democratisation process. However, as we have indicated above, there may be a lot to learn from those experiences. But there is a lot also that democratic transition theory can glean from the unique, but instructive Moroccan experience.

60 Georgina Waylen, 'Women's Movements and Democratisation in Latin America', *Third World Quarterly* 14(3) (1993): 573–87.

9

RETHINKING RELIGION AND DEMOCRATIC TRANSITION: LESSONS FROM THE ARAB WORLD

Khalil Al-Anani

Religion has been at the crux of the public debate in the aftermath of the so-called Arab Spring. While the Arab uprisings were not about religion per se or raised religious slogans and demands, the role of religion, particularly Islam, in the public sphere has been one of the most contested and debatable issues over the past few years. The rise of Islamist movements and groups to power in countries like Egypt, Tunisia and Morocco raised fears of their political and religious agenda. It deepened the fears of secular forces of what they perceive as an 'Islamist hegemony' and control over state and society. Those fears, whether imagined or real, have created significant disagreement and divisions among political forces and weakened democratic transition in most of the Arab countries. Furthermore, political actors, who once collaborated to topple autocratic regimes in Egypt, Tunisia, Libya and Yemen, were dragged into an identity politics battle over the state's identity, how Islamic should be the post-uprising constitution, the role of Sharia in public life, and freedom of religion and religious beliefs. This battle has resulted in the failure of democratic transition in Egypt and made the Tunisian transition weak and fragile.

To be sure, the role of religion during democratic transitions is not unique or limited to the Middle East. During the different 'waves of democracy', religion and its relationship with politics, was a highly debated issue in Europe during the nineteenth century,[1] and Latin America,[2] the southern

Mediterranean[2] and or Eastern Europe during the twentieth century.[3] As José Casanova puts it, ']T[he resistance to the secular differentiation of religion and politics is neither uniquely "Muslim" nor peculiarly characteristic of non-Western religions.'[4] In all of these cases, political actors were divided and disagreed on what role, if any, religion should play during the transition and whether religious parties and groups should be involved in politics and contest power. More importantly, religion is not the only factor that determines the outcome of the transition from authoritarianism into democracy. As the late Alfred Stepan and Juan J. Linz point out, 'Conflicts concerning religion, or between religions, did not figure prominently in either the success or failure of third-wave attempts at democratic transition.'[5]

This chapter explores the role of religion, namely Islam, in the aftermath of the Arab Spring and to what extent it shaped the outcome and trajectory of the Arab uprisings. By doing so, the chapter helps to better understand three key issues: (a) the role of religion during political upheavals and whether it hinders or facilitates democratic transition; (b) the impact of the Arab Spring on Islamist groups and movements during and after the Arab Spring; and (c) some theoretical conclusions that can go beyond the Arab World and improve our understanding of the relationship between religion and democratic transition. The chapter proceeds as follows: I begin by revisiting the literature on the relationship between religion and democratisation

[1] For more on the debate of religion and democracy in Europe during the nineteenth century, see, e.g., George H. Sabine, 'The Two Democratic Traditions', *Philosophical Review* 61(4) (1952): 451–74; Owen Chadwick, *The Secularization of the European Mind in the Nineteenth Century* (Cambridge: Cambridge University Press, 1975); Paul E. Sigmund, 'The Catholic Tradition and Modern Democracy', *Review of Politics* 49(4) (1987): 530–548; Philip Nord, *The Republican Movement: Struggles for Democracy in Nineteenth-Century France* (Cambridge, MA: Harvard University Press, 1995).

[2] See, e.g., José Casanova, 'Modernization and Democratization: Reflections on Spain's Transition to Democracy', *Social Research* 50(4) (1983): 929–74.

[3] For a comparison between Islam and Catholicism with regard to democracy, see, e.g., Ateş Altınordu, 'The Politicization of Religion: Political Catholicism and Political Islam in Comparative Perspective', *Politics & Society* 38(4) (2010): 517–51; José Casanova, 'Catholic and Muslim Politics in Comparative Perspective', *Taiwan Journal of Democracy* 1(2) (2012): 89–108.

[4] Casanova, 'Catholic and Muslim Politics', p. 90.

[5] Alfred Stepan and J. Juan Linz, 'Democratization Theory and the Arab Spring', *Journal of Democracy*. 24(2) (2013): 15–30.

and how it shaped our understanding over the past few decades. I also examine the assumptions about Islam/Muslims and democracy and to what extent they are relevant to the Arab Spring. I then explore the role of Islamist movements and groups during the transition and explore how their strategy and calculations affected the political trajectories in their countries and how they were affected by the transition. The chapter ends with some theoretical conclusions and findings that enhance our thinking of democratisation in the Arab World.

Religion and Democratisation: An Enduring Debate

The question of whether religion has an impact, either positive or negative, on democratisation and democratic transition is perennial. Transitologists and scholars of democratisation have greatly disagreed on answering that question. While some of them do not consider religion to be a determinant factor in transition to democracy,[6] others believe that religion can play a role in democratic transition.[7] Furthermore, apart from the conventional argument that dismisses the role of religion in public life as a result of modernisation, which dominated social theory over the second half of the past century, scholars have disagreed on the influence of religion on democratisation. Whereas some scholars argue that certain religions and religious traditions impede democratic transition because of their anti-democratic, anti-rationalist and anti-relativist attitudes,[8] others believe religion has a positive influence on

[6] For more on this point, see, e.g., Seymour M. Lipset, *Democracy and Working-Class Authoritarianism* (Berkeley: Institute of Industrial Relations, University of California, 1959); Dankwart A. Rustow, 'Transitions to Democracy: Toward a Dynamic Model', *Comparative Politics* (1970): 337–63; Thomas Carothers, 'The End of the Transition Paradigm', *Journal of Democracy* 13(1) (2002): 5–21.

[7] For more on this point, see, e.g., Jeffrey Stout, '2007 Presidential Address: The Folly of Secularism', *Journal of the American Academy of Religion* 76(3) (2008): 533–44; Liz Fawcett, *Religion, Ethnicity, and Social Change* (New York: St. Martins, 2000); Mirjam Kunkler and Julia Leininger, 'The Multi-Faceted Role of Religious Actors in Democratization Processes: Empirical Evidence from Five Young Democracies', *Democratization* 16(6) (2009): 1058–92; Robert D. Woodbury, 'The Missionary Roots of Liberal Democracy', *American Political Science Review* 106(2) (2012): 244–5.

[8] See, e.g., Bryan S. Turner and Oscar Salemink, *Routledge Handbook of Religions in Asia* (London: Routledge, 2015); T. Kuran, 'The Political Consequences of Islam's Economic Legacy', *Philosophy and Social Criticism* 39 (2013): 395–405.

democratisation, such as the case with Protestantism in Western democracies or Roman Catholicism in Poland, Chile and Brazil.[9]

The inconclusive arguments regarding the impact of religion on democratisation prompted scholars to investigate the intricate relationship between religion and politics particularly during times of upheaval. To bypass this analytical and theoretical polarisation, Alfred Stepan introduced the term 'twin tolerations', which he contends can resolve the tensions between state and religion. According to Stepan, state and religion can coexist if they recognise, respect and tolerate each other's spheres.[10] As he and Juan Linz put it, 'In a country that lives by these two tolerations, religious authorities do not control constitutionally empowered democratic officials, while these officials do not control religion as long as religious actors respect other citizens' rights.'[11] However, as Abdelwahab El-Affendi (Chapter 3, this volume) argues, Stepan's theory of the 'twin tolerations' advocates "a liberal conception of democracy, which trumps religion". Furthermore, the 'twin tolerations' presumes that the state and religiously-motivated actors have the same perception and understanding of religion as a prerequisite.

Similarly, Jocelyne Cesari provides another analytical approach that explains the relationship between religion and democratisation, focusing on examining the state–religion relationship from an institutional perspective.[12] As Cesari puts it, 'An institutional approach shifts the perspective from a polarized state–religion focus to complex sets of interactions between the two spheres, including adaptation, cooperation, and competition.'[13] According to her, this approach 'considers state–religion relations an element conditioning the democratization process, because of its impact on the behavior of actors with various goals, both sacred and profane'.[14] While the institutional approach provides useful insights to examine state–religion relations, particu-

[9] See, e.g., Daniel Philpott, 'Christianity and Democracy: The Catholic Wave', *Journal of Democracy* 15(2) (2004): 32–46; Jocelyne Cesari, 'Religion and Democratization: When and How It Matters', *Journal of Religious and Political Practice* 2(2) (2016): 131–4.

[10] Alfred Stepan, 'Tunisia's Transition and the Twin Tolerations', *Journal of Democracy* 23(2) (2012): 89–103.

[11] Stepan and Linz, 'Democratization Theory and the Arab Spring'. p. 17.

[12] Cesari, 'Religion and Democratization'.

[13] Ibid., p. 132.

[14] Ibid.

larly during transition periods, it does not compellingly explain how and why religion becomes a highly contentious issue that can affect democratic transition. Also, it overlooks how political actors use and sometimes manipulate religious sentiment in order to advance their political agenda. As the chapter shows, the secular–religious polarisation has significantly affected the quality of democratic transition after the Arab Spring. In Egypt, for example, the debate on the role of religion in the public sphere started as early as the uprising. Islamist groups used religious sentiment and slogans to invigorate the public towards specific political choices that served their agenda. Also, it is worth mentioning that the chapter will focus on religious actors, that is, Islamists, and how they interact and engage with other political forces during transition. But the role of religious institutions is beyond the scope of this chapter.

Islam and Democracy after the Arab Spring

The rise of Islamist movements after the Arab Spring has renewed the debate on the compatibility of Islam and democracy.[15] The debate was intensified after the 'failure' of the transition in Egypt, Syria, Yemen and Libya. Essentialist arguments such as 'Arab exceptionalism' and similar claims have resurfaced again with the failure to produce sustainable democracy. Even before the Arab Spring turned into a long winter after the collapse of transition in Egypt in the summer of 2013, the spread of chaos in Libya and Yemen, and the civil war in Syria, some scholars questioned its motivation and dubbed it an 'Islamist Revolution'. They argued that the Arab uprisings would do nothing but enable Islamists to achieve their long-standing dream of establishing an Islamic state.[16] They also believe that the Arab Spring was nothing but a mirage and 'false dawn'.[17] Some scholars, however, considered

[15] This debate goes back to the late 1970s, particularly after the Iranian Revolution as many Orientalists argued that Islam and democracy are incompatible. For more on this debate, see, e.g., Asef Bayat, *Islam and Democracy: What is the Real Question* (Amsterdam: Amsterdam University Press, 2007)

[16] For more on this point, see, e.g., H. Fradkin, 'Arab Democracy or Islamist Revolution?' *Journal of Democracy* 24(1) (2013): 5–13.

[17] Steven A. Cook, *False Dawn: Protest, Democracy, and Violence in the New Middle East* (New York: Oxford University Press, 2017).

these claims 'essentialist' and irrelevant to the experience of the Arab Spring, particularly with Islamists' commitment to the rules of the game in Tunisia, Morocco and Egypt. Olivier Roy, for example, considers the idea of 'Islamic exceptionalism' to be an illusion. He argues that 'political and the religious changes in Muslim societies are in tune with global trends . . . [and] a profound alteration of traditional Islam, which is now giving way to a more open and diverse religious field'.[18] In fact, the Arab Spring has invalidated the key assumptions of the incompatibility of Islam and democracy through the protest of millions of Arabs and Muslims against autocratic regimes in the Arab World. Those who took to the streets did not call for a 'religious state' or for Islamic law (Sharia) to be applied; this included Islamists who participated in the popular protests against dictatorship. Rather, they aspired to universal civil and political values such as freedom, justice and dignity. Islamist groups were keen to play down the fears of their liberal and secular counterparts, emphasising their commitment to democracy and freedoms. Furthermore, to attribute the failure of democratic transition in the Arab World in the aftermath of the Arab Spring to Islam or Islamists is to reaffirm the reductionist and essentialist approaches that failed to predict the Arab Spring in the first place. This also ignores the complexities of the region and the role of regional and international players in shaping the outcome of the Arab uprisings, particularly in Libya, Yemen and Syria. True, Islamists were key players in these cases, however, they were not the only key actors.

Furthermore, most analyses and arguments of the 'failure' of the Arab Spring have focused on a number of factors, internal and external, where the role of Islam is nominal, if at all. For example, Jason Brownlee, Tarek Masoud and Andrew Reynolds argue that the 'modest harvest of the Arab Spring' can be explained by the dynastic character of the Arab autocratic regimes and their ability to buy loyalty.[19] For them, the individualist and personal regimes are more resilient in defying change because of these two characteristics. Another line of scholarship investigated the role of regional and international players in affecting the Arab Spring. Hinnebusch, for

[18] Olivier Roy, 'There Will Be No Islamist Revolution', *Journal of Democracy* 24(1) (2013): 19.

[19] Jason Brownlee, Tarek E. Masoud and Andrew Reynolds, 'Tracking the Arab Spring: Why the Modest Harvest?' *Journal of Democracy* 24(4) (2013): 29–44.

example, stresses the role of global powers in shaping the outcome of the Arab uprisings. According to him, 'The Uprisings provided a new context for competitive interference by global powers that blocked any straightforward export of democracy.'[20] In fact, the failure of transition in most countries was clearly the result of external interference by different powers and a reflection of regional and international competition in the region. The Saudi–Iranian rivalry has significantly impacted and shaped the outcome of the Arab uprisings in places such as Bahrain, Yemen and Syria. Similarly, the Russian intervention in Syria in 2015 was a turning point not only in the Syria, but in the entire region. True, Syria's civil war was affected by the Sunni–Shia division; however, this division was intensified by the political and geo-strategic conflict in the region.

Islamists during Transition: What Went Wrong?

Like their counterparts, Islamists were surprised by the eruption of the Arab Spring. After decades of repression and exclusion, Islamists were able to normalise their political status and engage in formal politics. In Egypt, as well as in Tunisia, Morocco, Yemen, Syria and Libya, they became key players. Their strategy and political behaviour, along with other players, have shaped the outcome of the Arab transitions. However, their roles and performance were uneven due to their different contexts and circumstances. Whereas they succeeded in gaining and holding to power in Tunisia and Morocco, they failed to do so in Egypt, Libya, Syria and Yemen. Without delving into the details of each of these cases, one can say that Islamists' strategy and behaviour were not primarily driven by religion, but rather by political and circumstantial calculations. In Egypt, for example, the Muslim Brotherhood (the Brotherhood hereafter) emerged as a key player in the post-Mubarak era. After decades of operating in the shadows, the movement came to power for the first time in its long history. However, the Brotherhood's decision to contest power after Mubarak was problematic and highly contested within the movement itself. During the uprising, the Brotherhood pledged not to take power or seek full

[20] Raymond Hinnebusch, 'Globalization, Democratization, and the Arab Uprising: the International Factor in Mena's Failed Democratization', *Democratization* 22(2) (2015): 340.

control of the state.[21] Moreover, a few days before the Mubarak's ouster, it announced it would not field a candidate in the presidential elections, and embraced the slogan of 'participation, not domination'.[22] However, one year later, the Brotherhood shifted its position and contested the 2012 presidential elections. Its candidate, Mohamed Morsi, became Egypt's first freely and democratically elected president. The Brotherhood justified this change of position as by the need to protect the revolution from the threats of the old regime.[23]

The Brotherhood's decision to contest the presidential election came in the midst of a standoff with the Supreme Council of Armed Forces (SCAF), which had assumed control of the country after Mubarak's fall. Following a short honeymoon, a clash of interests surfaced between the Brotherhood and SCAF. While the Brotherhood sought to secure more power after the removal of Mubarak, SCAF was reluctant to relinquish its control over the state. Therefore, when Morsi eventually became president, his authority was significantly undermined, and he was left with no real powers. The standoff between the two sides was not based on views over democracy, achieving the uprising's objectives or meeting the demands of the people, rather, it was over each side's share of power and political privileges.[24] After reneging on its promise to hand over power within six months, SCAF sought to secure as much power as possible from the emerging political order. For the junta, the military's long-standing independence and privileges were a red line and therefore not a topic for negotiation with any civilian regime. On the other hand, the Brotherhood obsessed over the possibility of the old regime's return. For them, the only way to prevent this regression was to step in and take power themselves. When the Brotherhood and SCAF failed to identify a 'consensus' candidate who could secure their interests, the clash between

[21] 'Muslim Brotherhood: "We Are Not Seeking Power"', *CNN*, 10 February 2011, available at: https://cnn.it/2xyQSgK, last accessed 3 May 2020.

[22] Nathan J. Brown, *When Victory Is Not an Option: Islamist Movements in Arab Politics* (Ithaca, NY: Cornell University Press, 2012).

[23] Kristen Chick, 'In Major Reversal, Muslim Brotherhood Will Vie for Egypt's Presidency', *Christian Science Monitor*, 1 April 2012, available at: https://bit.ly/2YtE0mV, last accessed 3 May 2020.

[24] David F. Gordon and Hani Sabra, 'The Muslim Brotherhood's Dangerous Missteps', *Reuters*, 11 April 2012, , available at: https://reut.rs/3fftqWH, last accessed 3 May 2020.

the two sides became inevitable.[25] Following a short period serving as a government-in waiting,[26] the Brotherhood became the new ruler of Egypt with all the powers, aspirations and challenges involved. The group's failure to make the needed transition from a vocal opposition movement to a ruling force became glaringly evident during Morsi's tenure, as the Brotherhood, ironically, assumed both identities. In addition, the Brotherhood encountered tremendous political, social and economic challenges that required fundamental changes in the movement's discourse and strategy. After only a year in power, Morsi was toppled in 3 July through a military coup backed by popular protests on 30 June 2012, and the revolution and transition was aborted.

In contrast, the Tunisian Ennahda movement played a key role in the success of Tunisia's democratic transition. The fall of the Ben Ali regime resulted in a great political void and at a time when most political parties and forces were not sufficiently prepared and qualified to rule individually. This may have been fortunate for the Tunisian revolution, as political forces and parties were forced to work together to manage the transition. After the Constituent Assembly elections, and after winning the first place in the elections rather than the majority, [27] Ennahda sought to establish a political coalition with other non-Islamic forces. It agreed to enter into a political partnership with two ideologically different factions, the Congress for the Republic, led by the secular figure of Moncef Marzouki and The Democratic Forum for Labor and Liberties, led by Mustapha Ben Jaafar. The three parties shared power as a 'troika' after the elections of 2011.[28] The experience of the troika seemed to be an important indicator of the spirit of compromise and partnership embodied by the revolution and demonstrated by most political forces. It also reflected the desire of the participating powers not

[25] Khalil Al-Anani, 'Upended Path: The Rise and Fall of Egypt's Muslim Brotherhood', *Middle East Journal* 69(4) (2015): 527–44.

[26] Tom Perry, 'As the Government-in-Waiting, Egypt's Muslim Brotherhood Finds Its Voice', *Reuters*, 28 February 2012, available at: https://reut.rs/2SvL6DP, last accessed 3 May 2020.

[27] 'Tunisia's Islamist Ennahda Party Wins Historic Poll', *BBC*, 27 October 2011, available at: https://bbc.in/2VW1qQe, last accessed 3 May 2020.

[28] For more on the dynamics of the Tunisian troika, see, e.g., Amel Boubekeur, 'Islamists, Secularists and Old Regime Elites in Tunisia: Bargained Competition', *Mediterranean Politics* 21(1) (2016): 107–27.

to monopolise power and exclude others. The troika succeeded in saving Tunisia from the problems that plagued other Arab Spring countries by agreeing on the policies and steps of the transitional period, which began with the writing of a new constitution followed by parliamentary and presidential elections. The mere participation of Islamists and secularists in one governing body was impressive, and sometimes surprising, given the state of hostility and ideological rivalry between the two blocs. However, the troika faced many crises that almost toppled it, with the most serious being the assassinations that targeted important political figures. Key victims included the Marxist leader Shukri Belaid, gunned down on 6 February 2013, and the Nasserite politician Mohammed Brahimi, killed on 25 July 2013. Ennahda withdrew from power, handing over to a government of technocrats to run the rest of the transition. At a time when some expected Ennahda to stick to its ideological positions, particularly on sensitive religious issues such as the provision of Sharia as a source of legislation, certain aspects of gender equality and freedom of conscience and belief, etc., everyone was surprised by the consensual position of the movement, which coincided with the positions of other forces participating in the Constituent Assembly. Perhaps the most significant feature of Ennahda's approach was its pragmatism and political realism. Ideology was not the prime driver of the movement's decisions or calculations. In order to preserve its gains, and protect the nascent democratic experience, Ennahda adopted a very pragmatic approach, particularly after the fall of Morsi in Egypt.

The Impact of Transition on Islamists

The French sociologist, Olivier Roy, argues that Islamism is shaped by politics rather than vice versa.[29] This was evident after the Arab Spring, which reshaped Islamist politics drastically. The contexts in which Islamists were operating played an important role in shaping their choices and strategies. Here, we can talk about three important contexts in which the choices of Islamists have varied over the past few years. The first is the transitional or reformist context, in which Islamists enjoyed some degree of integration and acceptance within the political game, as in Morocco and Tunisia. The

[29] Roy, There Will Be No Islamist Revolution', p. 15.

inclusion of Islamists contributed to their ideological and political transformation, particularly with regard to thorny issues such as the relationship between religion and politics, issues of individual freedoms, human rights, relations and attitudes towards women and minorities, without forgetting that these contexts are not necessarily fully democratic, or ruled by Islamists in full. The second context is the authoritarian and repressive context whose interactions range from the partial exclusion of Islamists (the case of Jordan) to total exclusion and eradication (Egypt and Syria). This context led to divisions and schisms within Islamist movements and parties, including the emergence of conservative voices and wings within these movements. This has led the Islamists to confront contradictory choices between acceptance, coexistence, rejection and confrontation, both politically (Egypt and Jordan) and militarily (Syria). The only beneficiaries of this context were violent radical movements such as ISIS and al-Qaeda, which have dominated the Islamic landscape in these countries over the past years. This served the interests of the repressive authoritarian regimes, which benefited from increasing regional and international support in the name of the war on terror.

The third context is characterised by armed conflict and civil wars (Yemen, Libya and, of course, Syria) that swept Islamists in its dynamics, fearing being discarded or beaten by rival parties. This context has produced a mix of strategies and tactics among Islamists, depending on the circumstances of each country. In the Yemeni case, for example, the Yemeni Islamist party, the Congregation for Reform, was forced to engage in a multiple negotiating processes, sometimes with the late President Ali Abdullah Saleh, sometimes with the Houthis and sometimes with a third party against both, such as Saudi Arabia and United Arab of Emirates (UAE). The party was forced to join the ranks of the popular resistance to confront the Houthis and stop their march towards key Yemeni cities, especially Aden and Taiz. In the Libyan case, the Islamists engaged in a military confrontation through militias and armed groups to counter the rebellion led by Khalifa Haftar in the eastern province. Despite the openness of Islamists to the options of international and regional solutions, there is a determination by regional countries such as Egypt and the UAE to eradicate them completely from the Libyan political scene. In Syria, the situation is not very different. Not a single Islamic movement refused to take up arms in the face of the war crimes and genocide waged by Bashar Assad against the Syrians. Past experience and political context may not be the sole determinants of Islamist responses to political challenges, to the exclusion of agency and choice. But the Islamists do not work in a vacuum, and their decisions and movements remain governed by the nature of the context in which they are active. It should be noted that the relationship between these contexts and the behaviour of the Islamists is not linear or mechanical, but is an interactive dialectical relationship in which many factors overlap. There is no room here to elaborate on this in more detail, however.

Furthermore, the involvement of Islamists in the formal process had a substantial impact on their ideology, discourse and behaviour. To take advantage of the new political space, Islamists had to adapt and alter their political language and tactics. Functioning in an open and free environment prompted Islamists to change their tactics and calculations. Therefore, instead of acting in the back seat of politics as opposition, Islamists moved to the forefront of Arab politics as power holders. The heavy legacy of the deposed regimes constitutes a challenge to Islamists' political and economic policies. The enduring problems of unemployment, poverty, corruption, etc. hampered their ability to rule easily. Since the unfolding of the Arab Spring, Islamist scene has witnessed several transformations and changes. First, new Islamist actors emerged while the old ones had to alter their tactics and ideological views. In fact, the Arab Spring ended the old 'Islamist architecture'. The new Islamist scene in the Arab World was far from monolithic. Rather it was fluid, dynamic and, most notably, divisive. In addition to established Islamists, such as the Muslim Brotherhood in Egypt and Libya, El-Nahdda in Tunisia, the Party of Justice and Development (PJD) in Morocco, new Islamist actors emerged. They came from different ideological and political backgrounds, ranging from ultra-conservative to reformist and from moderate to extremist, for example, political Salafis, ex-jihadists, independent Islamists, Sufis, etc. In Egypt, for instance, some fifteen Islamist parties, official and unofficial, have been founded since the ousting of Mubarak. They were spawned from different Islamic ideologies. Most strikingly, Salafis, who had persistently shunned politics as religiously prohibited (haram), became key players in Egyptian politics. They rushed into electoral politics and won almost 25 per cent of seats in the new Egyptian parliament in

2012. The second remarkable change in the Islamist landscape was the emergence of 'informal' Islamists. For decades, Islamist parties, movements and organisations were the only representatives of Islamism. However, since the Arab Spring a new strand of Islamist actors has emerged and can be dubbed 'informal' Islamists. They are not officially affiliated with any of the Islamist movements or associations, nor are they keen to establish their own parties or organisations. Ironically, they eschewed joining the new Islamist parties that have been founded since the Arab Spring. Thus, they are free from organisational and hierarchical burdens. 'Informal' Islamists rely heavily on social networks, kinship, friendship links and new technology to disseminate their ideology and widen their influence. They have followers from different social strata; urban and rural, poor and rich, schools and universities, etc. For them, street vendors are as important as university professors. In Egypt, for example, many 'informal' Islamists emerged after the January uprising. Three of the four Islamist candidates who ran in the presidential election come from among the 'informal' Islamists: Hazem Salah Abu Ismail, who was a front-runner in the elections before he was disqualified for legal reasons pertinent to his mother's dual citizenship; Abdelmoniem Abul Fotouh, who was eliminated in the first round; and Mohamed Selim al-Awa, the second Islamist candidate who lost the election. All were outspoken, charismatic and influential preachers with numerous followers and supporters. In addition, many 'informal' Islamist networks have emerged since the uprising, including the Salafi Front, the Hazemoon network and the Jurisprudence Commission for Rights and Reform.[30]

The third change in Islamist politics concerns Islamist discourse, ideology and tactics. Islamists' involvement in electoral politics affected their ideological and political views. For instance, many Islamists avoided religious 'absolutism', halal and haram dichotomy, and adopted 'relativism' and pragmatism. They shifted their discourse from the ideological fringes to the political centre. Thus, the language of politics is overshadowed their religious rhetoric. Before the Arab Spring, terminology like democracy, elections and citizenship were alien to some Islamists, particularly the Salafis. However,

[30] Al-Anani Khalil, 'Islamist Parties Post-Arab Spring', *Mediterranean Politics* 17(2) (2012): 466–72.

after the Arab Spring they began to use these terms in everyday discourse, suggesting that the 'secularisation' of Islamists has started, albeit subtly. During the election campaigns in Egypt, Tunisia and Morocco, Islamist candidates abandoned religious and dogmatic propaganda. They did not promise 'paradise' as a reward for those who would vote for them, but rather pledged to improve the economy, fight corruption and attract foreign direct investment (FDI). Islamists have increasingly realised that their legitimacy does not stem from the 'mosque' but rather from their performance in public office. Finally, the fourth change in Islamist politics is inter-Islamist conflicts. The Arab Spring has rebuilt the relationship between (and within) Islamist movements to become more complex, fluid and sometimes confrontational. In addition to theological and ideological differences, Islamists' divisions are now drawn over various lines and fronts. For instance, the Ennahda party in Tunisia is struggling with conservative Salafis over issues of public freedoms and the role of religion in the public sphere. Likewise, in Egypt the relationship between the Brotherhood and Salafis was tense and contributed to the removal of the Brotherhood from power in 2013. The organisational cohesiveness and discipline that seemed to characterise Islamist movements are now fading away.[31]

Whither Islamism?

The Arab Spring was a tough test for Islamist movements and groups, whether those who took power through elections or those who remained in opposition as they had been for decades. While some Islamists succeeded in adapting to the new political environment, as in Tunisia, Morocco, Kuwait and Yemen, others remained unchanged and could not cope with the new changes, as in Egypt, Jordan and Libya. While some Islamists still deal with what happened over the past few years as if nothing has changed, others have undergone significant changes in their ideology, organisation and strategy. The experience of the past decade has revealed how diverse the Islamists' responses are to changes locally, regionally and internationally. This makes it very difficult to make sweeping generalisations about these responses, or to presuppose a degree of conformity or similarity among Islamist groups as if

[31] Ibid.

they were reproductions of each other. The intra-Islamist differences are similar to those between other currents and political parties in the Arab World. One of the experiences of the past years has also been the difficulty in turning slogans into reality, especially in the context of a rapidly changing world of mistiness and uncertainty. The slogans chanted by these movements, such as 'Islam is the solution', the establishment of the 'Islamic state', 'the application of the Sharia', etc., all remained just that, slogans.

Islamists' political experience also reveals the difference between being in opposition and holding power. The lack of experience of many Islamists in governance made them less competent and unable to meet the aspirations of their constituencies. This is as much as the authoritarian regimes that did not allow them to share power even at municipal level which affected their governance skill, particularly in addressing key problems such as poverty, unemployment and corruption. The experience of the Islamists also revealed that the issue of mixing politics and preaching (*daw'a*) not only harms them, their organisation and performance, but also the political situation in their countries as a whole. While some Islamists separate religious and political activities such as in Tunisia and Morocco, their counterparts in Egypt and Jordan have yet to catch up. Additionally, Islamists had to rethink and clarify their positions on critical issues such as citizenship, individual and personal freedoms, the nation-state and democracy. Some have done so, becoming more progressive, while others are still figuring out how to deal with these issues. Furthermore, the emergence of nihilistic organisations such as the Islamic State (known as *Da'esh*/ISIS) put the rest of the Islamists in an unprecedented defensive position. The emergence of the extreme right in the West, and its ignorance of the vast differences between various Islamist groups, has turned them into a new 'enemy' that has to be destroyed, as President Donald Trump and his Arab authoritarian allies insist.

Conclusion

The relationship between religion and democratic transition is rather complex, involving different elements, such as the mode of transition, identity conflicts, the civil–military relationship, trust between political parties, calculations of political actors, etc. As the chapter shows, religion was not the main determinant of the outcomes of the Arab Spring, neither was it the driving force of protests and upheavals in the region. Rather, the decisive factors in determining the outcomes of the transitions were the political calculations of political actors, the role of the old regime (the 'deep state') and counter-revolutionary forces (internal and external, mainly the latter).

Several theoretical conclusions and lessons can be drawn from the Arab Spring when it comes to the relationship between religion and democratic transitions. First, religion does not play a crucial role in transition insofar as political actors invoke and employ it in the political arena to legitimise their behaviour and advance their agenda. The disputes and divisions among political actors in the Arab World after the Arab Spring were not about religious issues or whether religion should have a role in the public space. Rather, the contests were over how to regulate and organise that (acknowledged) role, particularly under the significant impact of unprecedented political openness.

Second, religious actors, that is, Islamists, encountered several challenges after the Arab Spring that were not primarily related to their religious ideology, but rather to their governance competency and capabilities. In most Arab countries, Islamists fared poorly or indifferently against their secular counterparts in facing the problems of poverty, unemployment or corruption. Their discourse, strategy and policies were contested and attracted public attention instead of remaining in the shadows. Therefore, Islamists' popularity has been significantly affected and people could judge their performance by worldly rather than by religious or spiritual criteria.

Third, as the chapter shows, the lingering mistrust and disputes between Islamists and secular forces greatly affected the transition process. The failure of these forces to reach consensus or agreement over several contested issues, such as the post-revolution constitution, societal identity, foreign policy, the role of the military, etc., jeopardised the transition process and diminished the opportunities for establishing a successful transition. Some issues relating to the role of religion in the public space, including demands for the protection of women's rights and non-Muslims' rights, were also matters of contention. Whereas Islamists could not provide guarantees to ensure pluralism and to protect personal and individual freedoms, their secular and liberal counterparts could not avoid the temptation of allying with non-democratic forces, that is, the military and deep state, as allies against Islamists, as was the case in Egypt, Tunisia, Libya and Yemen.

Finally, the political and ideological polarisation in the post-uprising phase was often toxic, helping to derail or disrupt the transition process. Not only did it deepen the mistrust between political forces and diminish the possibilities of building cross-ideological alliances; it also permitted old regime forces to exploit the fear of Islamists to fracture the democratic coalition and find a way back into the political process and sabotage the entire transition. The case of Egypt provides a clear example of how the military and the *ancien régime* exploited political divisions between Islamists and non-Islamists in order to reassert their hold on political life, and later to execute the coup that ended the democratic transition in 2013.

To sum up, these lessons and conclusions take us back to where we started: while religion seems to dominate the public debate after the Arab Spring, the contest was primarily a reflection of fears and mutual insecurities among political factions.

10

DEMOCRATIC TRANSITION IN RIVALRY CONTEXTS

Marwan Kabalan

Introduction

Except for Tunisia, in most Arab countries where a popular uprising has taken place in pursuit of better living conditions and political rights, chaos and instability have prevailed. Syria, Libya and Yemen have all been embroiled in protracted civil conflicts since the beginning of the 2011 Arab revolutions, with massive external interventions. In Egypt, forces of the old regime, supported and funded by key regional powers, mobilised to remove the democratically elected president and restore autocratic rule. In Bahrain, the regime requested intervention by the Gulf Cooperation Council (GCC) 'Peninsula Shield Force' to suppress the protest movement. In most, if not all, of these cases, foreign interventions, and the network of alliances of the incumbent regimes or their oppositions, played vital role in shaping the outcome of the conflict. External factors acted here as the independent variable par excellence in rendering the transition from autocratic rule to democracy a failure. Regional alignments, competition for power and influence, and the security dilemma faced by most of the states concerned during the course of the Arab revolutions, transformed domestically driven, largely peaceful popular uprisings into violent conflicts with varying degrees of regional and international involvement.

This chapter assesses the role of the external environment in facilitating or inhibiting change during the course of the 2011 Arab revolutions. It argues that domestic conditions, no matter how ripe and promising, do not alone guarantee successful democratic transition. The right domestic environment is an essential, but is not a sufficient condition for establishing democracy, especially in rivalry contexts. In fact, the likelihood of a successful democratic transition diminishes in rivalry contexts. Here, revolutions and domestic instability invite rival external powers to intervene in favour of maintaining the status quo, or in support of change, transforming the domestically originated protest movements into wider geo-political conflicts. In contrast, liberal integrative contexts provide incentives and channels of support for democratic transition. Transition processes in Southern and Eastern Europe support this assertion, particularly after the EU changed from being 'a "club" of democracies to a "school" of democracy'.[1] Even in Turkey, the desire to qualify for membership of the EU contributed significantly to political reform and democratisation.[2] The absence of regional rivalry contexts in these cases made the transition process smooth and less painful.

In the Arab world, regional and international dynamics played instrumental role too, but towards inhibiting rather than facilitating democratic transition. Here regional and international rivalries made it almost impossible for any meaningful transition to take place. Except in the early stages of the Libyan revolt, wherein a regional and international consensus emerged to stop an incumbent regime from suppressing a protest movement, external powers were deeply divided on the other Arab revolutions. With extremely divergent views, ideological depositions and geopolitical interests, some powers intervened to prevent change, suppress the revolution and maintain the status quo; others went in the opposite direction. But even those who supported change did so in pursuit of their own interests, not because they favoured democracy.

In Egypt, Syria, Bahrain, Yemen and post-Ghaddafi Libya, the conflict between the status quo powers and revisionist powers has turned the people's

[1] Democratic Progress Institute, *The Role of European Union Accession in Democratisation Processes* (London: DPI Publications, 2016).

[2] Meltem Müftüler Baç, 'Turkey's Political Reforms and the Impact of the European Union', *South European Society & Politics* 10(1) (2005): 16–30.

battle for rights and liberties into violent local, regional and international entanglements. In rivalry contexts, this outcome proved unavoidable.

The conclusion is that although all Arab revolutions are homegrown phenomena, external powers have attempted, and will always attempt, in rivalry contexts, to shape and influence the outcome. States usually intervene when they find a window of opportunity to maximise their gains, protect their national interests and ensure survival.[3] In regional rivalry contexts, the prospect of democracy transition is therefore dim. Any efforts in that direction will be almost always be inhibited by power politics, balance of power and a chronic security dilemma. We therefore believe that the move from a rivalry context into a more integrative context, wherein all states can ensure their security regardless of the domestic settings of any given state within that system, is a prerequisite for successful democratic transition in the Arab region. A cooperative security model, akin to such bodies as the OSCE in Europe, could act as a catalyst for democratic change in the Middle East.

Revolution and Change in Rivalry Contexts

Rivalry context is a complex situation in which states disagree over issues, or interests, for an extended period, to the extent that they engage in relatively frequent diplomatic or military challenges, directly or indirectly.[4] Rivalry context intensifies at times of regional instability, unrest or change; wherein rival powers perceive the emerging situation as either a threat or an opportunity to expand their interests and roles, alter balances of power and consolidate themselves domestically.[5]

In this context, the 2011 Arab revolutions were a watershed event in the Middle East, and with the presence of several interstate rivalries they quickly transformed from being largely local protest movements about political rights

[3] Fred Halliday, *Revolution and World Politics: The Rise and Fall of the Sixth Great Power* (Basingstoke: Macmillan, 1999).

[4] D. Scott Bennett, 'Democracy, Regime Change, and Rivalry Termination', *International Interactions* 22(4) (1997): 369–97 at 370–1.

[5] See K. Rasler and W. R. Thompson, 'Rivalries and the Democratic Peace in the Major Power Subsystem', *Journal of Peace Research* 38(6) (2001): 659–83; William R. Thompson, 'Identifying Rivals and Rivalries in World Politics', *International Studies Quarterly* 45(4) (2001): 557–86..

and economic opportunities into regional and international events, exacerbating old rivalries and creating new ones.

Indeed, a revolution is a native phenomenon usually caused by local factors and occurs within local social and political contexts and settings.[6] Yet once a revolution starts, it ceases to be a local event; it, rather, becomes a matter of interest for outside powers, which try to shape the course of events in their favour. States have the propensity to intervene in the internal affairs of other states and particularly when these other states are weakened, or struck, by internal strife, revolution or uprising in a rivalry context. '[I]f revolutions are nothing if they are not international, the same goes for their opposite, counter-revolution, and for their failures.'[7]

Foreign intervention in the internal affairs of states facing revolution or civil strife is therefore unavoidable in rivalry contexts. When a revolution or internal strife occurs in a certain state, a prime opportunity arises for some powers and risks arise for others. Therefore, in most cases, competing foreign powers intervene to decide the fate of a revolution.[8] States seek to maximise their power by helping their friends, whether through a central authority or a rebel movement. Likewise, they will oppose their foes, regardless of whether they are in government or outside it.

A revolution entails the transfer of power within a state to new elites. But because this often leads to shifts and changes that affect the foreign policy of a given state, revolutions have a deep impact on the regional balance of power, on alignments and hence on the security of other states.[9] In fact, there are instances where revolutions have led to broader conflicts, even wars. After the removal of the *ancien régimes* of France 1789, Russia 1917, China 1911, and Iran 1979, the revolutionary states were subject to attacks from foreign outside powers.[10] In other cases, revolutions led to civil war, with different external powers involved, supporting different local parties, with the Yemeni

[6] T. Skocpol, *States and Social Revolutions: A Comparative Analysis of France, Russia, and China* (Cambridge: Cambridge University Press, 1979), p. 4.

[7] Halliday, *Revolution and World Politics*, p. 6.

[8] Stephen M. Walt, *Revolution and War* (Ithaca, NY: Cornell University Press, 1996), pp. 32–3.

[9] Halliday, *Revolution and World Politics*, pp. 226–33.

[10] Walt, *Revolution and War*, pp. 32–3.

revolution of 1962 being a prime example in the Arab World. These cases, among many others, illustrate the casual link between revolution and foreign intervention especially in rivalry contexts.

In addition, when states face social revolutions, usually in the short term their defence capabilities become affected, most often greatly weakened. This tends to alter the balance of power between states in the regional or international system.[11] Foreign intervention occurs here as it provides what Stephen Walt calls 'a window of opportunity' for two reasons. First, the weakness of the revolutionary state is often interpreted by other states as a chance to improve their positions: either by seizing territory or by seeking diplomatic concessions. Second, social revolutions can increase security competition among other states, where foreign powers compete against each other to improve their position in the system. This could happen either by taking advantage of the instability inside a third state to change the balance of power in favour of a particular state (e.g., to instal a friendly regime in the revolutionary state or oppose the removal of a friendly one), or/and by preventing rival states from doing the same.[12]

Under certain conditions, other states might act out of fear that the potential capabilities of a post-revolutionary state might become greater and more threatening if it succeeds in stabilising the country post-revolution. This could act as a prime motive for intervention. Following the Iranian Revolution, which ousted the shah in 1979, Iraq eyed an opportunity to attack, as Iran was plunged into post-revolutionary chaos. Using both qualitative and quantitative methods, Carter, Bernhard and Palmer found that usually a revolutionary state has greater capabilities, and can mobilise more resources than when the state was under the command of the *ancien regime*. Under the command of a revolutionary state, elite coherence, the revitalisation of the state bureaucracy, and the shared revolutionary ethos of both elites and the population at large, allows post-revolutionary regimes to exercise a greater degree of command and control over society. This makes it possible to raise larger armies and extract greater

[11] Halliday, *Revolution and World Politics*, p. 6.

[12] Walt, *Revolution and War*, pp. 32–3.

resources.[13] This situation alarms neighbouring states and leads them sometimes to act pre-emptively.

Rival states could intervene directly, using proxies or help remnants of the old regime to recapture the state and reinstate the old regime. Between 1918 and 1920, the Allies sent forces to fight against the Bolsheviks, and supported local forces too against the Russian revolutionary regime.[14] In 1961, the United States sponsored a counter-revolutionary military group, made up mostly of Cuban exiles who fled to the United States after Castro's takeover of power in 1959, but also of some US military personnel.[15]

In some cases, a government under threat by domestic turmoil or revolution might seek assistance from neighbours and allies to ensure its survival. The protest movement may do the same if that proves vital to achieving its objectives. In fact, the success of a protest movement depends more than regime survival on external support.[16] Regimes are usually better equipped to fight rebellion or suppress a protest. They control the media and the armed forces, and usually have better financial resources.

The likelihood of revolution spreading to other states also encourages intervention.[17] The fear of a domino effect, real or imagined, following a revolution compels states to act.[18] Ideological factors also play a role in the calculus of states at times of revolution. Like-minded regimes tend to sympathise with each other. Here aggressive liberals would argue in favour of intervention to promote liberal values as much as realists would favour intervention for security reasons.[19]

The outcome of the Arab revolutions can be, to an extent, explained

[13] J. Carter, M. Bernhard and G. Palmer, 'Social Revolution, the State, and War: How Revolutions Affect War-Making Capacity and Interstate War Outcomes', *Journal of Conflict Resolution* 56(3) (2012): 346–7.

[14] Patrick J. Conge, *From Revolution to War: State Relations in a World of Change* (Ann Arbor: University of Michigan Press, 2000), p. 16

[15] Peter Kornbluh, *Bay of Pigs Declassified: The Secret CIA Report*, National Security Archive Documents Readers (London: New Press, 1998)

[16] Onora O'neill, 'The Dark Side of Human Rights', *International Affairs* 81(2) (2005): 427–39.

[17] Walt, *Revolution and War*, p. 30

[18] Halliday, *Revolution and World Politics*, pp. 230–3.

[19] Ibid., p. 227.

through rivalry contexts, wherein outside powers, hostage to their security dilemmas, national interests and ideological dispositions, have been compelled to intervene and shape the outcome in their favour. In fact, during the course of the Arab revolutions, regimes and rebels alike have sought foreign backing to champion their cause and tip the balance in their favour. In rivalry contexts, outside powers rush to answer the call for intervention. The external dimension is key to understanding the course and outcome of a revolutionary process. Whether it ends up as a democracy like Tunisia, or develops into chaotic situations like Libya, Yemen and particularly Syria, depends largely on which outside actors won the intervention game, the pro-change or the pro-status quo.

The Rivalry Contexts of Arab Revolutions

Revolutions are primarily domestic events but have implications for the external environment, that is, in intensifying regional rivalries, disrupting the balance of power and exacerbating the security dilemma for the concerned states. These factors play a key role in deciding the fate of a revolution and whether it succeeds in removing a sitting regime and replacing it with a democracy. Theda Skocpol sees revolutions largely as a domestic phenomenon. They emerge from political and socio-economic crises caused by the structures and local environments of the old regimes.[20] Yet a revolution could hardly succeed in replacing an incumbent regime, let alone building a democracy, without the right external conditions.

In fact, most revolutions, especially in rivalry contexts, attract foreign intervention in support of one side or another in a domestic conflict. The absence of foreign intervention can also affect the course of a revolution and the likelihood of establishing democratic rule as an outcome. When the United States declined to intervene in support of Ferdinand Marcos in Philippines in 1986, the revolution succeeded in forcing him to step down. The departure of Marcos allowed free elections and the establishment of democratic government. In this particular instance, it was clear that when foreign backing was withdrawn from a regime, which lacked domestic legitimacy and popular support, the regime collapsed, provided that the military stays neutral. Although the Cold War was in its height, the United States was

[20] Skocpol, *States and Social Revolutions*.

not concerned about a communist takeover, and hence declined to support an old ally, knowing that the new government would maintain its alliance relationship.[21] In contrast, in 1973, the United States intervened to overthrow the democratically elected, leftist, pro-Soviet government of Salvador Allende in Chile, replacing it with a military regime. In a rivalry context, the fate of the revolution and the likelihood of it leading to the establishment of a democracy or a dictatorship is decided by the external environment more than anything else.

The Arab revolutions of 2011 were not an exception in this regard. Despite the variability of their outcomes – civil war, military coup, foreign military intervention or a combination of these – they have all largely been shaped by external factors. Throughout this chapter, we seek to explain how foreign powers have sought to dictate the course of Arab revolutions in order to guarantee certain outcomes. With little regard to the wishes of the people who initiated these revolutions, hoping for better living standards and more representative government, external powers, attentive mainly to the impact of these revolutions on the regional balance of power and their security requirements, have turned them into violent competitions for power and influence.

Given its vulnerability, state fragility and social divisions, the Arab World has been a great deal more open to foreign intervention than other regions around the world. Indeed, this also varies from one Arab country to another. But overall, the geo-political importance of the Arab World, its vast oil and gas reserves, and the rivalry context, wherein rival powers vying for gains and influence compete, makes the Arab World a more attractive place for outside intervention

In fact, the Arab state system itself was charted by foreign powers. During the First World War, the allied powers (France and Britain) divided the possessions of the Ottoman Empire in the Levant and ruled the conquered countries for most of the inter-war period. Following the Second World War, the Soviet Union and the United States inherited the positions of France and Britain, wherein the Arab World became part of the global ideological and geo-political rivalry of the Cold War.

[21] Gary Hawes, 'United States Support for the Marcos Administration and the Pressures that made for Change', *Contemporary Southeast Asia* 8(1) (1986): 18–36.

The end of the Cold War did not affect the propensity of the outside powers to intervene in the Arab World. It, in fact, led to the exact opposite. Military intervention in the Arab region increased after the collapse of the Soviet Union. In 1991, the United States led an international collation to end the Iraqi occupation of Kuwait. In 1992, the United States intervened in Somalia on humanitarian grounds. In 2003, the United States invaded Iraq and overthrew the regime of Saddam Hussein. In 2011, NATO intervened in Libya and helped to remove the regime of Mummar Ghaddafi. In 2014, the United States formed and led an international coalition to eliminate the Islamic State (ISIL). In 2015, Russia intervened in Syria in support of the Bashar al-Assad regime.

The end of the Cold War did not ease regional rivalries either, nor did it reduce competition over regional leadership. On the contrary, competition between regional actors increased, especially after the US withdrawal from Iraq in 2011. The actors may have changed, but the game remained the same. Before the end of the Cold War, three centres of Arab power were competing for Arab and regional leadership: Egypt, Iraq and Syria. The 2003 US invasion of Iraq removed a formidable regional contender. The Arab Spring neutralised the other two: Egypt and Syria. As a result, the centre of gravity in Arab politics shifted towards the Gulf region, wherein Saudi Arabia, UAE and Qatar have become key players in regional politics. Indeed, Iran and Turkey have always been important regional powers, but particularly after the US withdrawal from Iraq in 2011, they gained further influence and their competition to fill the vacuum left behind by the United States increased.

These five regional actors have played vital role in deciding the fate of the 2011 Arab revolutions. In Libya, Egypt, Syria, Yemen and Bahrain, rivalry and competition between these powers have turned domestic protest movements into civil conflicts, war by proxy or direct military interventions. The lack of US leadership allowed these regional actors, and also an outside power (Russia) to play a more important role, particularly in the case of Syria.

The Case Studies

In this part, we examine the role played by foreign actors – in a rivalry context – in transforming what was meant to be peaceful democratic transitions into violent conflicts in most of the 2011 Arab revolutions. We examine the role of these actors in five cases: Egypt, Libya, Bahrain, Yemen and Syria. All of which had, or continue to have, extensive foreign interventions; with different outcomes, none has produced democratic rule.

Egypt

Tunisia may have been the trigger for the 2011 Arab revolutions, but Egypt was the engine that drove and guided them through. Given its size and regional weight, Egypt unleashed a wave of change that altered the political landscape of the Arab region. It was the model that Arab protesters tried to emulate in every single Arab revolution that followed.[22]

The 25 January 2011 revolution started on 'police day' in a protest against increasingly authoritarian practices, rampant corruption, poor economic conditions and possible hereditary rule, as Mubarak was grooming his son, Jamal, to succeed him. After eighteen days of continued pressure, Mubarak decided to step down and the supreme council of the armed forces took control.

Throughout almost three weeks of peaceful protest, regional and international reactions varied. Western countries, including the United States, Britain, France and Germany, called for reforms and expressed concern over the use of violence against protesters.[23] At a later stage, as the situation began to look increasingly untenable, US President Barak Obama urged Mubarak to step down.[24] When Mubarak bowed to pressure, Obama praised the achievement of the Egyptian people, and encouraged other activists in the region to follow suit: 'Let's look at Egypt's example,' he urged.[25] Russia and

[22] David Ottaway, *The Arab World Upended: Revolution and Its Aftermath in Tunisia and Egypt* (Boulder, CO: Lynne Rienner, 2017).

[23] Alan Silverleib, 'World Leaders Denounce Attacks on Egyptian Protesters', *CNN*, 2/2/2011, available at: https://goo.gl/4JmTq1; Jeremy M. Sharp, 'Egypt: The January 25 Revolution and Implications for U.S. Foreign Policy', *Congressional Research Service*, 11 February 2011, available at: https://goo.gl/vEK42u, all last accessed 3 May 2020.

[24] 'Obama says Egypt's Transition "Must Begin Now"', *CNN*, 2 February 2011, available at: https://goo.gl/hMTpzW; Helene Cooper and Mark Landler, 'White House and Egypt Discuss Plan for Mubarak's Exit', *The New York Times*, 3 February 2011, available at: https://goo.gl/LWB6fx, all last accessed 3 May 2020.

[25] William Branigin, Thomas Erdbrink and Liz Sly, 'Obama Urges Mideast Allies to "Get Out Ahead" of Protests, Denounces Iranian Crackdown', *Washington Post*, 14 February 2011, available at: https://goo.gl/kBRou8, last accessed 3 May 2020.

China viewed the revolution differently, seeing it as a Western attempt to sow the seeds of division and chaos in the region and beyond.[26] However, it was on the regional level that the battle for Egypt was about to begin. Regional powers differed on interpreting the impact of the revolution on their national interest and the regional balance of power; with Turkey, Qatar, the UAE and Saudi Arabia in the forefront; assuming a leading role.

Qatar and Turkey were amongst the staunchest supporters of the Egyptian revolution. Fanning the winds of change, which blew throughout the Middle East, the Al Jazeera news channel offered uninterrupted live coverage of Tahrir Square, the hub of protests and sit-ins from the beginning of the revolution until Mubarak agreed to step down. Qatar also provided financial support for the post-Mubarak regime.[27] It hailed the first democratic presidential elections, which brought the Muslim Brotherhood to power in Cairo. Turkey too viewed the collapse of the Mubarak regime as an opportunity to change the regional political landscape in its favour. Furthermore, Ankara interpreted the electoral victory of the Muslim Brotherhood in the 2012 presidential elections as a success for its model of government.[28]

By contrast, Saudi Arabia and the UAE opposed the Egyptian revolution and expressed support for Mubarak. The state-run Saudi Press Agency quoted King Abdullah as telling the Egyptian president in a phone call that the organisers of the demonstrations were 'infiltrators', trying to destabilise Egypt in the name of freedom of expression.[29]

[26] Fiona Hill, 'How Russia and China See the Egyptian Revolution', *Foreign Policy*, 15 February 2011, available at: https://goo.gl/m9XMte, last accessed 3 May 2020.

[27] Borzou Daragahi, 'Qatar gives Egypt $3bn Aid Package', *Financial Times*, 10 April 2014, available at: https://goo.gl/bSVFkm, last accessed 3 May 2020.

[28] Peter Kenyion, 'The Turkish Model: Can It Be Replicated?' *NPR*, 6/1/2012, available at: https://goo.gl/sQC9yh; Zenonas Tziarras, 'Turkey–Egypt: Turkish Model, Political Culture and Regional Power Struggle', *Strategy International*, No. 4 (2013), available at: https://goo.gl/HMaaD6; Banu Dağtaş, 'Constructing the "Arab Spring": News Discourses in Turkish Newspapers', *Global Media Journal* 6(2): 19–, available at: https://goo.gl/wRixoz; Saeed al-Haj, 'Turkish Influence on Arab Islamist Movements', *Al Jazeera*, 24 October 2016, available at: https://goo.gl/opxQNL; Soner Cagaptay and Marc J. Sievers, 'Turkey and Egypt's Great Game in the Middle East', *Washington Institute*, 8 March 2015, available at: https://goo.gl/wtUYYn, all last accessed 3 May 2020.

[29] Caryle Murphy, 'Fall of Mubarak Deprives Saudi Arabia of Closest Local Ally', *The National*, 14 February 2011, available at: https://goo.gl/iZKvJW, last accessed 3 May 2020.

Saudi opposition to the post-Mubarak regime mounted after the ascendance of the Muslim Brotherhood's candidate, Muhamad Mursi, to power. Saudi Arabia interpreted this as a threat to its conservative model of authoritarian governance, even to the survival of the Saudi regime. It also feared that this would help to expand Turkish and Iranian influence. Riyadh became particularly nervous in February 2013 when Mahmoud Ahmadinejad became the first Iranian head of state to visit Cairo since the 1979 Iranian Revolution.

Saudi Arabia and the UAE, on the one hand, and Qatar and Turkey, on the other, entered into a fierce competition to sway the events in Egypt in their favour. Eventually, Saudi Arabia and the UAE helped to stage a military coup that ended Egypt's short-lived democratic rule.[30] The two countries threw their weight behind the military regime and offered billions of dollars of aid to help it survive and buy public consent.[31]

In that way, regional rivalry led to the failure of democratic transition in Egypt, affecting other Arab revolutions.

Libya

Inspired by the revolutions in Tunisia and Egypt, Libyans rose up in February 2011 to remove the regime of Mummar Ghaddafi. The regime acted swiftly to suppress the rebellion, threatening extreme force to regain control of Benghazi, Libya's second largest city, where the revolt originated. At the early stage of the revolution, it seemed almost impossible for the rebels to win against the regime. It was not until the intervention by NATO forces, with political support from the Gulf Cooperation Council (GCC)-led Arab League, did the rebels stand a chance of toppling the regime.

Foreign intervention led to the removal of Muammar Ghaddafi from power. Outside powers took advantage of the domestic grievances of the Libyan people and backed the revolution to oust Ghaddafi. They provided military, financial and political support to help overthrow an authoritarian

[30] Dexter Filkins, 'Saudi Prince's Quest to Remake the Middle East', *The New Yorker*, 9 April 2018, available at: https://bit.ly/3c1cXn4, last accessed 3 May 2020.

[31] Patrick Werr, 'UAE Offers Egypt \$3 Billion Support, Saudis \$5 Billion', *Reuters*, 9 July 2013, available at: https://reut.rs/2Stwfda, last accessed 3 May 2020.

regime. Most of these countries had problems with Ghaddafi, and seized an opportunity to remove him.

The UN Security Council (UNSC) provided the legal framework that permitted the use of force to protect the civilians in rebel areas. On 26 February 2011, only days after the protest movement broke out, the UNSC passed Resolution 1970. It condemned the use of lethal force against civilians by the Libyan government, imposed an arms embargo, a travel ban, and placed an asset freeze on Ghaddafi, his family and closest political allies.[32] The Arab League suspended Libya's membership, and later called on the UNSC to impose a no-fly zone, which was enforced by NATO.[33]

Regional and international consensus emerged that the civilians must be protected, and that the regime must be stopped. The United States, France, the United Kingdom, the Arab League and the GCC countries, seemed all to be in agreement on that goal. A second UNSC resolution was adopted and served that purpose. Resolution 1973 authorised the use of all 'necessary measures to protect civilians'. The resolution was passed by a vote of ten in favour with five abstentions.[34]

Without outside support, it would have been impossible for the rebels to bring down a well-armed and well-funded regime. By funding, arming and fighting with the rebels, outside powers virtually guaranteed the fall of Ghaddafi, even though that objective was never explicitly stated. The ultimate goal was to establish a friendlier government in Libya, an oil-rich country with strategic importance.

France, Italy, Britain and the Arab Gulf states in particular stood to gain the most from the revolution in Libya, which they helped to fund and arm and provided political support. They were directly involved in the military intervention as well. Qatar was the first Arab state to recognise the

[32] 'Security Council Committee Established Pursuant to Resolution 1970 (2011) Concerning Libya', United Nations Security Council, 2011, available at: https://goo.gl/9yiCLs, last accessed 3 May 2020.

[33] 'Arab League asks UN for No-Fly Zone over Libya', *The Washington Post*, 12 March 2011, available at: https://goo.gl/oMifYR, last accessed 3 May 2020.

[34] 'Security Council Approves "No-Fly Zone" over Libya, Authorizing "All Necessary Measures" to Protect Civilians, by Vote of 10 in Favour with 5 Abstentions', United Nations Security Council, 17 March 2011, available at: https://goo.gl/Evfrwj, last accessed 3 May 2020.

Libyan rebels.[35] The UAE also played a key role in the war efforts against Ghaddafi.[36]

Yet the moment the Ghaddafi regime started to unravel the consensus that led to its demise collapsed. Rival actors, vying for power and influence, began arming and funding different rebel groups. The two regional powers that were often pitted against each other in the course of the Arab revolutions were Qatar and the UAE. Libya was a prime example of the competition between these two GCC countries, aspiring to the formation of a friendly regional structure. After the 2013 military coup, Egypt, in alliance with the UAE, also began to play a key role in supporting local proxies in the Libyan conflict. The two countries supported a coalition led by former Libyan army officer, Khalifa Haftar, in his bid to take over power by military force. France, Italy, Saudi Arabia and Turkey have also been involved in supporting different Libyan factions.[37]

The post-revolution rivalry context has made it extremely difficult for Libyans to transit towards democracy. Not only does democracy seem to be as distant eventuality, but also Libya's territorial integrity is today threatened. The presence of two governments (in the east and west of the country) and two parliaments, each claiming legitimacy, and each supported by rival external powers, is an indication of the destructive role of rivalry contexts for post-revolution democracy transition.

Bahrain

Like other Arab revolutions, Bahrain's uprising was caught up in the midst of regional rivalries. The small Arabian Gulf island is sandwiched between two big regional powers: Saudi Arabia and Iran. The situation is further

[35] Regan E. Doherty, 'Qatar Recognizes Libyan Rebel Body as Legitimate', *Reuters*, 28 March 2011, available at: https://goo.gl/Ngu4Um, last accessed 3 May 2020.

[36] Ishaan Tharoor and Adam Taylor, 'Here are the Key Players Fighting the War for Libya, All Over Again', *The Washington Post*, 27 August 2014, available at: https://goo.gl/N7bE5R; Giorgio Cafiero and Daniel Wagner, 'How the Gulf Arab Rivalry Tore Libya Apart', *The National Interest*, 11 December 2015, available at: https://goo.gl/PyxDmP, all last accessed 3 May 2020.

[37] Ben Fishman, 'Shifting International Support for Libya's Unity Government', *The Washington Institute*, 19 January 2017, available at: https://goo.gl/GtP2H3, last accessed 3 May 2020.

complicated by sectarian divisions within Bahraini society, a Sunni-ruled country where the Shia make up the majority of the population. The Bahraini regime hence depends largely on foreign backing, mainly from Saudi Arabia, to maintain power and ward off an opposition that seeks support from Iran. Therefore, when Bahraini activists, inspired by the success of their peers in Egypt and Tunisia, took to the street on 14 February 2011, demanding political and economic reforms, the government accused them of acting on instructions from Iran. Iran fuelled suspicions about possible involvement when it publicly backed the uprising, claiming that it was part of an Islamic revival movement inspired by its 1979 Islamic revolution. Iranian leaders openly called for the overthrow of the Bahraini government.[38]

The government almost lost control as the protests persisted. Protesters in the capital Manama camped for weeks at the Pearl Roundabout, which became the centre of the protest movement. Security forces could not handle the situation against increasingly emboldened young Bahrainis incensed by rampant corruption, unemployment and political authoritarianism. Yet, unlike the case in Libya, foreign intervention here came in support of the regime, not the rebels. As mass protests grew, the Bahraini monarch requested intervention from his GCC allies. On 14 March 2011, 'Peninsula Shield Force', led by Saudi Arabia, rolled into the country to 'restore order'.[39]

GCC governments would not take any chances. Any change of government, they feared, would turn Bahrain into a surrogate of Iran on the western shore of the Arabian Gulf, shifting the balance of power decisively in Iran's favour. Iran was already boosting its regional stature as a result of the 2003 US-led invasion of Iraq. The removal of Saddam Hussein put Iran's allies in

[38] Geneive Abdo, 'The New Sectarianism: The Arab Uprisings and the Rebirth of the Shi'a-Sunni Divide', The Brookings Institution, April 2013, available at: https://goo.gl/5jk9sJ, pp. 51–6, last accessed 3 May 2020.

[39] Rachel Bronson, 'Saudi Arabia's Intervention in Bahrain: A Necessary Evil or a Strategic Blunder?' Foreign Policy Research Institute, March 2011, available at: https://goo.gl/TBmyf6, last accessed 3 May 2020; Michael Slackman and Ethan Broner, 'Saudi Troops Enter Bahrain to Put Down Unrest', *The New York Times*, 14 March 2011, available at: https://goo.gl/tfhwH2, last accessed 7 May 2020.

power in Baghdad. The withdrawal of the US forces from Iraq by the end of 2011 rendered Iran the main power broker in Baghdad, altering the regional balance of power.

The association of the Bahraini protest movement with Iran was a very effective tool in the hands of the government in winning foreign support. The admission of 2,000 troops, mainly from Saudi Arabia and the UAE, ended a month of protests and sit-ins that almost shocked the GCC.[40] The revolt in Bahrain was stifled at birth. It was prevented from developing into a fully-fledge revolution by the swift and decisive military intervention of Bahrain's GCC allies to prevent what was portrayed as pro-Iran Shiite rebellion from toppling the Sunni-led government.

The regional rivalry context led almost instantly to the transformation of the pro-democracy Bahraini protest movement into a geo-political conflict between rival powers, triggering foreign military intervention. The GCC countries assumed that the success of the revolution would almost certainly bring to power a pro-Iran Shiite government. This would affect Bahrain's foreign policy and regional alignments, strengthening Iran's hand in the region. Foreign intervention, in this case, was provided to prevent change and maintain the status quo. Indeed, by not giving Iran the chance to contemplate further intervention in support of the rebellion, Bahrain narrowly avoided a Syria-like scenario. Civil war was averted as a result of the GCC intervention. Yet the burgeoning pro-democracy movement was also crushed and silenced almost on the spot.

Yemen

In February 2011, thousands of Yemenis took to the streets demanding that Ali Abdullah Saleh step down after more than three decades of authoritarian rule. The trigger for the protest was a proposed amendment to the constitution that would have allowed Saleh to stay in power indefinitely. The swift toppling of Zain El Abidine bin Ali in Tunisia and Hosni Mubarak in Egypt emboldened protesters, the majority of whom were young Yemenis calling

[40] 'Threat to Domestic Stability Divides Gulf States over Arab Intervention', *DW*, 20 April 2011, available at: https://goo.gl/EVP5iM; 'Gulf States Send Forces to Bahrain Following Protests', *BBC*, March 2011, available at: https://goo.gl/KXYDVB, all last accessed 3 May 2020.

for better living conditions and an end to the rule of Ali Abdullah Saleh and his family.

After months of protests, the GCC tried to broker an agreement between Saleh and his political opponents. After several assassination attempts, Saleh did eventually bow to pressure and accepted a GCC plan to step down in exchange for immunity from prosecution.[41] He handed over power to his vice president, Abd Rabo Mansour Hadi, in November 2011. Hadi's weakness, and the inability of the different political factions to agree on a power-sharing formula, led to a prolonged political crisis.

Saudi Arabia, the regional status quo power, which took a negative attitude towards Arab revolutions in general, interpreting them as a threat to its conservative monarchical political system, was not enthusiastic about any sort of democratic transition in Sana'a. It sought to keep a dominant position in Yemen by trying to work out an agreement that would keep the old traditional political structure in place, but without Saleh. The pro-Iran Houthi movement took advantage of the political stalemate and seized the capital in September 2014.

Al Houthi rebels used the talks, sponsored by the UN special envoy to Yemen and resulting in the signing of the Peace and National Partnership Agreement (PNPA), to buy time to realise their main objective – capturing the capital and taking control of the state. The PNPA demanded the formation of a national unity government, and a re-examination of the make-up of the national committee to oversee the implementation of the recommendations of the 2014 National Dialogue Conference (NDC) agreement. The NDC was supposed to pave the way for legislative and presidential elections, and start a democratic transition.[42]

The fall of the capital to Al Houthi forces on 21 September 2014 dashed

[41] Mohammed Al Qadhi, 'Yemen Accepts GCC Plan for Saleh to Depart', *The National*, 24 April 2011, available at: https://goo.gl/gFqCEQ; 'Yemen's President Accepts Deal To Step Down', *NPR*, 24 April 2011, available at: https://goo.gl/MCdmZM, all last accessed 3 May 2020.

[42] 'Yemen National Dialogue Conference participants', *The National*, 18 March 2013, available at: https://goo.gl/hiaZbU; 'Outcomes of Yemen's National Dialogue Conference: A Step toward Conflict Resolution and State Building?' Arab Center for Research and Policy Studies, 27 February 2014, available at: https://goo.gl/PE6Cdx, all last accessed 3 May 2020.

these hopes. Given its strong ties with Iran, Saudi Arabia interpreted the Houthi takeover as a game changer, planned and executed at instructions from Tehran. Iranian MP, Alireza Zakani, made a very provocative statement when he said that Sana'a had become the fourth Arab capital, after Beirut, Damascus and Baghdad, to fall to Iran, in a reference to the Al Houthi seizure.[43]

On 26 March, 'Operation Storm of Resolve' was launched to torpedo what Riyadh regarded as a grand Iranian plan to close the circle around it from the south in Yemen after having established its influence in the north of the Arabian Peninsula in Syria and Iraq. Indeed, had it not been for the Saudi-led intervention, Al Houthis would have certainly succeeded in controlling Yemen and changing its foreign policy and regional alignments, most probably towards rapprochement with Iran and further away from Saudi Arabia. Riyadh intervened to prevent this probability and a major shift in the balance of power. Yemen was hence another Arab revolution country to have fallen victim to Saudi–Iranian rivalry. Its democratic transition was crippled by external forces and regional rivalry contexts.

Syria

No other Arab Spring revolution was affected by regional rivalry contexts more than Syria. In March 2011, the Syrian revolution started as a peaceful protest movement. Young Syrians overcame their fears and took to the streets, demanding political reforms, an end to corruption and job opportunities. The protest movement was faced with extreme force. In the face of well-armed regime forces, the opposition called for foreign intervention to protect civilians. They had watched NATO intervention in Libya, and hoped for similar military action that would eventually lead to toppling the regime of Bashar al-Assad.

In fact, when the Syrian uprising broke out, the prevalent regional settings were very attractive for foreign intervention. Syria is an important middle-size power in the Levant. The outbreak of the 2011 uprising put it at the centre of regional conflict, which escalated after the US-led invasion of Iraq.

[43] 'Sanaa is the Fourth Arab Capital to Join the Iranian Revolution', *Middle East Monitor*, 27 September 2014, available at: https://goo.gl/cwiF4J; 'How Iran Views the Fall of Sana'a, Yemen: The Fourth Arab Capital in Our Hands', *Jerusalem Center for Public Affairs* 14(36), 3 November 2014, available at: https://goo.gl/kEQZQb, all last accessed 3 May 2020.

Since the 1979 victory of the Islamic revolution in Iran, Iraq had acted as a bulwark against the export of the revolution and the expansion of Iran's regional influence. The removal of Saddam Hussein regime in 2003 by the United States provided Iran with an opportunity to expand westward. The US withdrawal from Iraq in late 2011 enabled Iran to establish an arc of influence that stretches from its eastern borders with Afghanistan to the Mediterranean via Iraq and Syria. Both Turkey and the Arab Gulf states, particularly Saudi Arabia, watched nervously the rise of Iran's power and influence in the region. Hence, when the Syrian uprising broke out in 2011, an opportunity loomed to roll Iranian influence back.

As the use of violence against protesters increased in intensity and brutality, the opposition intensified its efforts to garner support for foreign military intervention to help oust Assad. In late 2012, the Syrian protest started to look very much like a civil war, with Turkey, the GCC countries and the Western powers supporting the opposition, with Iran and Russia (and, to an extent, China) supporting the regime. The conflict started to transform into a war by proxy.

While Iran increased its economic aid to the Syrian regime to level out the sanctions imposed by the Western powers and the GCC, Russia provided diplomatic cover in the UN, along with China, by frequently using its veto power to block a Libya-like scenario in Syria.

In 2013, Russia helped to avert US military action against the regime of Bashar al-Assad after violating a red line drawn by the Obama administration on the use of chemical weapons in the conflict. Russia brokered an agreement to remove the Syrian regime's stockpile of chemical weapons in exchange for cancelling US plans to take military action against the regime.[44]

As significant gains were made at the expense of the regime by an opposition emboldened by a Turkish–Saudi rapprochement initiated by the ascent of King Salman to the throne in Saudi Arabia in early 2015, the Syrian regime requested direct Russian military intervention. In September 2015, Russia threw its weight behind the regime and the Iranian-backed militias to prevent a victory by the opposition.

[44] Ben Rhodes, 'Inside the White House During the Syrian "Red Line" Crisis', *The Atlantic*, 3 June 2018, available at: https://bit.ly/2WqHeoE, last accessed 3 May 2020.

The rise of ISIL in Iraq and Syria in the summer of 2014 forced a reluctant US administration to undertake its own military intervention in Syria. Following the establishment of the US-led anti-ISIL international coalition, the United States began supporting the so-called Syria Democratic Forces, a loose coalition of mainly Kurdish fighters, who were US trained and armed to contain and defeat ISIL.

By the end of 2017, it was clear that the two great powers had achieved their objectives in the Syria conflict: the United States by defeating ISIL, and Russia by defeating the Syrian opposition and rescuing the regime of Bashar al-Assad.

The early protesters, who demanded political and economic reforms, had been crushed. Regional rivalry contexts turned yet another peaceful revolution into a failed attempt for democratic transition.

Conclusion

With its relatively more successful transition to democracy, Tunisia avoided the fate of the other Arab revolutions mainly because it is a fringe state of much less interest to rival powers. The lack of a rivalry context played in favour of making the transition there smoother. In the other Arab revolutions, the outcome was completely different. The regional and international environment overcame the will of the people, and inhibited the transition to democracy. In Libya, the UN imposed strict sanctions on the regime, while NATO and the GCC funded, supported and provided military aid that enabled the rebels to take control. The collapse of the old regime ended the consensus between the intervening powers, igniting rivalry between them and provoking civil conflict. In Bahrain, the exact opposite occurred. Foreign intervention was invited to support the ruling regime and suppress the rebellion. The protest movement was crushed on the spot by the GCC 'Peninsula Shield Force'. In Yemen, the 2011 GCC initiative facilitated the removal of former president, Ali Abdullah Saleh, but failed to reach agreement on a power-sharing formula. Factional conflict and elite divisions paved the way for the pro-Iran Houthi takeover, which has in turn unleashed a Saudi-led military intervention. In Egypt, weak democratic rule was established following the 25 January revolution. A Saudi-sponsored military coup returned the country to autocratic rule. In Syria, the peaceful protest movement ended up as one of the most violent proxy wars in recent history, involving all of the key regional and international powers. Syria represented a Hobbesian state of war of all against all, wherein different powers supported different proxies involved in different wars.

All of these cases show that the will of the people to bring about change and end tyranny was not enough to achieve that goal. It needed the right external conditions: an integration context, wherein all the powers concerned would ensure their security and guarantee that the change in the domestic settings of a given country will not affect them negatively. The absence of cooperative regional security concepts and mechanisms made the failure of the Arab revolutions to establish democracy almost inevitable. The Middle East rivalry context and the return to the Cold War atmosphere between Russia and the West rendered the long-awaited wave of Arab democracy transition into fierce conflicts. Unless this environment changes, the possibility of democratic change in the Arab World will remain a remote possibility.

11

THE 'ARAB SPRING' AND THE CHALLENGES OF SECURITY SECTOR REFORM

Omar Ashour and Dana El Kurd

The Arab Uprisings were principally sparked by the brutality of security actors in almost every country in which they occurred. In Tunisia, Mohammed Bouazizi's self-immolation following an insult by the police in December 2010 triggered the revolution. In Egypt, the June 2010 murder by two policemen of internet activist Khaled Said, followed by the brutality of police during the fraudulent parliamentary elections of November–December 2010, set the revolution's context. In Libya, the arrest in February 2011 of Fathy Terbil – a human rights lawyer who had represented the families of the victims of the June 1996 Abu Selim prison massacre, in which more than 1,236 political prisoners were gunned down by Moammar Gadhafi's security forces – sparked that country's revolution. In Syria, abuses committed in March 2011 by Assad's security forces, which included pulling out the fingernails of children and teenagers in Deraa, triggered the protests that ignited that country's ongoing civil war. In many ways, the Arab Spring was a region-wide reaction against violations by the security services.

Throughout the decades prior to the 2011 revolutions, Arab security establishments behaved more like organised crime syndicates than professional security services. Concepts such as human rights, human security, democratic control, civilian oversight and accountability were absent from the lexicons of Arab interior and defence ministries, and any attempt to introduce them was met with brutal repression—as, for example, during the January 1992 coup against Algeria's reformist president, Chadli Bendjedid,[1] and the June 1989 coup against Sudan's democratically elected prime minister, Sadeq al-Mahdi. Indeed, Egyptian opposition activists unsurprisingly chose to stage the massive protests that began Egypt's revolution on 25 January: Egypt's 'Police Day', intended to 'honour' the security services. '[We] wanted to ruin their party like they ruined our lives,' a young Egyptian revolutionary told us. 'We had to break them . . . I wish there was another way but there wasn't.'

Following the removal of dictatorships in Tunisia, Egypt, Libya and Yemen, security sector reform (SSR) has become an immediate objective of both revolutionary and reformist forces, regardless of ideological or political affiliation. How this reform process plays out will be decisive in determining the future of Arab democracy.

SSR can be described as the transformation of a country's security apparatus – including the roles, responsibilities and actions of all the actors involved – so that it is managed and operated in a manner consistent with democratic norms and sound principles of good governance, and thus contributes to a well-functioning security framework. Ideally, the reform process should embrace all branches of the security sector, from the armed forces to the customs authorities. The focus here will be on post-conflict or transitioning security bureaucracies affiliated with interior ministries, as opposed to those affiliated with defence ministries or under the direct command of the top executive, such as the president in Egypt and the prime ministers in Tunisia and Libya. In Egypt, Libya and Tunisia, security bureaucracies under the interior ministries include the police; paramilitary forces, such as the Central Security Forces in Egypt and the Intervention Forces in Tunisia; domestic intelligence services, such as the National Security Apparatus in Egypt; and temporary irregulars, such as the Supreme Security Committee in Libya. In Palestine, the security sector has undergone a number of changes and overlapping jurisdictions. Today, the security forces under the interior ministry include the Preventive Security Services, intelligence (split into

[1] Omar Ashour, 'The Algerian Tragedy', *Project Syndicate*, 2 January 2013, available at: https://bit.ly/2zQQz1o, last accessed 4 May 2020.

General Intelligence, Military Intelligence and Military Police Intelligence), and the various types of police.

Two core objectives of SSR are critical in the case of Arab states in general and Arab Spring countries witnessing post-authoritarian transitions in particular. These are, first, the establishment of effective governance, oversight and accountability in the security system; and, second, the improvement of the delivery of security and justice services. The challenges of SSR are numerous, however, beginning with the technical, organisational, and administrative dimensions of the process. In addition, SSR is a highly political process involving powerful anti-reform factions within the relevant bureaucracies, as well as amongst external powers. Indeed, this political dimension can dictate the direction and success of the entire project.

Literature Gaps

Security Studies and democratic transition literature has focused on a number of key variables that determine the success – or failure – of the transition process. Following waves of democratisation and the latest events of the 'Arab Spring', the role of the security sector has become well-established as a crucial determinant of successful democratic transition. Moreover, aside from democratic transition, scholars of civil–military relations have long recognised the importance of professionalised armies, subservient to civilian control, in minimising repression and coups.[2]

In terms of transition studies, such as seminal work by O'Donnell and Schmitter, the issue of elite negotiations was highlighted as crucial for the success of democratic transition.[3] As such, the armed forces and security sector were recognised as important players amongst a number of political actors. Moreover, the manner by which the armed forces were convinced

[2] Azmi Bishara, *Army and Politics: Theoretical Problems and Arabic Models* (in Arabic) (Doha: Arab Centre for Research and Policy Studies, 2017); Omar Ashour, 'Collusion to Collision: Islamist–Military Relations in Egypt, *Brookings Papers* 14 (2015): 5–8; Mehran Kamrava, 'Military Professionalization and Civil–Military Relations in the Middle East', *Political Science Quarterly* 115(1) (2000): 67–92; Morris Janowitz, *The Professional Soldier: A Social and Political Portrait* (New York: Free Press, 1968); Michael Makara, 'Coup-Proofing, Military Defection, and the Arab Spring', *Democracy and Security* 9(4) (2013): 334–59.

[3] Guillermo O'Donnell and Philippe C. Schmitter (eds), *Transitions from Authoritarian Rule* (Baltimore, MD: Johns Hopkins University Press, 1986).

to 'return to the barracks' was considered a major determinant of successful political reform.[4]

More recently, democratisation literature has focused specifically on a 'bottom-up' approach, that is, with a focus on the agency of political actors and the impact of protest.[5] This is particularly the case for much of the scholarship that emerged following the Arab Spring.[6] It was recognised that the armed forces in these states were important – in a similar fashion to the democratisation literature of the third wave – but it was unclear just *how important* this political actor would be. There was a substantial level of disagreement in the literature on how to classify the Arab regimes in the first place. And this included confused assessments of how powerful the armed forces were in each case.

Take, for instance, the case of Egypt. For many years, the major classification schemes in comparative political science simply denoted Egypt as a 'hybrid regime', with some works making no assessment as to whether the executive, the party (i.e., the National Democratic Party) or the armed forces were the most powerful.[7] And, in many of the cases across the Arab World, we also had instances of strong internal security forces, separate from military institutions. Before 2011, these developments were not previously prominent – with notable exceptions – on the radar of political scientists and security studies scholars studying democratic transition, authoritarianism and the security sector.

During and after the 'Arab Spring', a body of research focused on

[4] Zoltan Barany, *How Armies Respond to Revolutions and Why* (Princeton, NJ: Princeton University Press, 2016).

[5] Michael Bratton and Nicolas Van de Walle, *Democratic Experiments in Africa: Regime Transitions in Comparative Perspective* (Cambridge: Cambridge University Press, 2002).

[6] See, for instance, Nouri Gana, *The Making of the Tunisian Revolution: Contexts, Architects, Prospects* (Edinburgh: Edinburgh University Press, 2013), chs 5–8. See also Bahgat Korany and Rabab El-Mahdi, *Arab Spring in Egypt: Revolution and beyond* (Cairo: American University in Cairo Press, 2014), part 2; Neil Ketchley, *Egypt in a Time of Revolution: Contentious Politics and the Arab Spring* (Cambridge: Cambridge University Press, 2017); Donatella Della Porta, *Mobilizing for Democracy: Comparing 1989 and 2011* (Oxford: Oxford University Press, 2014).

[7] Barbara Geddes, 'What Do We Know about Democratization after Twenty Years?' *Annual Review of Political Science* 2(1) (1999): 115–44.

dissecting and analysing the Arab security sectors.[8] These works proffered a complex map of the sectors and their impacts on political authorities and local economies. Bishara framed and analysed the various relationships between different types of Arab armies and political regimes, how these relationships have historically developed in the post-colonial period and how they impacted the 'Arab Spring'. This was done with an in-depth empirical focus on Syria and Egypt.[9] Ṣāyigh dissected Egypt's military economy and showed how the Egyptian army became the major economic player in the aftermath of the 2013 coup. The economic activities of the military include 'delivering massive infrastructure projects, producing consumer goods ranging from food to household appliances, manufacturing industrial chemicals and transporting equipment, and importing basic commodities for civilian markets'; with major enterprises in steel production, pharmaceutics, gold prospecting, and managing religious endowments and pilgrimage.[10] Chaitani, Ashour and Intini produced the first United Nations report that comparatively dissected Arab security sectors across several Arab countries and analysed the main issues facing them during political transitions.[11] The report found that parts of the security sector in Arab states (specifically and more dominantly military institutions) directly control parts of the economy. For example, 'following the privatisation of many public companies in the late 1980s, the Egyptian military essentially took control of some state-owned enterprises'.[12] The ramifications skewed the free market dynamics. To put it briefly, the military–economic complex had low-to-no oversight, benefited from preferential customs and exchange rates, tax exemption, free land ownership and

[8] See, e.g., Bishara, *Army and Politics*; Ashour, 'Collusion to Collision'; Yazīd Ṣāyigh, 'Above the State: The Officers' Republic in Egypt', Carnegie Middle East Centre, Carnegie Endowment for International Peace, 2012; Yazīd Ṣāyigh, 'Dilemmas of Reform: Policing in Arab Transitions', *Carnegie Paper*, March 2016; Yazīd Ṣāyigh, 'Owners of the Republic: An Anatomy of Egypt's Military Economy', *Carnegie Paper*, November 2019.

[9] Bishara, *Army and Politics*, pp. 37–101, 105–37, 150–99.

[10] Ṣāyigh, 'Owners of the Republic', pp. 1–2, 121–5.

[11] Youssef Chaitani, Omar Ashour and Vito Intini, 'An Overview of the Arab Security Sector amidst Political Transitions: Reflections on Legacies, Functions and Perceptions', *United Nations' Economic and Social Commission for West Africa (UN-ESCWA)* (New York: United Nations Publications, 2013).

[12] Ibid., p. 16.

confiscation rights (without paying the treasury), and an army of almost-free labourers (conscripted soldiers); thus creating unfair competition with the private sector.[13]

However, the involvement in the economy via corrupt or skewed privatisation processes is non-uniform among Arab Spring states and among different institutions of the security sector within the very same state. Clear cases would be the security bureaucracies under interior ministries that we focus on in this chapter. For example, during the Arab Spring, Omar Ashour wrote two reports on SSR for the Defence and National Security Committee of the Egyptian People's Assembly (lower house in 2012) and the National Security and External Affairs Committee of the Egyptian Consultative Council (upper house in 2013). The report exclusively focused on the institutions of the Egyptian Ministry of Interior (as opposed to the Ministry of Defence). Within these limitations and compared with state-funded issues, corrupt privatisation had a lower impact as a hurdle to reforms. Even back then, Egypt's Ministry of Interior was a massive bureaucracy employing more than one million people, including officers, petty officers, soldiers, conscripts and civilian administrators. Its labour force included more than 831,000 full-time jobs (that is about seven times the entire police force of the United Kingdom, including Northern Ireland and about ten times the British standing army). This was in addition to complex networks of more than 300,000 paid informants and ex-convicts; all paid by the state. Elements and networks in the 'part-time' segment could be hired by the state, ruling party bosses and businessmen loyal to the regime during election periods. Some of the former officers (mainly from the counter-terrorism combat units of the State Security Investigations) became hired assassins for loyalist businessmen. But, overall, these issues – as serious and shocking as they are – are relatively minor compared with the seven critical challenges outlined below.

Security sectors behave dynamically differently during uprisings and transitions. This was evident during the 'Arab Spring', as whole militaries or military factions defected across the region. Makara, for instance, assesses

13 Ashour, 'Collusion to Collision', pp. 17–18, available at: https://www.brookings.edu/wp-content/uploads/2016/06/collusion-to-crackdown-english.pdf. For more details on the case of the Egypt – the most startling in terms of military–economic activities in comparison with other Arab Spring countries – see Ṣāyigh, 'Owners of the Republic'.

coup-proofing measures in three countries – Egypt, Yemen and Syria – and pinpoints which employed successful strategies.[14] Countries which built parallel security institutions or distributed material incentives to control the security apparatus were less successful in keeping the security forces 'in the barracks' than countries that exploited communal ties. Still others argued that timing is the most important factor; coup-proofing strategies are not likely to succeed in the event of excessively long periods of rule, in which incumbents become vulnerable 'lame ducks'.[15] Such conditions, argues Albrecht, are likely to spark the intervention of the security sector in politics. The studies that emerged following the Arab Spring thus not only recognised the variation in security sectors across these states, but that previous analysis had not fully anticipated the impact of internal security services on the transition process.

Some scholars argue that most of the theories on democratic transition focused solely on the domestic dimension and the agency of actors, even though there remained some disagreement over how each actor would behave. However, a few notable exceptions made the argument that 'structure' had been neglected in research on the subject. This included studying the historical legacy of security apparatuses across the region. According to this line of argument, this missing aspect explained to some degree why political scientists were caught unaware by the uprisings. Scholars also did not have the tools for understanding why some transitions succeeded while others failed. Arguments focused on 'structure', that is, the historical context of each state and its development, would be more useful, these scholars argued, as structure was the key determinant of transition success or failure.

Specifically, Brownlee, Masoud and Reynolds argued that while no structural preconditions determined where the uprisings occurred, two important structural preconditions determined whether they succeeded or failed: oil wealth and hereditary succession.[16] The success of democratic transitions in

[14] Makara, 'Coup-Proofing, Military Defection, and the Arab Spring'.

[15] Holger Albrecht, "The Myth of Coup-Proofing: Risk and Instances of Military Coups d'État in the Middle East and North Africa, 1950–2013', *Armed Forces & Society* 41(4) (2014): 659–87.

[16] Jason Brownlee, Tarek Masoud and Andrew Reynolds, *The Arab Spring: Pathways of Repression and Reform* (Oxford: Oxford University Press, 2015).

the region can be predicted by those two factors alone, as they have cascading effects on a variety of important variables – including the state of the security sector. Oil wealth has the effect of providing a way to buy off important actors as well as a 'repression effect' that enables regimes to strengthen their security apparatuses vis-à-vis any opposition. Hereditary succession has a similar effect on agents of repression, according to the authors, in that it 'indicates heightened loyalty to the executive'. The mechanism by which this happens remains opaque. Nevertheless, Brownlee et al. make the argument that, if a case has either one of these conditions, then democratic transition becomes much less likely.

One aspect acknowledged briefly in this assessment was the factor of international involvement. Citing the case of Libya, the authors argue that international involvement acted as a '*deus ex machina*', in that it facilitated transition in a case in which the regime would not have succumbed to popular pressure, given its oil wealth. Nonetheless, the 'structure' that these authors consider ignores the international dimension in a fuller sense. In particular, if we are to examine the structure of Arab countries, we cannot ignore the impact of international involvement in creating and supporting 'agents of repression' across the region, in the long term and not just during a critical juncture as a *deus ex machina*.

A number of studies, for example, highlight some negative impacts of US aid in the Middle East, unlike other regions because – arguably – it is tied to authoritarian durability.[17] Similarly, some of the studies on the effect of American military bases in areas of high strategic value argue that these bases had an 'autocratising' effect.[18] This autocratising impact occurs through a variety of mechanisms, most important of which, for our purposes, has to do with providing regimes and their security forces with the technical knowhow and financial capacity to repress the opposition. American military basing decisions have this effect precisely because public opinion in the Middle East is ambiguous towards, or even hostile to, American military basing. Thus, in these cases, the United States values stability and empowers 'agents of

[17] Erin Snider, 'US Democracy Aid and the Authoritarian State: Evidence from Egypt and Morocco', *International Studies Quarterly* 62(4) (2018): 795–808.

[18] Andrew Stravers and Dana El Kurd, 'Strategic Autocracy: American Military Forces and Regime Type', *Journal of Global Security Studies* 5(3) (2020): 427–42.

repression' to make sure public opinion is not acted upon. The Middle East's high strategic value, and America's overarching strategic goal of naval predominance, makes this the natural outcome of its involvement in the region.

Such effects of international involvement, and particularly US involvement as the global hegemon, merits more focus in theories of democratic transition focused on structure. Similarly, in some of the theories focused on actor agency, the international dimension is minimally engaged with. This limits crucial research that shows international involvement in the security sectors of Arab states, and how that plays a critical role in both the historical development of each case, as well as during moments of critical juncture when change becomes possible. As we will see in the coming sections, the international dimension can help to explain why certain cases of security sector reform in the region neglected key objectives of human security, and often helped to empower authoritarian governments.

Second, many of the studies focused on the official armed forces and their role which, though important, neglected the impact of interior security forces on the transition process. Only recently have studies acknowledged the rivalries that existed between different parts of the security sector in many of these states and have begun to examine the effect this had on the outcome of democratic transition.

And, finally, it is difficult to speak of de-militarisation in cases of occupation or active warfare – in which the official state is unable to exercise full control of its territory or maintain order, and/or groups cannot be guaranteed safety vis-à-vis their opponents without maintaining armed forces. This is the case for parts of the Arab World specifically, as we shall see in the coming section. Thus, de-militarisation and civilian control over armed forces/militias can be the wrong framework to impose on certain populations prior to cessation of political negotiations.

Attempted Reforms

In this section, we will focus on certain cases before and after the Arab Spring uprising to illustrate how security sector reform has been attempted across the region. These cases will highlight some of the critical challenges faced by security sector reformers, including situations of occupation, ongoing armed conflict, numerous security institutions with overlapping jurisdictions and other contextual factors. We shall start with the pre-Arab Spring case of Palestine and then with three Arab Spring cases of Tunisia, Egypt and Libya.

Reform Attempts before the Arab Spring: The Case of Palestine[19]

The international dimension, particularly the involvement of the United States, has been a crucial factor in attempted security sector reform across the region. This was especially the case following the Cold War. To stave off the threat of intra-state conflict and mitigate its impact on civilians, international organisations adopted the concept of 'human security'.[20] Human security meant that international actors, with the United States at the forefront, began focusing on the interplay between insecurity, poverty and civil wars, with the argument that civil conflict was the key driver of overall insecurity.

As such, the United States (among other actors) focused on state-building, security sector reform and rule of law programmes as the priority in many post-conflict zones. The argument was that securing these populations would lead to economic development, and thus less conflict overall. But, of course, some critics have pointed to flaws in this logic and its implementation, particularly since programmes such as security sector reform often took precedence over other forms of peace-building addressing underlying structural problems.[21]

Security sector reform in Palestine is a case in point. With the signing of the Oslo Accords in 1993, Palestinians were expected to stabilise their population and provide security for Israel, even while the occupation was ongoing.

[19] Although considered an atypical case given the ongoing Israeli occupation, many studies have found it helpful to examine the Palestinian case in the context of comparative politics, as its dynamics are replicated in other states across the region (i.e., international intervention, authoritarianism, etc.). See, e.g., Amaney Jamal, *Of Empires and Citizens* (New York: Cambridge University Press, 2012) and Dana El Kurd, *Polarized and Demobilized: Legacies of Authoritarianism in Palestine* (Oxford: Oxford University Press, 2020). Moreover, ongoing violent conflict and weak state institutions are not a feature of Palestine alone, but can be found in other cases in the Arab World. As such, while we recognise the aspects of the Palestinian case that are unique, and address them in this section, we still find it useful to use the case as a point of comparison.

[20] Mary Kaldor, *Human Security: Reflections on Globalization and Intervention* (Cambridge: Polity Press, 2008).

[21] Mandy Turner, 'The Peacebuilding–Counterinsurgency Nexus in the Occupied Palestinian Territory', *Review of International* Studies 41(1) (2015): 73–98.

International donors, with the United States at the forefront, penalised the Palestinian Authority (PA) repeatedly when they believed Palestinian leadership behaved in a way that betrayed this original goal. There were repeated complaints about corruption and a lack of professionalisation under Yasser Arafat, even as scholars pointed out that the parameters by which the PA was judged were not suitable to its unique status.[22] Thus, as Palestinian leadership attempted to navigate their newfound position of building a state while also dealing with the realities of occupation, the security sector developed in a way that donors deemed to be 'unprofessional'. Specifically, donor countries, with the United States at the helm, complained that the security sector was not taking security coordination seriously, and that it had metastasised to over seventeen different organisations under Arafat's direct command – although the original Oslo Accords granted the PA the right to establish only six specified organisations.[23]

With the eruption of the second *intifada* in 2002, parts of the PA's security forces splintered and actively resisted Israeli military occupation.[24] US officials accused Arafat of orchestrating the *intifada*, or at the very least turning a blind eye to armed resistance.[25] As a result, he was eventually placed under siege in his Ramallah compound, where he remained until his death. Members of General Intelligence and Preventive Security were particularly targeted.[26] The organisation was accused of facilitating the *intifada* alongside Fatah-affiliated militias, and many of its members were assassinated by Israeli forces during this period.[27]

22 Mushtaq Husain Khan, 'Introduction', in Inge Amundsen, George Giacaman and Mushtaq Husain Khan (eds), *State Formation in Palestine: Viability and Governance during a Social Transformation* (New York: Routledge, 2004), pp. 1–12.

23 Roland Friedrich, Arnold Luethold and Firas Milhem (eds), 'The Security Sector Legislation of the Palestinian National Authority', Geneva Centre for the Democratic Control of Armed Forces (DCAF), 2008, available at: https://bit.ly/3dduV5Z, last accessed 1 June 2019.

24 For more information on the disarmament, demobilisation, and reintegration process following the second *intifada*, see 'Ruling Palestine II: The West Bank Model?' International Crisis Group, 17 July 2008.

25 Neri Zilber and Ghaith Al-Omari, 'State with No Army; Army with No State', Washington Institute for Near East Policy, March 2018, available at: https://bit.ly/3ddjYRS, pp 20–4, last accessed 1 June 2019.

26 Ibid.

27 Ibid.

The events of the second *intifada* led the United States and its allies to place security sector reform as their top priority. The United States tightened control over aid money spending, training security personnel received and who could serve in these capacities. Furthermore, they supported the appointment of Salam Fayyad as prime minister, and provided targeted aid to the PA security forces, while simultaneously cracking down on opposition elements deemed unacceptable to Israeli security.[28]

To combat the growing support for Islamists following the victory of the Islamist party, Hamas, in the 2006 parliamentary elections, the United States circumvented Palestinian institutions and provided financial aid directly to the president's office. This was done in order to facilitate the expansion of a security force specifically tasked with repressing the opposition.[29] Indeed, the United States and its allies encouraged Fatah, the outgoing party, to essentially launch a coup against Hamas, thus leading to the split in governance between the West Bank and Gaza which persists to this day.

Security sector reform in Palestine meant that, while the occupation was ongoing and settlements only increasing in number and size, the PA leadership was spending a full third of its budget on its security forces to reassure their Israeli counterparts, leading to one of the most intense levels of policing in the entire world.[30] In the West Bank, there is one security/police officer for every forty-eight Palestinians, compared with one police officer for every 384 Americans.

Moreover, under the guise of security sector reform, the United States and its allies essentially became embroiled in internal Palestinian politics, cementing particular dynamics. First, supposed security sector reform created a situation in which the executive branch, and particularly the president himself, became more and more insulated from public pressure, or even pressure from other parts of the government.[31] This helps to partially explain why Mahmoud Abbas, the current Palestinian president, has overstayed his term

28 'Ruling Palestine II: The West Bank Model?' pp. 2–6.

29 David Rose, 'The Gaza Bombshell', *Vanity Fair*, April /2008, available at: https://bit.ly/2WlkfeM, last accessed 2 July 2019.

30 Alaa Tartir, 'The Palestinian Authority Security Forces: Whose Security?' *Al-Shabaka*, 16 May 2017.

31 El Kurd, *Polarized and Demobilized*, pp. 45–67.

limits and increasingly acts with impunity. And this is in spite of the many attempts to reform the security sector so that other parts of the government – including the legislature and the judiciary, as well as a body called the National Security Council – could exercise some control as well. When political developments went in a direction that the United States and its allies did not approve of, these attempted reforms were ignored and/or reversed.[32]

Second, security sector reform in Palestine greatly facilitated the hyper-polarisation we see in the territories today, specifically the split between the PA and its opposition. This polarisation is reflected in the wider society, generating lower levels of trust as well as inhibiting the ability of Palestinians to coordinate and engage in collective action.[33]

Increased authoritarianism as a result of security sector reform also facilitated increasingly negative outcomes in quality of life. The split between the West Bank and Gaza has been catastrophic to Palestinian national ambitions, and it was essentially spurred by policies intended to 'professionalise' the security sector and 'stabilize' (i.e., subjugate) the Palestinian population. The meddling in Palestinian politics and, more pertinently, the Bush administration's backing of particular armed groups over others, has cemented the division between Palestinian factions. Thus, instead of working as a united front to end the siege on Gaza and address the impact of occupation on Palestinian freedom of movement and economic conditions, the PA and its Hamas counterpart in Gaza remain gridlocked. This is aside from the increased levels of anxiety, distrust and helplessness generated by 'reform' policies with the wrong objectives.

Finally, as mentioned in the previous section, there is the issue of demilitarisation and civilian control being an inappropriate objective for the PA and Palestinian society. Pursuing security sector reform following the second *intifada* did not increase the safety of Palestinian citizens, nor even help the PA exercise greater control over its territory. Instead, it has provided cover for further retrenchment of the Israeli occupation, and greater levels of insecurity for the Palestinian people. Much as particular economic policies have been criticised as inappropriate for the context of Palestine following the Oslo

32 Friedrich, Luethold and Milhem, 'The Security Sector Legislation of the Palestinian National Authority', p. 24.

33 El Kurd, *Polarized and Demobilized*, pp. 67–90.

Accords, security sector reform policies also need to be interrogated in terms of their objectives and impact, especially in cases where violence remains the main mode of politics.

In sum, security sector reform in Palestine strengthened dynamics considered to be the opposite of good governance and rule of law, including increased insulation and personalisation of the security sector, decreased civilian oversight, greater levels of social and political polarisation, and lack of representativeness. The Bush administration involvement was a key facilitator of these dynamics, but it is indeed difficult to imagine a scenario in which the Palestinian security sector was truly reformed given the context of occupation. For the security sector to be reformed in Palestine, security forces need to be subordinated to representative Palestinian institutions and afforded the necessary tools for professionalisation. This would necessitate that the security forces in Palestine help to protect Palestinians from threats of violence, and not help perpetrators of such violence, such as the occupation forces and/or Israeli settlers. Obviously, the Israeli government would never allow such dynamics to emerge. As such, security sector reform in Palestine is only reform by name.

Reforms During and After the 'Arab Spring': Tunisia, Egypt and Libya

Following each (initially) successful revolution of the Arab Spring, various SSR initiatives were put forward by governmental and non-governmental institutions, as well as by independent experts. In Tunisia, SSR efforts started as early as June 2011, a few months after President Zine el-Abidine Ben Ali fled. In November 2011, the Ministry of Interior laid out a roadmap for reforming Tunisia's security sector in a white paper. It discussed transforming the security sector from a police order to a police service, one that could respond urgently to the new challenges of crime. Tunisia's elected leaders in 2011, however, saw this white paper as the product of former regime elements within the Ministry of Interior, who were not necessarily pro-reform. 'There are some good elements [in the white paper]. But it offers no comprehensive reform,' Amer Larayedh head of the Political Bureau of the Ennahda party, the lead party in Tunisia's ruling coalition, told Omar Ashour.[34] Meanwhile,

[34] Amer Larayedh, Head of the Political Bureau of the Ennahda Party, interview by Omar Ashour, Doha, 30 May 2012.

in December 2011, Ali Larayedh, a civilian who was himself a torture victim during the sixteen years he was jailed by the Ben Ali regime, became the interior minister (later also prime minister from March 2013 to January 2014).

In Egypt, more than ten SSR initiatives have been proposed since March 2011, varying significantly in terms of quality and comprehensiveness. The proposals have been put forward by a range of stakeholders, including independent experts, civil society groups, disenchanted police officers, the Ministry of Interior and parliament. Civil society organisations offered various initiatives focused on legal reform, oversight and civilianisation of the security sector. Disenchanted police officers were able to form several independent organisations, such as the General Coalition for Police Officers (GCPO), which lobbied for official recognition as a police union with an elected leadership. The initiatives proposed by GCPO and others were focused on cleansing the police force of corrupt generals; improving work conditions, training, media relations and public relations; plus, increasing salaries and pensions. Several independent SSR experts were consulted by both the presidency and the parliament regarding implementation of the various proposals, including first author of this chapter.[35]

But perhaps the boldest step towards civilian control over the security sector was taken by the Egyptian presidency. In August 2012, a massacre of Egyptian soldiers in Sinai by an armed group permitted the newly elected President Mohamad Morsi to get rid of the top brass of Egypt's Supreme Council of the Armed Forces (SCAF), including its head, Field-Marshal Hussein Tantawi, and his deputy, Lt General Sami Anan. The Sinai incident also sparked a purge of some of the most powerful generals across the security sector.[36] These included the head of the General Intelligence Directorate, Murad Muwafi; the head of the Presidential Guard, Nagib Mohammed Abd

[35] In 2012 and 2013, Omar Ashour advised two Egyptian parliamentary committees: the Defence and National Security Committee in the People's Assembly (Lower House) headed by Major-General Abbas Mukhaimar, and the National Security and External Affairs Committee in the Consultative Council (Upper House). The latter's subcommittee on SSR was headed by Major-General Kamal Amer. Ashour also advised the Libyan General National Congress – among a group of experts – on demobilisation and redesigning security sector governance. Parts of this chapter are based on these experiences.

[36] For a full background of Sinai's crisis, see Omar Ashour, *How ISIS Fights: Military Tactics in Iraq, Syria, Libya and Egypt* (Edinburgh: Edinburgh University Press, 2021), pp. 160–76.

al-Salam; the head of the Military Police, Hamdy Badin; the head of the Cairo Security Directorate, Mohsen Murad; and the head of the Central Security Forces, Emad al-Wakil. Based on previous fieldwork by the first author, these generals all shared an anti-reform stance, defiance of elected civilian rule and a desire to maintain as many Mubarak-era policies and practices as possible. Two of them, Badin and Murad, were specifically accused by several revolutionary and reformist groups, including the GCPO, of organising a campaign of repression against activists.

In Libya, security sector change of leadership in hopes of reforms began with the appointment of Salem al-Hasi as the head of the Libyan intelligence agency, the Foreign Security Apparatus (FSA) in February 2012. Al-Hasi, who was a member of the armed wing of the National Front for the Salvation of Libya (NFSL), had spent more than two decades in exile in the United States and defected from the NFSL. He became the first civilian opposition figure to lead an Arab intelligence service. 'All of the Arab intelligence services', al-Hasi said upon taking his post, 'were there to protect the regime and oppress citizens. I will change that. The Libyan intelligence will be under the control of the elected executive, and the direct oversight of the legislative assembly.'[37] Al-Hasi faced criticisms early for allegedly tapping phones and electronically monitoring Gadhafi loyalists, using the interception equipment inherited from his regime. He was removed by parliament in February 2015, against the background of a surge in the presence of ISIS in Libya. This highlighted the need for crafting laws for oversight and control of the security and intelligence apparatuses, as well as a clear mechanism for enforcing that control, with support from the UN Support Mission in Libya (UNSMIL), as well as independent experts and international actors.

Critical Challenges

Seven major hurdles faced the achievement of the core SSR objectives of effective security sector governance in the early phases of post-Arab Spring democratisation process, following the successful overthrowing of despots in Tunisia, Egypt, Libya and Yemen. They also apply elsewhere in the Arab

[37] Salem al-Hasi, interviewed by Khaled Mahmoud, *Al-Sharq al-Awsat*, 8 February 2012, p. 6.

World. First, was extreme political polarisation, which led to the politicisation of the SSR process, even political violence; second, was internal resistance and spoiler tactics by anti-reform factions within the security sector; third, was the limited capacity and resources of the newly elected governments; fourth, was weak democratic institutions; fifth, was limited knowledge and experience of SSR requirements among stakeholders; sixth, which mainly applies to Libya and Yemen, was the incomplete demobilisation, disarmament and reintegration (DDR) of former anti-regime fighters; and, seventh, was international involvement that undermined attempts at security sector reform, and empowered anti-reform factions or spoilers.

Political polarisation per se should not be a hurdle to SSR. Diversity in the political spectrum, heated debates, intense arguments and general differences of opinion should be celebrated as gains of the revolutions. Indeed, this freedom of opinion and expression should be aimed for in other Arab countries. Polarisation in the cases of Latin America has been found to be a key determinant for the formation of strong political parties, and thus a robust democratic system.[38]

However, not all polarisation has the same impact. In the Arab World, where hyper-polarisation had been spurred by pro-authoritarian international intervention, polarisation had a more negative impact on governance generally, and on SSR processes in particular. In the aforementioned transitioning countries, leaders in charge of the process, such interior ministers and intelligence chiefs, complained that the chaos following the revolutions, and the soaring attacks on security agents and government offices, made it difficult to tackle the reform process. This problem was made even more difficult by lack of consensus among political actors.

In that sense, post-Arab Spring interior ministries face a dilemma. On the one hand, they are responsible for defending state institutions, which are constantly under attack by violent groups from various backgrounds. On the other hand, if any members of these attacking groups should be killed or injured, the interior ministry will be accused of brutality. On top of

[38] Steven Levitsky, James Loxton and Brandon Van Dyck, 'Introduction: Challenges of Party-Building in Latin America', in Steven Levitsky, James Loxton, Brandon Van Dyck and Jorge Dominguez (eds), *Challenges of Party-Building in Latin America* (New York: Cambridge University Press, 2016), pp. 1–49.

that – structurally – all these ministries have limited experience in non-lethal tactics of riot control.

A major in the Egyptian Central Security Forces who witnessed the attacks on the presidential palace on January 2013 summarised the problem to Omar Ashour as follows: 'the pattern we have here is that the officer gets attacked with shotguns and Molotov cocktails. If he flees, he gets accused of negligence, and then he gets tried. If he fights back, he gets accused of brutality, and then he gets tried as well. What exactly is he supposed to do?'

Intense political polarisation over the SSR process also proved to be a hindrance. On talk shows, political figures called for SSR to be implemented and for police brutality to end. At the same time, the very same political figures continued to praise generals known for their support of brutal tactics. Some politicians even called on these generals to intervene in the political process by cracking down on their political rivals. As comparison with other cases makes clear, the unity of political forces regarding the very particular demands for depoliticising the security sector and imposing civilian control over the armed forces is key for the success of both security sector reform and democratisation. In the Palestinian case, security sector reform was equally hindered by political rivalry. Politicians called for security sector reform, only to reverse their positions when they felt threatened by it (Mahmoud Abbas before and after the 2006 legislative elections is a case in point). As a result of the politicisation of security sector reform, many Palestinians across the political spectrum also viewed it as a tool or weapon to be wielded, rather than a process to serve clear and professional objectives.

A second challenge was the strong resistance within the security sectors in post-Arab Spring countries to several critical elements of the reform process. Many of the leaders of Arab interior ministries understood the reform process to mean increasing the material capabilities and budgets of their respective institutions. Whereas this is a part of the SSR process insofar as it aims to enhance the performance of these security institutions, Arab interior ministries do not usually welcome other elements of SSR. These included effective civilian oversight, procedures ensuring transparency, the introduction of merit-based as opposed to seniority-based promotion criteria, and even revisions of the police academies' curricula – though there is lesser resistance to this last element compared with others.

Accountability in particular faces strong resistance. One example from Tunisia is the case of Colonel Moncef al-Ajimi, the former director of the Tunisian Intervention Forces. Al-Ajimi was officially accused of firing on peaceful protestors in the towns of Thala and Qasarin during the Tunisian revolution. During al-Ajimi's trial in 2013, then-Interior Minister Larayedh attempted to remove him from his position. In reaction, hundreds of policemen from the Bouchoucha barracks physically blocked access to al-Ajimi, and then organised a strike to protest his attempted dismissal. Thousands of Intervention Forces members withdrew from key locations in several Tunisian cities and returned to their barracks. 'We will not be a scapegoat for the families of the martyrs,' said one of the protesting policemen. As a result, Larayedh had to keep al-Ajimi in the ministry. In June, a military court found al-Ajimi not guilty. Though the military prosecutor appealed the verdict, the incident reflects the level of resistance to the process of accountability faced by newly elected, post-revolution governments.

In Palestine, when asked about security coordination with Israel, there is a strong sentiment among high-ranking members of the security sector that 'we know best' what Palestinians need. There were also repeated comments that Palestinian society should not call for democracy or accountability because society 'is not ready'.[39] Moreover, the security sector's targeting of Palestinian opposition groups is justified as work against treasonous elements.[40] This sentiment explains why, following the legislative elections of 2006, intra-Palestinian violence erupted, with members of the security sector engaging in street battles with Hamas and leading to many deaths.[41]

A third challenge is limited capacity and resources. The post-revolution, democratically elected governments in Egypt, Libya and Tunisia inherited serious economic challenges, with soaring national debt and limited resources available for a thorough SSR process. The economic crisis, however, did not prevent governments from allocating huge resources to the security sector.

[39] El Kurd, *Polarized and Demobilized*, p. 14, see also ch 2, 'Americans Have Taught Us: There is a Difference Between Democracy and Creating Problems'.

[40] Ibid.

[41] Khalil Shikaki, 'With Hamas in Power: Impact of Palestinian Domestic Developments on Options for the Peace Process', Crown Center for Middle East Studies, 2007, available at: https://bit.ly/3dhvH1W, p. 7, last accessed 1June 2019.

However, there was limited public information about how such resources were spent and with which outcomes, undermining both transparency and accountability.

The related fourth and fifth challenges to SSR in post-Arab Spring countries are weak democratic institutions, and limited knowledge and experience of SSR requirements among many of the stakeholders in the process. In Egypt, the lower house of the parliament, the People's Assembly, which was elected following the revolution, was dissolved by the SCAF following a Constitutional Court verdict that deemed parts of the electoral law unconstitutional in June 2012. Before dissolution, the lower house had approved amendments to a law governing the organisation of the police force. The new version of the law removed the president's right to act as the head of the Supreme Council of the Police, and amended articles relating to salary controls and the status of certain ranks in the force. This led to frustration among members of parliament and activists, who thought that the parliament had its priorities wrong. Clearly, there is a big gap between the revolutionary demands of eradicating torture, ending impunity and increasing transparency, on the one hand, and the limited knowledge of how to translate such demands into policies and procedures for SSR, on the other. A general understanding of such limitations in Tunisia led the government and the Interior Ministry to collaborate with an international organisation and SSR experts to identify necessary reforms as early as July 2011.

The sixth challenge to SSR, appearing mainly in Libya and Yemen – and to a much lesser extent in the Sinai Peninsula of Egypt – was DDR. The DDR process is key to the success of both the SSR and democratisation processes in these countries. If it fails, or succeeds only partially, armed organisations will emerge as a challenge to democratically elected governments, as the case of Libya currently demonstrates. Elected Libyan governments, and the current internationally recognised administration, had attempted to integrate militias into a national army. However, the capacity of the state to achieve this remained limited, while militias remain reluctant to give up arms. This has led to the current crisis, where the foreign-backed General Khalifa Haftar claims to lead a 'national army', itself composed of multiple militias and acting as one, in order to end the power of militias.

Moreover, collective reintegration of armed brigades has proved to be highly problematic, as it undermines the command-and-control structures within the military and security forces. 'Reintegrated' personnel take orders from the immediate commander of their own brigade, not from the minister of defence or interior. The Kufra events of February–June 2012, in which two tribes clashed in the southeast of Libya, leaving more than 100 people dead, not only exposed the limited capacity of the army and security forces to contain inter-tribal violence, but also the weak command-and-control structure within the Ministry of Defence. Such weakness is sensed by other non-state armed formations, which refuse to disarm when the state cannot guarantee their safety due to limited capacity, among other factors. This ultimately undermines the DDR process altogether and further complicates the related processes of SSR and democratisation. A very similar situation existed in Yemen, although there the forces of the old regime had not been initially undermined as they had been in Libya.

The seventh challenge is the anti-reform regional environment. The 'Arab Spring' – more reformist than revolutionary – still faced a similar reaction to the French Revolution, when European monarchies rallied to put an end to it. In an attempt to defend a regional status quo whose main feature is authoritarianism, several regional actors did not perceive SSR processes, as well as any meaningful democratisation process, as beneficial to their interests; more as threats to the security and stability of their regimes. As a result, most of the pro-continuity forces in Egypt and other Arab Uprising countries had strong, wealthy and aggressive regional backers – such as Saudi Arabia and the UAE – which bolstered their stances, morally, logistically and financially, as well as by intensive propaganda campaigns of deception and misinformation. Coups were encouraged and funded as in Egypt, while a military campaign was launched on Yemen – after a complicated chain of reactions to its uprising. Additionally, new militias were created and armed in Libya and Yemen, and encouraged to bid for power, thus reversing the whole democratisation process.[42] Confirming research on this topic, this has led to an escalation of violence and an overall more

[42] Ghaith Abdul-Ahad, 'Yemen on the Brink: How the UAE is Profiting from the Chaos of Civil War', *The Guardian*, 21 December 2018, available at: https://bit.ly/2xze3r7, last accessed 2 July 2019.

intractable situation with regard to armed groups and their future role in the state.[43]

On the other hand, most Western democracies as well as regional ones were hesitant to commit or to assist in a time-consuming, resource-draining, no-holds-barred conflict about the future of democracy in the Arab region. This stance differed from the support granted to Eastern European transitions during the 'third wave' of democratisation, and thus weakened most of pro-change and pro-reform Arab forces. Additionally, some of the technical support and resources for SSR from international democratic partners was neither effectively nor appropriately targeted. For instance, in Palestine, when the United States funnelled aid and weapons into the expansion of armed forces under the direct control of the president, this indirectly facilitated the Fatah coup attempt against Hamas and ongoing violence between the two factions. Also, anti-democratic forces manipulated Western support to foster a propaganda campaigns to delegitimise SSR as a 'foreign conspiracy' aimed at weakening or infiltrating the security services. Some of the local pro-democracy forces failed to counter that propaganda or even to launch a counter-narrative.

Conclusion: Security Reform Challenges and Democratic Deficiency

Most of the Arab Spring states suffered from the threat of a military/security takeover of the state. This existed due to three related factors. First, the continued and intensifying polarisation among key political actors along sectarian, ethnic, regional or political lines, some of which are related to the former (such as the secular–Islamist lines of polarisation). Second, the above highlighted patterns of anti-reform and spoiler regional intervention. And, finally, the failure to bring the security apparatus and other militarised actors (e.g., militias) under control.[44] Matters were made worse by the politicisa-

[43] See, e.g., Omar Ashour, 'Punching Above Weights: Combat Effectiveness of Armed Nonstate Actors in the Arab World and Beyond', *Strategic Papers* (Doha: Arab Centre for Research and Policy Studies, 2020), available at: shorturl.at/ryFH5, last accessed 27 September 2020; Patrick Regan, 'Third-party Interventions and the Duration of Intrastate Conflicts', *Journal of Conflict Resolution* 46(1) (2002): 55–73.

[44] On that transformation process, see Omar Ashour, 'Bullets to Ballots: Transformations from Armed to Unarmed Activism', *Strategic Papers* (Doha: Arab Centre for Research

tion of the security sector in countries like Egypt, and the militarisation of politics in countries where conflict descended into civil war, as in Libya, Syria and Yemen. This empowered the militias, turning them into armed political parties.

The impact of all this was to destroy the consensus over democratisation, opening the way for all sorts of local adventures and anti-reform regional powers, who took advantage of the chaos to change the rules of the game in their favour. The outcomes are now well-known: a coup in Egypt where the military subjugated all civil administrative power centre to its will, rather than the reverse; in Yemen, a takeover by the Houthi militia provoked a Saudi-led intervention in 2015; a similar attempt is under way in Libya, with a militia led by the rogue General Khalifa Haftar, but this time supported by the UAE, Saudi Arabia and their allies. Thus, all countries of the Arab democratic uprisings are currently arenas of civil wars, as unreformed security apparatuses are reasserting its unchallenged dominance, or foreign-supported regimes or militias are vying with each other to displace civilian, unarmed politics.

Although the repressive societal model known as the '*mukhabarat* state'(intelligence state) was severely undermined by the Arab revolutions in Tunisia, Egypt, Libya, Yemen and Syria, many of its subcultures survived. The success of SSR in post-transition polities is conditional on favourable political, institutional and legal provisions, including political consensus on SSR, civilian institutional oversight and new police laws. This in turn requires a strong national consensus, with unequivocal international support, on democratic goal and agendas. Little of this materialised in the Arab Spring countries discussed here. In all cases, no democratic transition is complete without targeting abuse, eradicating torture and ending the impunity of the security services while imposing effective and meaningful elected-civilian control of both the armed forces and the security establishments. Those objectives were at the core of the Arab revolutions of 2010–2011. They have yet to be attained.

and Policy Studies, 2020), available at: shorturl.at/fMNT9, last accessed 27 September 2020; Omar Ashour (ed.), *Bullets to Ballots: Collective De-Radicalization of Armed Groups* (Edinburgh: Edinburgh University Press, 2021).

CONCLUDING REMARKS: ON VIRUSES, PHANTOM ACTORS AND OTHER COLONIAL GHOSTS

Abdelwahab El-Affendi

A key chant of the 19 December 2018 Sudanese revolution (the inaugural event of the 'second wave' of Arab uprisings), was: 'You arrogant racist, all the country is Darfur'. It was a response to the arrest of students accused of being a 'cell' from a rebel Darfur militia planning acts of violence and sabotage. The regime of Omar El-Bashir had used this tactic before, accusing protesters from shanty towns of responsibility for violence. This ruse usually worked, as in September 2013, when protests lost steam almost instantly at the spectre of possible ethnic violence. However, the December 2018 protesters refused to swallow the bait. Like the vanguard of the 25 January protesters in Egypt, who created the Facebook page, 'We are all Khalid Said' (in solidarity with a victim of police brutality), the Sudanese protesters told the regime: 'We are all Darfurians!'

Corrosive Insecurity

This links to a theme that runs through the chapters of this book regarding the pivotal role of induced insecurity in discouraging democratic activism, a hypothesis for which the Arab revolutions were an important test. The revolutions succeeded as national collective action only by rejecting and neutralising such divisive narratives of insecurity and sectarianisation, as threatened dictators raised the spectre of some diffuse threat ('Islamism', sectarianism, foreign conspiracy, etc.) to rally domestic and international support. Ironically, this contradicted boasts by these same dictators that they had already banished these threats! Later, the mantra became: 'Do you want us to become like Syria (or Libya, Yemen, etc.)? Thank God for your brutal dictator!' However, the masses and activists were not interested. Many had bought into such narratives before, only to find themselves victims in turn. This sobering enabled the emergence of pro-democracy alliances that made the revolutions possible.

If the 2011 uprisings were non-sectarian, those of the 2018–2019 second wave were consciously anti-sectarian. In Sudan, devout 'Arab' Muslims revolted against the ethno-religious pretences of an 'Islamist regime' that often claimed to defend the urban elite against the 'barbarians' outside the walls. In Iraq, the Shia masses rose up against sectarian militias and parties ruling in their name. In Lebanon, a majority from all sects and all classes challenged elites claiming legitimacy as sectarian representatives. Algeria was not absent during the 2011 phase, but the protests failed to take off due to memories of the 'dark decade' of the 1990s, where the military reciprocated Islamist violence with some of its own generalised terror. All that changed in February 2019, when the insistence on keeping an unfit president in power convinced the public that enough was enough.

Similar instances of outrage at attempts by despots beyond their sell-by-date to perpetuate their intolerable rule were the link between the 2011 uprisings and their 2018–2020 sequel. Together with shocking acts of regime brutality, these attempts represented the last straw that prompted people to rise up and proclaim enough! (*kefaya!*, the name of a 2004 Egyptian protest movement), or 'We are disgusted!' (*Girifna!*, the label of a 2009 Sudanese youth protest group). The shout: 'Leave!' (*Dégage* – Tunisia; *Irhal* – Egypt) then reverberated, as did Algeria's 'Leave, every one of you!', and Lebanon's 'Everyone means everyone!'.

In Chapter 11, Ashour and El-Kurd sum up this insecurity–solidarity dynamic as they remind us that police brutality has been the trigger for almost every Arab Spring uprising. The same point is made by El-Affendi in Chapter 3, highlighting the revolutions as acts of solidarity with the victims of brutality. In all the Arab revolutions, acts of love, altruism and heroism shone like a warm spring sun. Many of those standing in the line of fire were not victims themselves, and could even count themselves among the privileged. This stands in sharp contrast to the insecurity of 'black hole states' that saw this altruism as a threat. The Syrian regime designates the 'White Helmets' volunteer rescue workers as 'terrorists', while journalists and human rights activists receive the label in Egypt and Saudi Arabia. Ironically, they are also the main victims of kidnappings and extra-judicial murders.

Here, a central defining dynamic emerges: the revolutions embody altruism, care and solidarity across divides; the regimes and their supporters promote narratives of fear, mistrust and imagined threats.

'Free-riders', Phantom Actors

The inspiring uniqueness and hybridity of the Arab 'refo-lutions' are emphasised by Asef Bayat in Chapter 4, who sees in them a novel and radically transformative model that inspired the world. However, they were limited in final impact, as their initial non-sectarian effervescence and astonishing rapid triumphs dissipated in the face of the hard slog of building new power structures. The pluralist tolerance of the refo-lutions allowed 'free-riders' (actors who had remained on the margin of the revolutionary initiative and battles) to take centre-stage. This enabled entrenched old regime partisans to retain/regain influence and initiate the counter-revolution.

This narrative was partly shared by Mady (Chapter 7), who deplores the displacement of revolutionary actors, mainly the non-partisan tech-savvy youth activists, by the weakened and divisive political parties. The latter dominated the transition, but failed to integrate the reticent youth. While not using the term 'free-riders', Mady reiterates Bayat's point about the revolutionaries having neither the will nor the capacity to take over the state as radical revolutionaries did elsewhere. This enabled 'traditional political actors' to appropriate and then mismanage the transition.

In Chapter 2, Bishara agrees that Arab uprisings were essentially more reformist than revolutionary, as shown by their pleas for reform. 'Revolutions oust regimes and do not *demand* that they be ousted,' or reformed. However, he sees the main problem in Egypt as the failure in reducing political polarisation, in contrast Tunisia's success saved democracy. As shown in an earlier work, however, Bishara does not buy the 'free-riders' thesis, dismissing as irrelevant rival narratives about 'who started the revolution' in contrast to 'who stole it'. As he pithily put it: 'Nobody stole the revolution from anybody.' Revolutions were not 'an [individual] intellectual property' to be stolen, but a diffuse socio-political phenomenon. The real question is not who started it, but who has the capacity to organise and lead. In Egypt, the revolution built on a series of youth insurrections within opposition (including Islamist) parties. This important insight is backed by Bishara's meticulous historiography highlighting the contributions of a broad range of actors to processes that paved the way for the revolution and then ensured its success.[1]

No less important was the reminder that democratic revolutions do not seek to monopolise power on behalf of a faction, but to lay the ground for an inclusive competitive democratic process. The youth activists did not want to rule the country. Indeed, it would be weird if they did!

Mady also highlights the crucial (and perverse) role of 'concealed' or 'secretive' actors during the transition; mainly semi-official actors, including military or security agents, members of the judiciary, party operatives or key political financiers. If pervasive, they could also be dubbed the 'deep state' (a deeply problematic term and a misnomer). Opposition groups could also have their puppeteers, as happened with the dual leadership of the Muslim Brotherhood and its official Justice and Freedom Party (JFP). In such an atmosphere, the real actors maintain 'plausible deniability', escaping responsibility for their actions, and depriving politics from its very essence: its publicity.

Colonial Ghosts

The ultimate 'phantom' actors are foreign powers hiding behind local agents, and there is an abundance of those here. In Chapter 10, Kabalan proposes that foreign intervention represents the key explanatory 'independent variable' for the failure of Arab transitions. This links to the point made by Bishara on the decisive impact of a country's geo-strategic significance to the success of transitions: Tunisia faced less disruptions to its democracy than Egypt, precisely because the latter mattered more to outside actors. In Chapter 7, Mady blames the marginalisation of the external dimension in mainstream transition theory for its limited relevance in the Arab region, where democracy is seen as a threat to US hegemony and regional allies. Both Mady and Kabalan

[1] A. Bishara, *Thawrat Misr, Part I, Min Al-Thawra ila Al-Inqlab* (*Egypt's Revolution: From Revolution to Coup*) (Doha: Arab Centre for Research and Policy Studies, 2016), pp. 366–7.

contrast the EU's positive role in democratisation in Southern and Eastern Europe to the negative influence on Arab democratisation of Western powers and their regional allies. The only partial exception, Libya, was dictated by political and economic interests, rather than partiality to democracy. Mady additionally highlights the resurgence of international and regional autocracies, and their role in undermining and obstructing the democratic revolutions in the region.

Dabashi (Chapter 5) takes the more radical step of dismissing both the modern nation-state and democracy as mythological notions camouflaging the inherent violence of the European-originating modern state, confirmed by its colonial history and neo-liberal present. Its colonial export to the Middle East had added racism to its multiple dysfunctions and pure violence, and is at the root of the present crisis and may be an indication that this model of state is in its death throes everywhere.

The point about the colonial pedigree of Arab despotism and its neo-liberal embeddedness raises the central question of the specific regime type sustaining this colonial persistence. The issue is approached by Luai Ali in Chapter 6 from the perspective of theories and typologies of authoritarian regimes, a possible alternative to the transition angle. The theories make their classifications and predictions according to factors that include the internal dynamics of autocratic regimes, their means of power maintenance or their mechanisms of ruler selection. However, when applied to Arab cases, these theories did not work well (except for one that partially did), having had problems in coding and/or classification. This test for the theories offers indications and directions for revision.

In Chapter 3, El-Affendi takes the issue further, identifying a unique Arab regime type: the 'black hole state', a multifaceted hybrid that had shown surprising adaptability, defying international and regional trends, while benefiting from them. Its features provide the explanatory link highlighting the persistence of the colonial legacy, given these regimes' reliance on foreign support due to their domestic isolation. The Syrian and Saudi regimes, for example, adopt a 'pay-to-be-colonised' approach, offering huge incentives to foreign hegemons (naval and military bases, billions of dollars in arms purchases, etc.) to ensure protection from their own people. In countries like the UAE, there are signs of this model further degenerating towards a totally privatised, politics-free model. In this 'Blackwater state' model, the military becomes a privatised militia attached to the warlord-leader, while the 'state' functions like a family firm, and where public space and the law virtually disappear.

Several major armies in the region are turning into semi-private (or autonomous) militias, with added sectarianisation and politicisation. Ashour and El-Kurd see in this a threat to a key demand of successful democratic transition: the subordination of the security sector to the elected government. This becomes impossible when the military doubles as a sectarian militia or as a business/political party. Even more so if Blackwater states engage in multiple and multifaceted regional interventions. Here, militias are formed and funded, so are political parties, civil society groups. This includes protest movements, such as Egypt's *Tamarrud* (Rebellion) that orchestrated the June 2013 protests against Morsi. Here, the phantoms become a real source of horror.

On Viruses, Enzymes and 'Moderate' Politics

Writing today under the shadow of the Coronavirus pandemic, the first genuinely global emergency, we can scarcely speak of 'normal' politics. With the focus in this volume on insecurity as a key factor in obstructing or disrupting democracy, such a universal agent of insecurity cannot be ignored.

In this respect, the 'medical' views of a prominent Arab democracy activist and transition actor acquire a new significance. Writing in 2004 during his forced exile, Tunisia's first democratically elected president, Moncef Marzouki (r. 2011–2014), likened dictators to viruses. As a simple nucleic acid molecule in a protein coat, a virus is a parasite that can reproduce itself only by infecting and taking control of living cells. It uses the cell to produce itself endlessly, with very destructive consequences for the organism. Dictators act in a similar fashion, parasitically taking control of the body-politic, and using its control mechanisms to their own interests, with comparable destructiveness.[2]

Contrast this to another tiny biological protein molecule, the enzyme,

[2] M. Marzouki, *'An Ayyi Dimuqratiyya Tatahaddathun?* (*Which Democracy are You Talking about?*) (Paris: Arab European Publishers, 2004), p. 17.

indispensable for the health of living bodies. Enzymes help to speed up the rate of chemical reactions within cells, making them vital for significant bodily functions, such as digestion and metabolism. Great and inspiring leaders, like South Africa's Nelson Mandela, function like enzymes, revitalising and energising communities, and enhancing the health of the body-politic. Tyrants like Iraq's Saddam Hussein, or Tunisia's own despot, Ben Ali, are destructive parasites who leave swathes of destruction in their trail.[3]

This takes us back to our starting point on the role of revolutionary forces in the Arab World as constructive agents of hope and solidarity, in contrast to the insecurity of forces of repression. Tourya Essaoudi's narrative (Chapter 8) about the pioneering democratising role of Morocco's vanguard women provides us with a snapshot of 'enzymes' in action. Women activists led intellectually, formulating concepts and narratives that indigenised and promoted democracy, politically, by assuming leadership positions in parties and within civil society and activists. They also played important roles in bridging the gap between polarised actors: regime and opposition, Islamists and secularists, left and right, international and national actors.

Many chapters have noted the constructive democratising contributions of 'moderate' actors, including moderate Islamists. Bishara and Mady emphasise the decisive role of trade unions and other civil society actors in promoting consensus in Tunisia, a contribution that earned them a Nobel Peace Prize in 2015. In this context, the above-cited criticism of Arab revolutions as too accommodating should be a cause for praise, instead. That this moderation was not reciprocated by anti-democracy forces, who even exploited and abused it, is not an indictment of the moderates, but of the international supporters of repression.

'Moderation' had not always been valued, often linked to traditional liberal aversion to popular mobilisation and wider political participation, seen by some as a threat to democracy. In Chapter 3, El-Affendi notes that moderation has usually been one-sided, accommodating dominant interests at the expense of their victims. The transition discourse itself embodies an intellectual shift from radicalism within the social sciences towards pro-system tendencies. However, this approach did have positive dividends, since compromises that

[3] Ibid., p. 18

looked like capitulation offered opportunities for more empowerment in the long term. But not always. Ashour and El Kurd remind us how the 'domestication' of the PLO ended disastrously for the Palestinians, whose 'liberation' organisation ended up as a policeman for the occupation. El-Affendi cites Turkey as a locus where 'moderation' was initially negative.

Moderation, like democracy itself, is a contextual reflection of existing balances and dynamics of power. Martin Luther King Jr is celebrated today as the epitome of moderation, but only after being murdered as a threat. The civil rights movement was accommodated only as larger threats loomed, including more radical challengers, and the embarrassment of racism at the height of the Cold War. In the Middle East, where the 'extremism' of the state became the new normal, moderation ceased to be a positive value. As genocidal regimes occupied centre-stage, moderation became neither desirable nor helpful. In a world dominated by viruses, enzymes can do little to help severely infected bodies.

The Science of Uncertainty

As an instance of moderation (domestication?) of political science, transition theory has been disparaged as a misleading 'hegemonic paradigm', which should cede to a realist acceptance of the durability of authoritarianism. Our contributors critically interrogate the theory, and its applications in the region's context, from different angles, while acknowledging its significant contributions. Bishara reminds us that major social transformations (modernisation, secularisation, the rise of capitalism, democratisation, etc.), are at the genesis of modern social science, raising key questions about origins, causes, trajectories, differentials, etc. At a meta-theoretical level, we note the interactive loop shaping the studies. Seminal events like the Arab Spring cause a shock and reactive theoretical modifications that in turn impact political practice. Theories inspire revolutions, which again reshape theory. Equally, theoretical scepticism and 'democracy-phobia', prevalent in Middle East Studies, can strangle democratic aspirations in the cradle. Theorisation is thus not a luxury. It is at times, like now, a life-and-death matter.

Hopefully, we will have a future, when this era of ours may be labelled the Coronavirus Age. In the meantime, what we need is certainly less viruses and more enzymes, more vanguard women and revolutionary youth and less tyrants and racists, more civil activism, and fewer and smaller armies, less credulous theorists and more probing ones. Let us hope this contribution belongs to the first set.

INDEX

Note: *italic* indicates images

EU representative:
Easy Access System Europe
Mustamäe tee 50, 10621 Tallinn, Estonia
Gpsr.requests@easproject.com

www.ingramcontent.com/pod-product-compliance
Lightning Source LLC
Chambersburg PA
CBHW070842300326
41935CB00039B/1360

* 9 7 8 1 4 7 4 4 8 3 2 2 3 *